I0613407

Catherine Mary Phillimore

Studies in Italian Literature, Classical and Modern

Catherine Mary Phillimore

Studies in Italian Literature, Classical and Modern

ISBN/EAN: 9783337178581

Printed in Europe, USA, Canada, Australia, Japan

Cover: Foto ©Thomas Meinert / pixelio.de

More available books at **www.hansebooks.com**

Studies
in
Italian Literature

Classical and Modern

ALSO

The Legend of "Il Cenacolo"

A Poem

BY

Catherine Mary Phillimore

WRITER OF "THE LIFE OF FRA ANGELICO," ETC., ETC., ETC.

London
SAMPSON LOW, MARSTON, SEARLE, & RIVINGTON
CROWN BUILDINGS, 188, FLEET STREET
1887

To

Enrichetta Caetani,

Duchessa di Sermoneta,

and

to the Honoured Memory of

her Husband,

Don Michelangelo Caetani,

Duca di Sermoneta,

these Pages

are Inscribed by the Writer

with

Reverence, Gratitude, and Affection.

———

" Or va', chè un sol volere è d'ambedue :
Tu Duca—tu Signore, e tu Maestro."
La Divina Commedia, Inf. c. ii, l. 109, 110.

PREFACE.

THE Essays which form this little volume have been reprinted, with additions, from the various magazines and
reviews where they were first published.[1]

They do not pretend to be other than studies, outlines
of thought, which may perhaps suggest how many a rich
spoil still remains to be gathered from the glorious page of
Italian literature. For to the student this can never cease
to glow with fascinating interest. Undimmed by the
course of centuries, it remains as vivid as the golden
ground of a picture by Fra Angelico, if indeed it may not
be said to gather from each succeeding age an added lustre,
like the glittering mosaic of San Miniato, mellowed in the
sunsets of 800 years.

The imagination which has passed in awe and wonder
before the sublime conception of the "Divina Commedia,"
may next pursue in the smooth numbers of Petrarch a
romance of such unrivalled constancy as would have sufficed to create the romantic age, had it had no other origin
or existence, and finally kindled to divine enthusiasm

[1] The *St. Paul's Magazine*, *Macmillan's Magazine*, the *Church
Quarterly Review*, the *Edinburgh Review*. The Legend of "Il
Cenacolo" is reprinted from the *Churchman's Companion*.

and led by Tasso, the Christian poet-knight, may follow
all the chivalry of Europe to worship at the Holy Shrine.

Again, when the drama of Italy in all its various forms
has supplied a manifold enjoyment, the eye and ear,
satiated with pleasure, may seek repose in the veiled light
and solemn hush of the great libraries, which served as
treasure-houses for the vast stores of learning till the art
of printing should one day disperse them over the world.

Here, in the still atmosphere, the manuscript folios
which line the walls, the glowing pages of some missal,
illuminated perhaps by Fra Angelico or Francia, jealously
guarded from the ravages of time, remain as silent witnesses
to the truth that " Labour is the price the gods have set
upon everything that is valuable."

What if the dust of centuries has accumulated round
the forgotten tomes ; what if the hands which traced
them have long since mouldered in the grave. Will not
the dust " hear and beat," the " wonted fires " quicken
into life at the approaching freedom of the " Patria Terra " ?

Favoured theme of Poetry, all-powerful to wing the
thoughts and dip the pen in fire, one after another the
sons of Italy pour forth their indefatigable lays and utter
the aspirations never to cease till the sword is sheathed in
the hour of victory, and the pen laid aside after celebrating
the song of triumph.

" Deh fossi tu men bella ! " is a lament which belongs
to a bygone age. Now that each one of her States.has put
her individual jewel into the circlet of freedom's crown,
rich in natural beauty, with every added treasure of
literature and art, let Italy reign " dalle Alpi al mar."

If there are any to whom the fair beauty of Italy has
ever appealed in vain, it is certainly not to the student of
her literature, when the time comes to tread the streets
that Dante trod, to touch the stone where he was wont

to sit, lost in thought, contemplating his beloved "San Giovanni," the "fonte del mio battesimo," where, alas! for his cruel fate, he was never to receive the poet's crown.

All around, in unchanging beauty, lie the scenes on which his eyes loved to rest—the soft, purple outlines of the mountains; the Arno rolling down its waters, now green with snow from the Apennines, now irridescent with every hue of the changing sky, "E cento miglia di corso nol sazia;"[2] the soft mists of the morning, the "dolce color d' oriental zaffiro"[3] gathered up into the zenith of the cloudless atmosphere, the white "Buoi di pari, a giogo,"[4] coming down from San Miniato, as the evening shadows fall and the familiar outlines of the Duomo and the Campanile, the Palazzo Vecchio and Santa Croce vest themselves in varying liveries of purple, red, and gold, till the sun sinks suddenly behind the last blue outline of the horizon, and the grey curtain of twilight falls on the fair scene; then across the gulf of centuries comes the echo of the

> Squilla di lontano
> Che parve il giorno pianger che si muore."[5]

If then these few studies should prove sufficiently attractive to tempt other students to search for themselves in the same mine of inexhaustible treasures, they will not have been written in vain.

It only remains to add that the translations of poetry [6] which bear the initials R. P. were supplied by the late Right Honourable Sir Robert Phillimore, and that it is from the recollection of the faultless taste and wise

---

[2] Purg. xiv. 1. 18.
[4] Ibid. xii. 1.
[6] Pp. 229, 233, 236.

[3] Ibid. i. 13.
[5] Ibid. viii. 6.

criticism which guided the revision of the Essays in their original form that their writer now derives the courage necessary to bid them once more

> " uscir del bosco
> E gir infra la gente."[7]

CATHERINE MARY PHILLIMORE.

THE COPPICE, HENLEY-ON-THAMES.
November, 1886.

[7] " Rime del Petrarca."   Canzone XIV.

CONTENTS.

STUDIES IN ITALIAN LITERATURE.

~~~~~~~~~~

THE "PARADISO" OF DANTE.

A Sketch.

"Qual alto seggio
T' abbia assegnato Dio ne le sue glorie,
Alighiero, non so. So che la tua
Italia ti locò nel più sublime.
So ch' ella sempre t' obliò nei giorni
De la viltà : ma ai dì de la speranza
Legge il tuo libro ; e ormai più non t' oblia." [1]

Perhaps of the three parts of the "Divina Commedia" the "Paradiso" is the least dwelt upon by English students of the great Italian poet. It has the just reputation of being the part most difficult of comprehension in the whole poem. Those who attempt to read it are deterred from doing so by the allegories and metaphors which, frequently employed throughout the work, occur in almost every line of the "Paradiso ; " by the arrangement of the heavenly spheres according to the now exploded Ptolemaical system ; and, above all, by the theological and philosophical expositions which, it must be admitted, are not entirely free from the scholasticism prevalent in the thirteenth and fourteenth centuries.

These appear to be some of the reasons why the "Paradiso," considered by Italian critics the greatest effort of Dante's mind. is so little appreciated by foreigners. With the exception of Cary, whose translation and

[1] "Canti di Aleardo Aleardi," p. 119.

B

whose notes are admitted by all to be equally good throughout the poem, the English commentators and essayists upon the "Divina Commedia," after criticizing in the most able and elaborate manner the " Inferno" and the " Purgatorio," scarcely mention the " Paradiso," and thus convey the impression that it is inferior to the preceding portions of the poem.

To cite one example, so important that no other is required, Lord Macaulay in his " Criticisms on the Principal Italian Writers," points out the best passages, dwells upon the beauty of the style, the unity and consistency of the poem, its minute details and powerful descriptions ; but only with reference to the " Inferno " and "Purgatorio." When he comes to the "Paradiso " he dismisses the subject in a few lines: " But among the beatified he [Dante] appears as one who has nothing in common with them, as one who is incapable of comprehending, not only the degree, but the nature of their enjoyment." And further on : " When we read Dante, the poet vanishes. We are listening to the man who has returned from 'the valley of the dolorous abyss.' We seem to see the dilated eye of horror, to hear the shuddering accents with which he tells his fearful tale." [2]

No mention is made of the reverse side of the marvellous picture presented to us by Dante, the spheres of eternal bliss, the ceaseless songs of praise, the heavenly hope, the blessed consolation of which he treats in the " Paradiso," and which the Italian critics, in their enthusiastic admiration, declare to be a kind of foretaste of the joys of il vero Paradiso.

The object of this paper is to endeavour to remove some of the difficulties which are to be encountered in the study of the " Paradiso," to give, if possible, a clue to the allegory which lies concealed in the poem, and thus to guide the reader to its manifold beauties.

It may also be urged in favour of so slight a sketch that few can really study the immortal poet without longing to add their contribution, however small it may be, to the livelong monument which every year increases to

[2] " The Miscellaneous Writings of Lord Macaulay," vol. i. pp. 62, 63.

one who may divide with Shakespeare his inheritance of fame.

Such is the double end proposed by a paper which has been compiled from the best Italian writers and commentators upon the subject. Among these standing ever foremost "sì come Sire"[3] is the late Duca di Sermoneta, upon whom his compatriot Dantophiles have unanimously conferred the title of the "Nestore dei moderni Dantisti."

Nowhere could this title have appeared more aptly conferred than when in the "Sala della Palombella" at Rome there fell from his own lips the exposition of the " Paradiso,"—

> " Facesti come quei che va di notte,
> Che porta il lume dietro, e sè non giova,
> Ma dopo sè fa le persone dotte;"[4]

and, out of the dark night of his blindness, the Duca, who, with the exception of some twenty lines, knew by heart the whole poem, shed beams of light which revealed every hidden depth of the author's meaning, seeing and telling

> " Of things invisible to mortal sight."

These expositions it was not given to all to hear, but all may study for themselves his " Tavole Topografiche," the work of an earlier period of his life, before the terrible visitation of blindness arrested his career as an artist.

" It is not possible," says De Witte, writing of these Tavole, " to place with greater clearness and precision before the eye of the reader the fabric of the Universe as conceived by Dante for the scene of his poem."[5]

The Duca was also the author of a treatise, entitled " Tre Chiose nella Divina Commedia di Dante," or "Three

---

[3] Inf. c. iv., l. 87.
[4] Purg. c. xxii., l. 67-9.
> " Thou didst, as one,
> Who journeying through the darkness bears a light
> Behind, that profits not himself, but makes
> His followers wise."
>
> *Cary, Trans.*
[5] " Carteggio Dantesco," p. 41.

Glosses upon three disputed points in the Divina Commedia," which created a great sensation in Italy, both on account of their wonderful research and erudition and for the translucent purity of the style.[6]

Besides these " lavori da me eseguiti," the Duca writes, " per giovare alla letteratura di Dante e non alla mia rinomanza," [7] but which certainly fulfilled both purposes, we can now refer to his Dante correspondence with such well-known commentators as De Witte, Giuliani, De Gubernatis, Carlo Troya, Trevisani, Ranieri, Alessandro, Torri, &c.

It is not necessary to enter into the many close and intricate speculations upon their great theme discussed in those pages, but there is one suggestion made by the " Nestore dei Dantisti " which should never be lost sight of by the student of the "Divina Commedia."

With apt illustration of the position he is about to advance, the Duca cites the passage in the " Inferno " where the Signor d' Altaforte, holding the severed head in his hand,—

> " Di sè faceva a sè stesso lucerna ;"
>
> *Inf.* c. xxix. l. 124.

and goes on to say, " The first, the best authority to refer to in the exposition of " Divina Commedia " is Dante himself, either in the poem itself, or in his other authenticated works. Among these I never could imagine why any doubt was cast upon the authenticity of his 'Epistola a Can Grande,' for who could possibly have invented or carried the fraud to such a pass ? If any one still entertains this doubt, I, for my part, question if he has ever understood a line of Dante, and of such there are not a few in the present day." [8]

---

[6] The third of the " Tre Chiose" was adjudged to be the " Commento Trionfale," because it revealed a special affinity of artist sentiment between the commentator and his subject. It dealt with the " Allegory of the Eagle of the Empire," Par. xviii. 76 *e seq* , and gave an interpretation pointing out the similitude between the Gothic M., the Florentine Lily, and the Imperial Eagle, which had hitherto occurred to no one of the many expositors of the " Divina Commedia."

[7] " Carteggio Dantesco," p. 57.

[8] Ibid., p. 56, 57.

Such is the advice of the last and noblest of the public exponents of the " Divina Commedia " in the Sala della Palombella at Rome in 1882, some five and a half centuries after the author had rested in an exile's grave, and the self-same introduction to the study of the " Paradiso " was employed by Filippo Villani, who succeeded Boccaccio in the office of public reader of the " Divina Commedia " within the first half-century of its appearance in the astonished world.

The advice bears especially upon the study of the " Paradiso " because it is that portion of the poem which is dedicated to Can Grande della Scala on account of his pre-eminence in Dante's opinion over the other potentates of Italy : because the most sublime cantica of the " Divina Commedia," the noblest effort of the author's genius, is the only fitting acknowledgment of the " Cortesia del gran Lombardo " which afforded him his first refuge and shelter in his exile.[1]

" Therefore," writes Dante in this epistle, " to show my grateful sense of the many benefits conferred upon me, I sought diligently among those things which it was in my power to give, passing even in review those which were most secret, in order to find for presentation what would be the worthiest, the most acceptable. Nor could I find anything more in keeping with the greatness of your station than this the most sublime cantica of the Commedia which is adorned with the title of the ' Paradiso.' This is my present epistle, signed with my own autograph, I inscribe, offer, and finally recommend to you." [2]

This remarkable letter proceeds to point out the links which connect the " Paradiso " with the two preceding portions of the " Divina Commedia." For the poem is framed on a plan of perfect symmetry, and one train of thought runs through it all. It must then be borne in mind that, among a variety of minor allegories, the two chief interpretations which the poem is capable of are these :—

1. Political, or, as Dante himself calls it, Historical ; and it is in truth an autobiographical narrative of historical events of Dante's age (1265—1321), chiefly those

[1] Par. xvii. 69.
[2] " Il Convito di Dante Alighieri e le Epistole," p. 511.

of his own country, but embracing also other nations, so far as they were connected with Italy, with constant allusions to ancient history, and that of the middle ages up to his own time. This is the first aspect which the poem presents to the reader.

2. Moral. The "Inferno" and the "Purgatorio" were intended by the poet to be representations of the active life of man. To trace the allegory from its beginning, Dante, that is to say, man, or a human being, endowed with reasoning faculties, mental and physical capacities of feeling, and the liberty of choice—having lost his way in the forest of human passion, vainly endeavours to escape from it and to climb the steep hill of virtue, but is hindered chiefly by three vices—envy, avarice, and pride. This is all related in the first canto of the "Inferno." He is so repeatedly foiled in his attempts that he is about to abandon the enterprise in despair, when Virgil, representing moral philosophy, appears to him. Virgil rescues Dante from the wood, and because he had fallen so far from virtue that it is necessary to show him the fearful consequences of vice, takes him down the Abyss of Hell, where he points out the certain punishment which overtakes each crime. This is the symbol of human reason directing the liberty of will and indicating the ruin which would result from the gratification of the natural appetites and passions.

In the "Purgatorio" Virgil conducts Dante up a steep and painful ascent, hardest in the beginning, but becoming gradually easier till it ends in the terrestrial Paradise at the summit. Thus moral philosophy or reason exercises its sway over the mind of man in another way, by the desire for good, showing him that in order to attain this good he must mortify his evil inclinations and correct his faults ; and this, although difficult and painful at first, becomes easier by degrees, until at length he finds that " her ways are ways of pleasantness, and all her paths are peace." As the " Inferno " and the " Purgatorio " are allegorical representations of the active life of man, so the :" Paradiso " would represent the contemplative life, the rest which the soul must find in God—to use Dante's own beautiful expression, " Nel vero in che si queta ogn' intelletto." [3] Dante takes for his guide in Paradise Beatrice, the lady whom he loved so passionately when on earth, and in whose honour the "Divina Commedia" was written, because, as he himself says, "Spero dire di lei quello, che mai non fu detta d' alcuna." In order, then, to render her due honour, he makes her to be the allegorical representation of the "Scienza Divina," or theology, endowing her with heavenly wisdom.

As moral philosophy applied to the mind of man cannot stretch beyond a certain point, but must give place to a higher knowledge—that is to say, theology—so Virgil cannot accompany Dante beyond the two first stages of his journey, but must yield his function of guide to Beatrice, in order to fit Dante's mind for the proper appreciation of the glories of Paradise.

With all the penetration and subtlety of an Italian mind, Dante perceived that only by degrees could he fathom, figuratively speaking, the depths of evil, or attain to the summit of perfection. Thus with the same art which led him to descend by degrees through the worst vices of the human race in their allotted place of punishment, till he reached their author at the bottom of the abyss; so, having previously purified his mind from all material corruptions in the cleansing fires of Purgatory, with a soul possessed of active and contemplative faculties, with science for his ladder, and theology for his guide, he passes from sphere to sphere in his "Paradise" until at length he reaches the culminating point of perfection, the "beauty of that holiness," in which with all the fervour of a deeply religious mind he longs to worship the vision of divine glory. Here, as Cary admirably renders the original,—

"Vigour failed the towering fantasy:
But yet the will roll'd onward like a wheel
In even motion, by the love impelled,
That moves the sun in heaven and all the stars." [4]

In the "Paradiso," the religious preponderates over the political or historical aspect of the poem; but it is impossible, and, indeed, a mistake, to attempt to define too

[3] Par. xxviii. l. 108.
[4] Cary's "Dante," Par. xxxiii. 131—135.

clearly where the one ends and the other begins, they are so closely intertwined that they are often merged entirely one in the other. Still, with the exception of the three cantos which Dante devotes to the historical account of his ancestor Cacciaguida, and one or two other episodes, the " Paradiso," true to the allegory which it is intended to convey, contains, for the most part, profound dissertations upon theology and philosophy.

That it was intended for minds of a more meditative class, who would not need the stirring incidents of the " Inferno " and " Purgatorio," with the historical interest attaching to them, Dante himself announces at the outset of the poem in the figurative language which he delighted to employ, having first warned the careless and superficial reader not to attempt to understand this part of the " Divina Commedia,"—

> "O voi che siete in piccioletta barca,
> Desiderosi d' ascoltar, seguiti
> Dietro al mio legno che cantando varca,
>   Tornate a riveder li vostri liti :
> Non vi mettete in pelago, che forse,
> Perdendo me, rimarreste smarriti.
>   *   *   *   *
> Voi altri pochi, che drizzaste 'l collo
> Per tempo al pan degli angeli, del quale
> Vivesi qui, ma non si vien satollo,
> Metter potete ben per l' alto sale
> Vostro naviglio, servando mio solco
> Dinanzi all' acqua che ritorna eguale." [5]

---

[5] " All ye, who in small bark have following sailed,
Eager to listen, on the adventurous track
Of my proud keel, that singing cuts her way,
Backward return with speed, and your own shores
Revisit ; nor put out to open sea,
Where losing me, perchance ye may remain
Bewilder'd in deep maze .   .   .
    *   *   *   *
Ye other few, who have outstretched the neck
Timely for food of angels, on which here
They live, yet never know satiety ;
Through the deep brine ye fearless may put out
Your vessel ; marking well the furrow broad
Before you in the wave, that on both sides
Equal returns."

CARY'S *Dante*, Par. ii.

To this latter order of student, and more especially to those who consider the two sciences, philosophy and theology, as only two different methods of arriving at the same conclusion, two different roads to one end, the " Paradiso " will always afford food for meditation of the highest order. And here the rare moderation which the author displays in keeping within the bounds of human capacity is worthy of especial remark. Having respect to the profound nature of his subject, he does not attempt to penetrate into hidden matters, or strive to comprehend what is purposely veiled from our eyes.

He is nevertheless determined that his poem shall contain all the sciences of the age, and therefore he founds it upon three systems, of which it is intended to be the exposition—philosophy, theology, and astronomy. With regard to philosophy, both natural and moral, that of Aristotle only was studied in the schools at that time. Dante was first instructed in it by his master, Brunetto Latini ; he afterwards pursued these studies in the schools at Bologna, and never ceased adding to them during all the long years of his exile from his country. The fruits of his immense research appear in the " Divina Commedia," but chiefly in the two first parts ; in the " Paradiso," however, philosophy gradually disappears, or rather expands into theology, the natural result of its teaching, and there this last and highest science finds its widest scope and attains its full development. Dante dwells upon the great truths of the Christian religion—the creation, the fall of man, the incarnation, the redemption and satisfaction, and the resurrection of the body ; he reasons upon them with an accuracy and with a depth of thought which drew from the learned Salvini, in his letter to Redi, the following encomium :—

> " Se volete saper la vita mia,
> Studiando io sto lungi da tutti gli uomini ;
> Ed ho imparato più Teologia
> In questi giorni, che ho riletto Dante,
> Che nelle Scuole fatto io non avria."

Aptly rendered by Cary—

> " And dost thou ask what themes my mind engage ?
> The lonely hours I give to Dante's page ;

And meet more sacred learning in his lines,
Than I had gained from all the school divines."

Perhaps in some respects this may be considered the
most remarkable feature in the poem, considering the time
in which the author lived. So far as the other sciences
were concerned, Dante was able, with the assistance of
the schools, to dive into their greatest depths and reproduce them in clear and concise forms in one of the noblest
epic poems that ever was composed. But with theology
it was different. Although it was professedly taught in
the schools with the other sciences, it was then the policy
of the Roman Church to keep men in profound ignorance.
Any attempt at reasoning would have been fatal to many
of her pretensions, and it was therefore immediately suppressed at the expense of justice and humanity. In her
sordid love of gain, even the exposition of the funda-
mental dogmas of the religion which she professed to
teach were neglected.

" Per questo [says Dante], l' Evangelio e i dottor magni
Son derelitti ; e solo ai Decretali
Si studia sì, che appare a' lor vivagni,
A questo intende 'l papa e i cardinali ;
Non vanno i lor pensieri a Nazzarette,
Là dove Gabriello aperse l' ali." [6]

Such being the state of things, not only is Dante's thorough
knowledge of the Bible a source of perpetual wonder to the
student of his works, but also that he should have had both
the discernment and the courage to place his finger upon
the real cause of the shortcomings of the Roman Church.
With a reasoning and philosophical mind, he discerned
then what liberal-minded members of the Roman com-
munion have only lately discovered—that the combination of the spiritual and temporal power was never
intended, that the exercise of the spiritual power was
crippled and thwarted by worldly motives attached to

[6] " For this,
The gospel and great teachers laid aside,
The decretals, as their stuffed margins show,
Are the sole study.   Pope and cardinals
Intent on these, ne'er journey but in thought
To Nazareth, where Gabriel ope'd his wings."
CARY'S *Dante*, Par. c. ix. 129—134.

temporal possessions, which choked up the fountain of the Church's life and poisoned its source. In some of the most famous passages of the "Paradiso" Dante protests against the corrupt state of the Roman Church, and this we find put into forcible language by a modern poet, who, apostrophizing Dante, observes:—

> "Tu saettasti il Vaticano, e i sacri
> Sardanapali da l' altar, ingordi
> De la caduca signoria del mondo,
> Inesorato giustizier." [7]

From century to century the echo of this passionate aspiration has been taken up in turn by the great sons of Italy and borne down the course of the world's history. Petrarch, Savonarola, Fra Paolo Sarpi, Rosmini, Gioberti, Minghetti, Curci, and Cavour, these, and many more, have striven for that grand idea of the position of the Roman Church first conceived by Dante, of her influence over the temporal affairs of the world, when uncontaminated by their touch, which would far exceed any yet achieved in the palmiest days of her worldly prosperity, when her throne was established upon ignorance and crime.

At last in 1870 the dream seemed about to be realized by the enforced severance of the temporal from the spiritual power of the Pope, that last link of the fetters by which Italy had so long been enslaved. Then the great Italian Liberals paused in final expectation, while upon the Duca di Sermoneta, the most prominent figure on that memorable occasion, devolved the task of presenting the result of the plebiscite to the king, which, by a majority of over one hundred and thirty thousand votes, gave Rome to be the capital of United Italy. But like all those who had preceded him in the great but hopeless cause, the Duca watched and waited in vain for any sign from the Vatican.

Clinging with sullen obstinacy to the shadow when the substance had been withdrawn, the Papacy would not divest itself of the "pompa Bisantina," which to his mind was so unfitting a robe for the Church of Christ.

He could only sadly compare the Papacy to the Basilica of San Paolo fuori le Mura,—

[7] "Canti di Aleardo Aleardi," p. 118.

" L'antica Basilica era ricca nella sua povertà;
Questa è povera nelle sue richezze." [8]

And when twelve more years had passed by recommend, as a faithful son of the Church, with his last
utterances the cause of truth and liberty to the Pope,
imploring him to recollect—

" Che la religione non si ottiene con gli sbirri." [1]

We now reach the last of the three systems which
form the groundwork of the poem—namely, astronomy.
Here, still pursuing his system of explaining invisible
things by things visible, Dante, by means of the material
heavens, endeavours to represent to our minds the unseen
world of bliss.   Perhaps of all the allegories and metaphors which have ever been employed for the purpose of
turning away our minds from the world and giving them a
glimpse of heavenly things, the elaborate composition of
the Italian poet, when carefully studied, is the most successful.   The beautiful choice of language, the carefully
selected metaphors, the vivid imagery suggested by a
brilliant Italian imagination, all these at first surprise our
minds into the belief of the wonderful conception presented to them, and the illusion once formed is preserved
with consummate art.   All the science the world was
then capable of is brought in to convince our reason, and
make a solid foundation on which to erect the fanciful
and marvellous conceit.   Even the method of progress
through the heavenly spheres is adapted to strengthen at
once the allegory and the illusion.   Beatrice is drawn
upwards by fixing her eyes first upon the sun, and afterwards, as she continues her ascending course, she lifts
them higher and higher up to the throne of God, and
Dante, by fixing his eyes upon hers, which at every stage
of their progress seem to shine with increased brilliancy,
is caught up together with her. [2]

Dante marvels at their rapid flight, and it is explained
to him by Beatrice in the following remarkable passage :—

" Le cose tutte quante
Hann 'ordine tra loro : e questo è forma,

---

[8] "Carteggio, Dantesco," p. 37.   [1] Ibid., p. 36.
[2] Convito, iii. 15.

Che l' universo a Dio fa somigliante.
Qui veggion l' alte creature l' orma
Dell' cterno valore, il quale è fine,
Al quale è fatta la toccata norma.
Nell' ordine ch' io dico sono accline
Tutte nature per diverse sorti
Più al principio loro, e men vicine :
Onde si muovono a diversi porti
Per lo gran mar dell' essere : e ciascuna
Con istinto a lei dato che la porti." [3]

That is to say, every created thing is destined for a distinct end, to which it gradually tends. With man this
destination is heaven. It is, therefore, as natural a consequence as that the smoke should mount upwards, that
when freed from all hindrances such as sin, and the
material incumbrances of the body which confine him to
earth, his spirit should ascend to God who gave it.

And here we would direct the attention of the student
of the " Divina Commedia" to the wonderful description
of the first disembodiment of the spirit which forms so
fitting an introduction to the theme of the " Paradiso :"—

" E quando Lachesis non ha più lino,
Solvesi dalla carne, ed in virtute
Seco ne porta e l' umano e 'l divino.
L' altre potenzie tutte quante mute :
Memoria, intelligenzia e volontade,
In atto, molto più che prima, acute.
Senz' arrestarsi, per sè stessa cade
Mirabilmente all' una delle rive :
Quivi conosce prima le sue strade," &c. [4]

---

[3] " Among themselves all things
Have order ; and from hence the form, which makes
The universe resemble GOD. In this
The higher creatures see the printed steps
Of that eternal worth, which is the end
Whither the line is drawn. All natures lean,
In this their order, diversely ; some more,
Some less, approaching to their primal source.
Thus they to different havens are moved on
Through the vast sea of being, and each one
With instinct given, that bears it in its course."
CARY'S *Dante*, Par. c. i. 104—109.

[4] Cary, Trans. Purg. xxv. 79 *e seq.*
" When Lachesis hath spun her thread, the soul
Takes with her both the human and divine

Almost startling in its simplicity, and yet how far more suggestive is this calm, direct statement, than the many elaborate theories which have since, from time to time, been advanced to solve the awful mystery, and satisfy the strongest longing of which the human soul is capable.

For many a long year Dante was absorbed in the sole contemplation of the world of spirits—a world, it is true, of his own framing—yet by the concentration of his great intelligence upon " the things which are not seen " instead of upon " the things which are seen," his words, when dealing with the invisible world, if they cannot be accepted as absolute authority have still a certain resistless power and weight.   They captivate and convince that spiritual side of our nature to which the whole of the " Divine Commedia " is addressed.

" The subject then of the whole composition, stated simply, is, the condition of the soul after death, because upon this the whole poem turns.

*   *   *   *

" The final object (of the poem), both in its part or as a whole, may be simple or complicated, obvious or remote ; but setting aside all subtle and close speculations, let it be briefly stated that the object alike of each part and of the whole is to rescue men from passing their lives in a state of misery, and to direct them into the way of happiness." [5]

To return to the astronomical side of the " Paradiso." It is scarcely necessary to observe that the Ptolemaical system of astronomy was the only one known in Dante's age.[6]   The " Paradiso " is, therefore, made to correspond exactly with that arrangement of the heavenly bodies.

Memory, intelligence, and will, in act
Far keener than before : the other powers
Inactive all and mute.   No pause allowed,
In wondrous sort self-moving, to one strand
Of those where the departed roam, she falls :
Here learns her destined path," &c.

[5] " Epistola a Can Grande della Scale.   Il Convito e le Epistole di Dante," p. 521.

[6] For further particulars respecting the Ptolemaical system, see Lewis's " Astronomy of the Ancients," chap. iv. sec. 10.

The earth is placed below, in the centre of the universe, and round it revolve, in perpetually increasing and ascending circles, the planets—the Moon, Mercury, Venus, the Sun, Mars, Jupiter, and Saturn. Beyond these he places the starry sphere, or sphere of fixed stars; then the crystalline sphere, called also " il primo mobile," being the primary cause of motion of the other planets; and, last of all, the empyrean, which, in the opening stanzas of the " Paradiso," Dante tells us, partakes more largely of the light of God's immediate presence, and is termed the " cielo quieto," or immutable sphere.

It would have been impossible, taking into consideration the limited knowledge of the age, with its imperfect system of astronomy, to have formed a grander idea of the heavens than that which Dante unfolds to us. Its perfect symmetry is even more manifest when we consider its allegorical and scientific meaning. Proceeding from the centre to the circumference, and gradually increasing in width and in height, the revolving spheres represent the various stages of heavenly bliss, showing the gradations by which the highest may be obtained; and it is a curious fact that this metaphor was adopted by the Jesuit preacher, Il Padre Segneri, in the seventeenth century. In his famous " Quaresimale," the sermon upon the text, " Domine bonum est nos hic esse," treats of the joys of heaven—" Al cielo, al cielo, fedeli miei devotissimo, al cielo, al cielo," are the opening words; and then, after pointing out to his congregation the " curioso viaggio che avete da fare nello spazio minore d' un ora," he exactly adopts the Dantesque arrangement of the spheres." [7]

It is hardly necessary to cite one of our most eminent divines to prove the truth of what Dante advances with respect to doctrine, although, with the characteristic difference between an English and an Italian mind, he does not attempt to describe the means by which these degrees of bliss will be established. Bishop Bull, in his sermon upon " the different degrees of bliss in heaven," observes : " There shall be degrees of bliss and glory in Christ's heavenly kingdom, and the more we abound in grace and good works here, the more abundant shall our

[7] Segneri, " Quaresimale." Predica x. s. iv.

reward be hereafter."[8]   Still more modern preachers have urged that "as the righteous may go from strength to strength here, so hereafter they may go from glory to glory, as one star differeth from another star in glory," which exactly coincides with the prevailing idea of the "Paradiso."

"For Thou rewardest every man according to his work." This text must have been ever before the mind which peopled those nine revolving spheres, and placed in the waxing, waning Moon the wills imperfect through instability ; in Mercury, more veiled from the solar rays than any other star, the wills imperfect through the love of fame ; in that last planet which can be reached by the shadow of the earth (Venus), the wills imperfect through excess of human love ; in the full blaze of the Sun, the centre of material light, the great spiritual and intellectual lights which have guided mankind along the path of knowledge ; in blood-red Mars, those martyrs, confessors, and warriors who have sealed their faith with their lives ; in the brilliant white light of Jupiter, the rulers and judges of the earth who ever kept unsullied the ermine of Justice ; and higher yet, in the calm, cold orbit of Saturn, those minds which rose to heavenly contemplation through the severest self-mortification when on earth.[9]

Dante's powerful mind and fertile imagination, not content with this one interpretation of his subject, took pleasure in working out also another theory, elaborately scientific. He makes the stages of good, whereby we ascend to perfection in the heavenly spheres, correspond with the various sciences which we use as steps in the acquisition of wisdom. Thus the seven first heavens answer to the "Trivio" and "Quadrivio," the seven sciences taught in the schools at that time. Grammar to the lunar sphere, logic to the planet Mercury, rhetoric to the planet Venus, arithmetic to the Sun, music to the planet Mars, geometry to the planet Jupiter, astrology to the planet Saturn. In the "Trivio" were comprised the

---

[8] Bishop Bull's Sermons. Sermon vii., p. 127.
[9] See Tavola vi., "Ordinamento del Paradiso" nella "Materia della Divina Commedia dichiarata in Tavole da Michelangelo Caetani."

three first sciences, which were looked upon as the minor sciences; in the "Quadrivio" the four last. The remaining spheres were allotted in the following manner:—Physics and metaphysics to the starry sphere; moral philosophy to the crystalline sphere (or "primo mobile"); theology to the empyrean. The reasons for this fanciful and curious arrangement are to be found in the "Convito," and, briefly stated, are these. There are three analogies between the planets and the sciences:—

1. Both revolve round an immovable centre. Each of the movable spheres revolves upon its own axis, which remains fixed, and each science presupposes a subject which is the centre of its learning and research.

2. The second similitude lies in the light cast by the one and the other. Each sphere illum'nates visible things, and each science throws additional light upon intelligible things.

3. Both conduce to the ultimate perfection of things. All philosophers agree in thinking that the heavenly bodies conduce to perfection in the generation of material things. In like manner it is by the aid of science that we are able to penetrate so far into speculative truth, in the attainment of which lies our ultimate perfection.

As we advance from one science to another in the pursuit of knowledge, the doubts and uncertainties which obscure our intellects vanish like the clouds before the sun. Dante employs the most delicate and transparent metaphor to describe this gradual unfolding of our minds to the truth, in representing the increased beauty of the expression and smile of his guide, Beatrice, as they mount from sphere to sphere. The light in her eye being the light which wisdom casts upon the mind, and the beauty of her smile the persuasions which wisdom employs, by pointing to the inward contentment and satisfaction arising from the acquisition of knowledge. This, moreover, has a double application when we consider that Beatrice is the impersonification of theology; and the metaphor which represents her increasing in beauty and perfection as she continues her upward flight into the Divine Presence, is intended to convey the idea that the nearer we approach the ineffable subject of our contem-

C

plation through the study of theology, the greater the peace and calm satisfaction which diffuse themselves in our souls.

Such is the brief outline of the general scope and plan of the "Paradiso." It can, however, only faintly indicate its real beauty, having skimmed but lightly over the surface of the vast depths of thought contained in the poem.

But let any one refer to the original, for the study of such dissertations as those on the Liberty of the Will,[1] the conviction of Divine Truth,[2] the folly of rash vows,[3] or of hasty judgments, illustrated by the famous comparison of the ship wrecked at the entrance of the harbour,[4] the inscrutable nature of Divine Justice to mortal intelligence, just as human sight may gauge the depths of the waters from the shore, but in mid-ocean the attempt is futile, still for all that the bed of the ocean is there;[5] the blessed spirits in the fulness of the joy of the Divine Presence compared to the cliff reflected in the waters;[6] the final vision of the Trinity which, as a dream

---

[1] "Lo maggior don, che Dio per sua larghezza," &c.—(*Par. v.* 20.)

[2] "Io veggio ben che giammai non si sazia
Nostro intelletto se 'l ver non lo illustra."
(C. iv. 124.)

[3] "Siate Cristiani a muovervi più gravi.
Non siate come penna ad ogni vento."
(C. v. 73.)

[4] "E legno vidi già dritto e veloce
Correr lo mar per tutto suo cammino,
Perire infino all' entrar della foce."
(C. xiii. 136.)

[5] "Però nella giustizia sempiterna
La vista che riceve il vostro mondo
Com' occhio per lo mare, entro s' interna;
Che, benchè dalla proda veggia il fondo
In pelago non vede; e nondimeno
Egli è; ma 'l cela lui l' esser profondo."
(C. xix. 59, *eseq.*

[6] "E come clivo in acqua di suo imo
Si specchia, quasi per vedersi adorno,
Quando è nel verde e ne' fioretti opimo;
Si soprastando al lume intorno intorno
Vidi specchiarsi in più di mille soglie,
Quanto di noi lassù fatto ha ritorno."
(C. xxx. 109 e *seq.*)

when one awaketh, eludes all power of description, and is
therefore, with consummate art, veiled as a climax too
sublime for human thought or speech,[7] and then judge
if these and other passages of equally unrivalled beauty
do not verify the saying of a brother bard in that same
" bella scuola " of Italian song, that—

> " Il vero condito in molli versi
> I più schivi, allettando, ha persuaso." [8]

---

[7] " All'. alta fantasia qui mancò possa."
                              (C. xxxiii. 139.)

[8] Tasso, " Gerusalemme Liberata," c. i. s. iii.

PETRARCH:

AN ESSAY ON HIS LIFE, TIMES, AND WORKS.

PART I.

" Voi ch' ascoltate in rime sparse il suono
Di quei sospiri ond' io nudriva il core
In sul mio primo giovenile errore
Quand' era in parte altr' uom da quel ch' i' sono;
Del vario stile in ch' io piango e ragiono
Fra le vane speranze e 'l van dolore,
Ove sia chi per prova intenda amore,
Spero trovar pietà, non che perdono.
Ma ben veggi' or sì come al popol tutto
Favola fui gran tempo: onde sovente
Di me medesmo meco mi vergogno:
E del mio vaneggiar vergogna è 'l frutto
E 'l pentirsi e 'l conoscer chiaramente
Che quanto piace al mondo è breve sogno." [1]
Le Rime di Francesco Petrarca, Sonn. i. Part I.

PERHAPS the attempt to compress so interesting a subject as the life and writings of Petrarch into a brief notice of a few pages may at first sight seem presumptuous; more especially when we consider that for the last five centuries there has been no lack of biographies of so remarkable a man. It would add another page to this essay merely to mention their names, and it would take many to enter into any details respecting them. Still, as the writer is more or less indebted for information to their labours, it is only right to mention, as briefly as possible, some of the most celebrated biographies of Petrarch. The Abbé de Sade divides them into five classes :—those who were his contemporaries and began to write before or immediately after his death. The first of these, and the earliest known, is Domenico Aretino. He was invited to Padua, by Francesco da Carrara, at the time when

---

[1] This sonnet and many other portions of the Canzoniere have been admirably translated by Barbarina, Lady Dacre. The collection was privately printed in 1836.

Petrarch, having attained his seventieth year, was living there. Domenico, notwithstanding the direct encouragement which he received from the poet himself, has only left us a short sketch of his life. Coluccio Salutati and Pietro Paolo Vergerio also wrote their biographies at this time, but their enthusiasm for the great genius who had just ceased to exist led them to fill up their pages with vague and indiscriminate praise, neglecting to investigate closely his life and history. They contented themselves with merely copying Petrarch's own " Epistle to Posterity," which source of information has been the natural refuge of all his biographers in every century. It is a curious autobiographical sketch, related with ingenious candour, dwelling more upon the motives which influenced his actions than upon the actions themselves, and describing with unaffected simplicity his abilities, his feelings, and even his personal appearance.

· The fame of Petrarch was at its height at the time of his death. It declined in the fifteenth century. The accomplished Latin and Greek scholars which this age produced set themselves the task of commenting upon the works of Petrarch. They despised his Latin style, and thus the depreciation of his works in that language may have helped to involve the famous Canzoniere in a similar fate. " The fourteenth century," observes Crescimbeni, " we have rightly called an evil century, on account of the cruel maiming of the Italian language by the critics of that time." The third order of biographers was headed by Lorenzo de' Medici, and to it Vellutello, Gesualdo, and Beccadelli also belonged. The coldness and indifference of the preceding century were now exchanged for the greatest enthusiasm. Editions of Petrarch were multiplied, academies formed for the purpose of explaining his works, and the critics of this age would acknowledge no defect in him nor any excellence to exist in a style different from his. But at the beginning of the seventeenth century the fame of the poet was again destined to receive a rude shock. It was at the hands of a certain Giovanni Battista Marina, who, while his own writings were filled with fantastical allegories and extravagant metaphors, cast ridicule upon the simple natural beauties of the poetry of

Petrarch. Unfortunately he had only too many followers.
Petrarch was despised and neglected, his works ceased to
be printed, and were scarcely read, while his biographers
dwindled down to a very small number, although Filippo
Tomasini published his "Petrarcha Redivivus," and
Tassoni critical remarks and observations upon his poems.
The historians of the eighteenth century—the age when
history, and especially the history of literature, was well
written—may be placed in the fifth and last class.
Among these are Muratori and, to mention no other names,
the Abbé de Sade.   His book, bearing the modest title of
"Mémoires pour la Vie de Pétrarque," has ever since its
publication in 1764 been the inexhaustible reservoir
whence the greater part of the information of subsequent
biographers has been drawn.   The value of this work is
especially enhanced by one circumstance, viz. that of the
author having finally decided the question concerning the
family and history of Laura, as to which he has succeeded
in bringing forward such satisfactory proofs that there
scarcely remains room for any further doubt upon the
subject.   This is admitted by Tiraboschi,[2] while, to justify
his countrymen for not having made the discovery before,
he ascribes the success of the Abbé to the free access
which, as a descendant, he had to all the archives of the
House of Sade ; that is to say, of Laura's husband.
Many writers also, not only of his own nation, such as
Tiraboschi, Maffei, Bardelli, Alfieri, and Professor Marsand
of Padua—who collected a "Biblioteca Petrarchesca,"
consisting of 900 volumes illustrative of his history,[3] but
of other nations besides have since written upon Petrarch,
and the subject has been fully treated by Ginguéné in his
"Histoire Littéraire de l'Italie."

The very fact of so much information having been
gathered together concerning him is almost enough to
discourage from the study of Petrarch those who have not
much leisure time at their disposal.   The design, there-

---

[2] Preface to vol. v. of "Storia della Litteratura Italiana."
[3] This collection has since been eclipsed by that of Professor
Willard Fiske at Florence, which numbers some 3000 volumes,
contains the rarest editions of Petrarch, and a copy of every work
which may bear directly or indirectly upon his Life and Times.

fore, of this essay is not to add to the number of
biographies which already exist, but to endeavour to call
attention to the more remarkable events of his life, to the
critical nature of the times in which he lived, and to the
twofold influence, political and literary, which he exercised
over his country.

Before we consider the peculiar aspect presented by the
romantic side of Petrarch's existence, it is well to cast a
brief glance over the times and circumstances of his
country at the time of his birth.

The Italian Republics, which had for a long period of
years been a prey to the violence of faction and the horrors
of anarchy, now sought to unite the discordant wills of
their citizens and to defend themselves from the attacks
of their enemies. Some thought the welfare of the State
was best provided for by giving full power to some one
powerful individual, who, uniting his own forces with the
collected strength of the " Comune," would have sufficient
power at once to repress factions within and repel
hostilities from without. These chiefs were always chosen,
either by force of arms or by the vote of the citizens, out
of the most illustrious families, and by degrees they
obtained complete possession of the cities which had
elected them. Thus, at the beginning of the fourteenth
century the Visconti ruled over turbulent Milan, the
Scaligeri governed Verona, the Carraresi Padua, the
Estensi Ferrara, the Gonzaga Mantua, &c , &c. The
Medici had not yet begun to rule over Florence, which
was, in common with many other of the Italian cities,
torn in pieces by the feuds of the Bianchi and Neri.

Meanwhile the Pontiffs, unmoved, beheld from afar the
discords and tumults by which Italy was agitated.
Bertrand the Goth, Archbishop of Bourdeaux, had,
chiefly through the influence of Philip IV. of France,
been elected Pope under the name of Clement V. ; and
the new Pontiff, out of gratitude to the French king,
transferred the Papal See and Court to Avignon, to the
detriment both of Rome and Italy. " Thus," says
Muratori,[4] " did the Apostolical See pass into France, and
remain there seventy years in captivity, like the captivity

[4] Ann. d' Italia, ann. 1305.

of Babylon, because of its slavish subservience to the whims of the kings of France."

At the beginning, then, of a century which augured most unfavourably for the future of his country, Petrarch was born " at Arezzo, July 20, 1304, on Monday, at the dawn of day, of honest parents, Florentines by birth, although exiled from their native city, of moderate fortunes, inclined, to speak the truth, to poverty." So Petrarch himself describes the fact in his " Epistle to Posterity." His father, called Petraccolo on account of the smallness of his stature, and his mother, " Eletta Canigiani," had been banished from Florence in 1302. It was the year also of Dante's exile, and together with him they had retired to Arezzo, whence on July 20, 1304, Petraccolo and Dante, with the other exiled Bianchi, made a night attack upon Florence, hoping to re-enter their native city by force. Thus the circumstances of Petrarch's birth are in accordance with the condition of his country and times, while they offer a curious contrast to the functions of a peacemaker universally assigned to him during the later years of his life. His early years were passed first at Incisa, in the Val d'Arno. Thence his parents moved to Pisa, where his father anxiously awaited the arrival of Henry VII., Emperor of Germany (the "Arrigo" for whom Dante prepares such an exalted throne in his "Paradiso"[5]), to restore the Ghibelline party at Florence. But the hopes of his party being crushed by the death of this prince, he fled to the Papal Court at Avignon, which soon became the refuge for exiled Italians.

During his father's lifetime Petrarch was compelled, sorely against the grain, to study the law, which in those times was considered the only road to honours and preferment. These studies were pursued at Carpentras, at Montpellier University, and finally at Bologna, then the great school of canon law. His progress, however, in this branch of learning was materially hindered by his early enthusiasm for the classics. His father was at first proud of his son's proficiency in this line, and encouraged his classical taste ; but when he discovered how much it

[5] Par. xxx. 135.

interfered with his more important legal studies, he threw
into the fire all the copies of the classics which Petrarch
possessed, till at length, moved by the tears and entreaties
of his son, he withdrew from the flames one copy of
Cicero and one of Virgil, which he allowed him to keep.

In 1326, the sudden death of his father summoned
Petrarch from Bologna to Avignon, and at the age of
twenty-two he found himself at liberty to abandon those
legal studies which had always been so distasteful to him.
He is, notwithstanding, anxious to explain that the antiquity of the laws, their authority and force, had not been
without attraction for him ; "yet," he adds, "their application had been so much marred and depraved by the
worldliness of mankind, that it distressed him to learn
them, because he would have scorned to make a dishonest
use of them, and an honest use it would have been very
difficult to make, as his integrity would have been attributed to ignorance." [6]   The death of Petrarch's father
was succeeded in a few months by that of his mother.
She died at the early age of thirty-eight, and the fact is
curiously preserved from oblivion by the number of
verses which Petrarch wrote in honour of her memory,
corresponding exactly with the number of her years.
And now Petrarch was to begin his life in Avignon.

. "Beside the banks of that river perpetually swept by
the winds of heaven I spent my childhood, under the
yoke of parental authority, and all my youth subject to
another yoke, that of my own passions," [7] he tells us himself, and the description of the river is borne out by the
old proverb : "Avenio ventosa, sine vento venenosa, cum
vento fastidiosa." The lofty walls of this curious city,
which, built by Clement VI., the fourth Avignonese
Pope, frown over the left bank of the Rhone ; the early
Romanesque architecture of its small but very peculiar
church ; and the tombs of its various Popes, still attract
the traveller who loves to have the past recalled to him,
and to linger over the outward expression of its history.
It is a strange fact that Petrarch was never able to tear
himself for any length of time from a place which is
nevertheless the object of his detestation.

---

[6] Epist. ad Post.   [7] Ibid.

" As for me, the abhorrence that I feel for this city is so great
that nothing can increase it." (Lib. xx. Lett. 14.)

"O my friends, who dwell in the most wicked of all cities." (*Ib.*
Lett. 9.)

" The Rhone swallows up all the honours which should belong to
the Tiber; and alas! what monsters are to be seen upon her banks!"
(Lib. i. Lett. 36.)

"I came on purpose to this most hateful of cities." (*Ib.*
Lett. 13)

" How sorely against the grain am I compelled to remain beside
the banks of the impetuous Rhone, and to sojourn in this most
ungrateful city." (Lib. xiv. Lett. 7.)

"It (Valchiusa) is too near to this Western Babylon, the worst of
all the habitations of men, and but little better than the infernal
regions from whence, with fear and loathing, I naturally seek to
escape." (Lib. xi. Lett. 6.)

Besides these passages from his letters, there are three
famous sonnets[a] against the Court of Rome established at
Avignon, and the first of these is directed against the
city itself :—

> " May fire from heaven fall upon thy head,
> O wicked Court! Thy former frugal fare
> Is now exchanged for luxury and pride,
> The spoils of others whom thou hast oppressed
> With evil deeds which are thy sole delight.
> O nest of treachery! in which is nursed
> Whatever wickedness o'erspreads the world," &c. &c.

Various attempts have been made to explain the abhorrence thus so strongly expressed. One is that Avignon
was connected, in Petrarch's mind, with the death of
Laura. It is observed that the maledictions against the
city date only from 1348, the year in which Laura died
of the plague at Avignon. But this would seem to be
hardly sufficient ground for so specific and continued a
condemnation; and probably a strong sense of the vices
which corrupted the Papal Court then established at
Avignon, to say the least, contributed largely to inspire
the loathing which his language has so fiercely expressed.

Petrarch and his brother Gherardo, the only two
children of Petraccolo and his wife, found themselves at

<hr>

[a] Sonnets xiv., xv., xvi., Part IV. As there are scarcely two
editions of Petrarch which are numbered alike, it is necessary to
state that the references to the Canzoniere quoted in this paper are
taken from the edition published by Bárbera at Florence, 1863.

the death of their parents in very narrow circumstances. The executors of the will had betrayed their trust and seized most of the property, and when the two brothers had collected what little remained to them of their inheritance, they found it absolutely necessary to embrace some profession as a means of livelihood. Imagining that at Avignon, the seat of Papal power and patronage, a means of subsistence would be most easily obtained, he and his brother submitted to the tonsure. They did not take holy orders, and in those days of laxity nothing further than the tonsure was required in order to obtain the highest ecclesiastical preferment. But Petrarch had no desire for riches. "Such is the nature of riches," he says, " that as they increase the thirst for them increases also, and consequently the more room is there for poverty." [9]

John XXII. had succeeded Clement V. in the Papal chair. The corruption of his court was imitated by the town; but in the midst of the general depravity which surrounded him, Petrarch remained uncontaminated. He was strikingly handsome when, at the age of twenty-two, he began life at Avignon: according to some biographers, he was vain of his personal appearance, but this failing lasted only a little while, and he was never tempted by frivolities to neglect his mental improvement.

Being now free to choose his own employment, he returned to his favourite study of the classics, which he pursued in peaceful content, his only anxiety caused by the extent of the vast field of knowledge which lay open before him, and which seemed to stretch to an immeasurable distance the further he advanced into it. He was universally courted by the rich and sought after by the learned, and it was at this time that he renewed the intimacy which he had formed at Bologna with Giacomo Colonna, one of that noble and ancient family whose well-known rivalries with the family of the Orsini make an essential part of the history of modern Rome. The first of the Colonna family in fame and spirit was Stefano, the father of Giacomo, whom Petrarch esteemed as a hero

---

[9] Epist. ad Post.

worthy of ancient Rome. In his distress, when his estates were confiscated and himself and his family banished, he was not an object of pity but of reverence. It is said that on being asked, " Where is now your fortress ? " he laid his hand on his heart and said, " Here." Doubtless this answer was present to Petrarch's mind when he addressed to him the sonnet " Gloriosa Colonna, in cui s' appoggia nostra speranza," [1] and others.

This year (1327) may be looked upon as the close of the first period of Petrarch's life. A new era was about to open upon him. The independence and pleasures of youth were now before him, with apparent liberty to choose whatever career he preferred ; but in the next year the whole aspect of his existence was changed by an accident which impressed a peculiar stamp upon his life, and without which, perhaps, he would never have obtained the fame of a great poet, whatever other celebrity he might have achieved as an orator, a philosopher, or a patriot.

Inside the cover of Petrarch's own copy of Virgil, which is now to be seen in the Ambrosian Library at Milan, we read the inscription to which so much importance has been attached by all his historians. The original is in Latin.

" Laura, illustrious for her own virtues, and long celebrated by my verses, first appeared to my eyes at the time of my early youth, in the year of our Lord 1327, in the morning of the 6th day of April, in the church of Santa Chiara at Avignon. And in the same city, the same month, the same sixth day of April, the same first hour of dawn, but in the year 1348, from this light of day that light was taken away, when I, alas ! was in Verona, ignorant of my fate. But the unhappy rumour reached me at Parma the same year, in the month of May, on the morning of the tenth. Her most chaste and fair body was laid in the burying-place of the church of the Cordeliers at vespers on the day of her death ; but her soul, I am persuaded, as Seneca said of Scipio Africanus, returned to heaven whence it came."

Some may think this simple and touching inscription

---

[1] Sonnets ii. xi. Part IV.

a more remarkable tribute to Laura than all the sonnets
which have immortalized her name. At all events it
strikes the very key-note of Petrarch's future life. It
reveals the source of that stream of beautiful ideas which,
though still the same, flows on in ever-varying metaphors.
All readers of Italian poetry have some acquaintance with
his Sonnets and Elegies, with what his countrymen have
called the "Canzoniere," and the names of Petrarch and
Laura have become inseparable in life and death. No
one can visit that Valchiusa which he immortalized without recalling the long period of years which Petrarch
suffered to be filled by one absorbing thought, one hopeless passion. The question always arises as to whether
his life was wasted ; but, on the contrary, to us it seems
as if the very fact of this all-absorbing interest made the
life of Petrarch an exception to the general rule applicable to the lives of learned men. As the romantic and
poetical sides of Petrarch's character are so interwined
that it is difficult, almost impossible, to examine them
separately, let us begin by considering the lady who
inspired so fervent an attachment that it has become a
matter of history.

Who was Laura ?

There appear to have been three theories respecting
her.

1. That she was not a person at all, but an allegorical
representation of Fame, her name Laura signifying "the
laurel wreath.' But this is at once demolished by
Petrarch's own letter to Giacomo Colonna.[2]

This theory is to be traced to the pedants of the
sixteenth century, who with heavy prolixity poured forth
their admiration by commentaries upon every word of
every sonnet. They sought to extract a hidden meaning
from the simplest language, to spiritualize his meaning, as
they supposed ; and the paradox of denying the reality of
Laura's existence was one result of these refinements.

2. That she was the daughter of Henri Chiabau
d'Ancezume, Seigneur de Cabrières, a little village about
three miles from Vaucluse (Valchiusa). It was the

---

[2] Lett. Fam. ii. 9.

custom of the inhabitants of Cabrières to make a pilgrimage
every Good Friday to visit the relics of St. Véran, which
are kept in the church of St. Véran at Vaucluse. Laura,
according to this custom, went there also, for the same
purpose. Petrarch saw her in the church, was struck by
her beauty, and from that day never ceased to love her.
This theory, first started by Vellutello, has no foundation
except some misunderstood verses of Petrarch, and it is
contradicted by other much clearer passages. It was,
however, believed for some time in Italy; and although
it has been entirely overthrown, there are some people
who still give it credit: witness the pamphlet published
in 1869 by Louis de Bondelon, called "Vaucluse et ses
Souvenirs," which is thrust into the hands of travellers
who visit Avignon and Vaucluse. It contains merely
Vellutello's theory slightly amplified, with the addition of
a good deal of French vehemence. But the best refutation
is to point out the grounds for belief on which the third
theory is founded.

3. That she was Laure de Noves, the daughter of
Audibert and Ermessende de Noves. The House of
Noves, which is of great antiquity, takes its name from
the village of Noves, situate about a mile from Avignon.
At the age of eighteen she married Hugues de Sade, on
January 16th, 1325. Two years afterwards, on April 6th,
1327, at the first hour, that is to say towards six in the
morning (for it was then the custom to count the hours
from the dawn), Petrarch saw her in the church of Santa
Chiara at Avignon, whither he had gone to pay his
morning's devotions. She was dressed in green, and her
gown was besprinkled with violets:—

> " Negli occhi ho pur le violette, e 'l verde,
> Di ch' era nel principio di mia guerra
> Amor armato sì, ch' ancor mi sforza " [3]

Her countenance and her aspect surpassed all human
beauty:—

> " Pensando nel bel viso più che umano."
> Canz. xii. Part I.

Her manner and carriage had a proud grace:—

[3] Canz. xii. Part I. See also Canz. ii.

" Il leggiadro portamento altero."—(Sonn. i. Part II.)

Her eyes were tender and brilliant :—

" Gli occhi screni, e le stellanti ciglia."—(Sonn. cxlviii. Part I.)

Her eyebrows were as black as ebony :—

" Ebeno i cigli."—(Sonn. cvi. *ib.*)

Her golden hair floated on her shoulders :—

" E il primo dì ch' i' vidi a l' aura sparsi
I capei d' oro onde si subit' arsi."

Her hands were whiter than snow or ivory :—

" Man ch' avorio, e neve avanza."—(Sonn. cxxix. *ib.*)

The sound of her voice was soft and sweet :—

" Chiara, soave, angelica, divina."—(Sonn. cxv. *ib.*)

And she was full of grace :—

" Atto gentile," &c —(Sonn clxxv.)

Such is only the outline of the portrait of Laura as delineated by Petrarch ; many finishing touches of exquisite
grace and delicacy are still to be found in his poetry.
That this was the lady who appeared in the church at Avignon, and that that lady was Petrarch's Laura, would seem
to be unquestionably proved by the manuscript inscription in the Virgil, whose authenticity has been further
established by a discovery made in 1795 by the Milanese
librarian, of a continuation of the inscription on the
cover of the book itself. This continuation contains
records, added from time to time in the same handwriting,
of the deaths of Petrarch's friends as they occurred.
When this note was first discovered in the Virgil, Vellutello, perceiving how entirely it overthrew his theory,
took refuge in saying that it was a forgery ; but the
later discovery of 1795 puts a stop to any imputation
of this kind, and the fact is now established by the
unanimous consent of the Italian *calligrafi*, by the
authority of De Sade, of Tiraboschi, and above all of
Bandelli, whose work, " Del Petrarca e delle sue opere,"
was published at Florence in 1837. One other curious
circumstance helps to maintain the truth of this theory
respecting Laura. In 1533, according to the Abbé de

Sade,[4] Girolamo Manelli, of Florence, Maurice de Sève, and Mgr Bontemps, Archbishop of Avignon, undertook to make investigations concerning Laura's family. In their search among all the ancient sepulchres at Avignon, they finally came to the church of the Cordeliers, where Petrarch says in his note Laura is buried. They found in the chapel of the House of Sade, which is in that church, among the tombs, a great stone, bearing no inscription, but two escutcheons obliterated by time, and a rose above the escutcheons. The stone being raised by order of the Archbishop, they discovered a coffin, inside which were a few small bones and a leaden box fastened down with a band of iron. The box contained a parchment folded and sealed with green wax, and a bronze medal, bearing on one side the figure of a woman with the initial letters, " M. L. M. J.," and nothing on the reverse. Maurice de Sève suggested the meaning of the initials to be " Madonna Laura morta *jace* " (the old form of Italian spelling having been used). A sonnet was written on the parchment, which was deciphered with some difficulty. It is supposed to have been written by Petrarch, and begins thus :—

" Qui riposan quei caste e felice ossa." [5]

The news of this discovery having reached the ears of Francis I., King of France, he stopped at Avignon on his way to Marseilles, caused the tombstone to be again raised, and re-opened the box to read Petrarch's verses. He then, himself, wrote Laura's epitaph, which was placed inside the box with the sonnet. If her fame had not already been firmly established, it would have been secured by these graceful lines of the chivalrous king :—

" En petit lieu compris vous pouvez voir
Ce qui comprend beaucoup par renommée,
Plume, labeur, la langue et le savoir
Furent vaincus par l'aymant de l'aymée.

" O gentil Ame estant tant estimée,
Qui te pourra louer qu'en se taisant ?

---

4 Vol. i. Note iv. p. 13.
5 Vol. ii. Note xi, " Pièces Justificatives," p. 41.

Car la parole est toujours reprimée,
Quand le sujet surmonte le disant." [5]

It is right to say that some Italian writers refuse to acknowledge that the sonnet was written by Petrarch, on account of its inferiority to his other poetry ; while others give full credit to the whole story. The arguments on both sides are too long to be cited here, but those who wish to find out minute particulars of the event, with contemporary evidence to support them, have only to look in the places already referred to in the Abbé de Sade's Memoirs. Assuming, then, that Laura's identity with Madame Laura de Sade is proved, it only remains to say a few words upon the character of Petrarch's passion for her.

At the epoch known to artists as the " Renaissance," after centuries of barbarism, despite the corruption and ferocity which still vitiated the manners of the age, there remained an exaggerated sentiment as to the passion of love. The empire acquired by women in the North, by contrast to the slavery of those of the East and South, had become exalted by chivalry into a kind of religion. The Troubadours were one consequence of chivalry, and the poet was as anxious to consecrate his verses to his mistress as the knight to lay at her feet the enterprises of his valour. Hence the " Corti d' Amore ;" and to these courts, which were held in Provence in the time of Petrarch, we owe the invention of his particular species of mystic lyrical poetry.

The manners and customs of the age gave a further stimulus to his already ardent passion, and to write of Laura became, with him, a kind of romance. He differs, however, from the early Troubadours of Italy, the character of whose poetry was often vague and undecided, in the precision of his language : every verse with him is a portrait, of Laura herself, of the places where she moved, of the little incidents of their intercourse. His romance is made up of the simplest events of her life : a smile, a look, an encounter, a passing cloud, a lost glove even, makes an object for his poetry, and enables him to

[5] Sade, " Mémoire·," vol. ii. note xii. p. 42.

D

present us with a series of exquisitely finished pictures. The air, the summer breeze, the water, the trees, the flowers, and the green sward, are, if the expression may be allowed, inspired with life, and personified by Petrarch in order that the most beautiful productions of nature may do honour to the object of his poetry and of his love.

Those who wish to be convinced of the high and noble character of his affection for Laura ought to consult Petrarch himself.

He says, in his "Dialoghi con S. Agostino:"—"Se fosse dato di mirare il mio affetto come si mira il viso di Laura, si vedrebbe che quello è puro, è immaculato al par di questo. Dirò di più; debbo a Laura tutto ciò che sono; salito non sarei in qualche fama, se ella non avesse fatto germogliare con nobilissimi affetti quei semi di virtù che la natura avea sparsi nel mio cuore, ella ritrasse il giovanile mio amore da ogni turpitudine e mi diede ali da volar sopra il cielo e di contemplare l'alta Cagione prima; giacchè è un effetto dell' amore il trasformare gli amanti e renderli simili all' oggetto amato."

The love of Petrarch was the glory, if it was also the torment of his existence; and although it may be scarcely credible that such an utterly hopeless love should have absorbed him nearly fifty years, the nature and constancy of it are painted with a charm, a loftiness of tone, and in such brilliant colours, that raise far above all vulgar and ordinary conceptions this the concentrated passion of his life. His Italian poetry was the result of these highly wrought feelings; and we must not forget that, in the estimation of Petrarch, it held a secondary place, and that he was even surprised at the success which it obtained during his lifetime. He trusted his reputation to his Latin works, and expected to win from those almost forgotten imitations of a dead language the immortality justly due to his poems in his native tongue. Posterity has passed a wiser judgment, and all who can thoroughly understand the Italian language will be of opinion that the "Rime del Petrarca" entitle their author to be considered as the prince of lyrical poetry.

In order to read the "Canzoniere" with proper atten-

tion and interest, the mind of the reader should accompany
step by step the mind of the poet, with reference to the
time, place, and circumstance which give occasion for his
poetry. It is a complete history of his life where it
touches by the very smallest incident the life of Laura.
According to most of the Italian commentators, the
" Canzoniere " may be divided into four parts.

In the first part are placed the " Rime in Vita di Madonna Laura.".

In the second, those " In Morte di Madonna Laura."

In the third, " I Trionfi."

In the fourth, the sonnets and compositions upon various
subjects. The Sonnets in the first part contain some of
the most famous " capi d' opera," but the Canzoni are
considered the jewels of the collection ; and the severest
of Petrarch's critics (Tassoni) is forced to own that
" there is not one of Petrarch's verses which would not
establish his reputation as a poet, but the 'Canzoni' are,
in my judgment, his best claim to honour and renown."
There are twenty-one in the first part : of these, Nos. viii.,
ix., x., xiv., and xv. are supposed to be the most celebrated. The first three of these are called by the Italians
the " Three Graces," and they affirm that there is no piece
of Italian poetry so pure, so polished, and so well sustained. They make altogether one poem, in three strophes
of fifteen verses. The grace and delicacy of Canzone xi.,
" Chiare, fresche, e dolci acque," is so well known that it
is only necessary to mention it by name. Voltaire translated it into French, because he said " ces monuments de
l'esprit humain délassent de la longue attention aux
malheurs qui ont troublé la terre." Canzone xii., apart
from its own merits, contains the description of the green
and violet dress in which Petrarch saw Laura for the first
time. The Sonnets in the first part are 207 in number,
far too numerous to attempt to describe in so small a
space. The two which relate to Laura's picture [6] are
addressed to the Siennese artist Simone Memmi, with
whose painting Petrarch was so enraptured that he exclaims,—

[6] Sonn. xlix. l., Part I.

D 2

"Sure Memmi mine in Paradise hath been,
    Whence came but late the lady of all grace,
    Whom on his canvas he hath sought to trace
    That we on earth might know fair Beauty's queen." [7]

The Ballati, Madrigali, and Sestini, the other varying
forms in which Petrarch clothes his poetical ideas, are
interspersed throughout the first part, but they are seldom
employed in the second, as not grave enough for so melancholy a subject.

If, as it is often said, all true poetry is tinged with
melancholy, the reason for the second part of the " Canzoniere" being preferred to the first is easily explained. We
can more readily sympathize with Petrarch now Laura is
dead. The exalted and romantic nature of his previous
sorrow was hard to understand, difficult to compassionate ;
but there are few who do not know what it is to mourn
a dead friend. Our tenderest sympathies and best feelings are enlisted as we follow Petrarch through his years
of mourning.

"To my belief,"

(he makes Laura say to him, when she appears to him in
a vision,)

"Long time on earth without me thou must live." [8]

And twenty-six years of constant love after her death did
Petrarch add to the twenty-one years which he had
already devoted to her during her lifetime. The Canzoni
of this part, eight in number, are all very beautiful, and
would fully repay a careful study of them, especially the
first, " Che debb' io far ?" Who has not felt the force of
the original lines—

,"Ah me ! that lovely face, prey to the worm !
    Which made earth heaven,
    Pledge of immortal hue.
    Unseen in Paradise now is her form ;
    The veil is riven
    Which o'er her youthful prime its shadow threw,
    Yet to be worn anew,

---

[7] Sonn. xlix., Part I. " Ma certo il mio Simon fu in Paradiso."
Prints of this picture are still -to be procured in the Libraria
Laurenziana at Florence.

[8] "Trionfo della Morte," cap. ii. " Al creder mio, tu stara' in
terra senza me gran tempo."

Radiant and glorified,
And never laid aside,
But everlasting, and mortals descry
That with Eternity Time cannot vie." [9]

And the same deep pathos is to be found in those two Sonnets [1] in which he bids farewell to Laura's earthly beauty. The idea also runs through the third Canzone of this part, disguised under various allegorical forms; and, apart from its own merits, this Canzone is still further interesting from having been translated by Spenser, in 1591, under the title of " The Visions of Petrarch."

The political Canzoni and Sonnets have purposely been passed by in order to speak of them in another place ; it only remains, therefore, to mention the Trionfi. These were visions, a kind of poetry in vogue at that time ; indeed, the whole of the " Divina Commedia " was framed upon this scheme. The Trionfi of Petrarch are six in number :—

1. Il Trionfo d' Amore.
2.   ,,   della Castità.
3.   ,,   della Morte.
4.   ,,   della Fama.
5.   ,,   del Tempo.
6.   ,,   della Divinità.[2]

In them the poet describes the various phases of existence through which a man must pass. In his first state of youth he is beset by the desires of the senses, which may all be comprised in the one term of self-love. But as his reason becomes gradually matured he perceives the unfitness of such a condition of life; he struggles against his desires, and overcomes them by the help of self-denial. In the midst of all these struggles, death comes upon him, and makes the victor and the vanquished equal, removing both from this world. Yet the power of death is not sufficient to destroy the memory of him who, by his noble and valorous deeds, has pur-

---

[9] Canz. i., Part II. " Oimè, terra è fatto il suo bel viso."
[1] Sonn. i. and xxiv., Part II.
[2] The " Trionfi del Petrarca" were painted by Andrea Vanni in the fourteenth century, and are still to be seen in the " Accademia delle belle Arti " at Siena. No. 152 e seg.

chased for himself an undying name.   He lives once more
by that fame—

" Which from the grave recalls the dead, bidding them live again." [3]

Only Time,

" Who with destroying venom blasts great names," [4]

gradually obliterates all remembrance of man's works,
however great or good, thereby teaching him not to hope
for any other undying existence than that blessed eternity
which is in the presence of God, and whose pleasures are
at His right hand for evermore.   Thus man at first falls a
victim to self-love, but self-denial will conquer self-love.
Death will triumph over both, Fame will rescue his
memory from death, but in its turn must succumb to
Time, while Time is finally lost in Eternity.   Of all the
Trionfi, the third, " Della Morte," is by far the most
poetical and the most full of interest.   In it the story of
Petrarch's love is retraced and explained ; and at last,
after the tempests by which his mind was agitated, and
the years of patient waiting, he seems to have found a
haven of peace and rest.   Who would grudge him the
consolation which he finally weaves for himself out of his
own vivid imagination ?   It is so full of power, so con-
vincing in its touching simplicity, that we feel to draw a
long breath of relief as we read it, while we rejoice in
thinking that comfort did come to him in the end.   It
has always been a favourite resource of the Italian poets
to call back the lost mistress from the grave.   Thus, in
the " Divina Commedia," Beatrice is constantly placed
before our eyes, acting and speaking as if in life.   Witness Tasso, when he summons back Clorinda after death
to console her faithful Tancredi ; witness the very instance
we have before us in Petrarch and Laura.   The idea
which runs through the second chapter of the " Trionfo
della Morte " is especially beautiful, and seems exactly to
touch the right chord, when the heart is aching, in times
of deep sorrow.   Not only does Petrarch insist in the

[3] Trionfo della Fama :—
    " Che trae l' uom del sepolcro, e 'n vita il serba."
[4] Trionfo del Tempo :—
    " E 'i gran tempo a' gran nomi è gran veneno."

most moving language upon the continuity of the existence
of his lost Laura in a blessed state of happiness, but he
also dwells upon her unchanged interest in the faithful
friend who is left behind to mourn her death. The following translation can only render in a very feeble manner
the beauty and force of the Italian, but it is inserted in
the hope that it may lead to the study of the original.[5]

" It was the night which closed that day of woe,
In which the sunlight of my life was hid,
And taken back to heaven, whence it came
To guide my erring steps. So I remain
As one deprived of sight, groping my way.
The air was filled, at that first hour of dawn,
With summer's softest breeze, whose gentle balm
Is wont, from off the shapeless dreams of night,
To lift the veil. And there came toward me
Advancing, as it were, from out a group
Of blest, rejoicing souls, a Lady fair
And lovely as the year in this his prime,
With all the fairest Eastern jewels crowned.

" She placed in mine that hand, which I so long
With fondest wish had coveted ; and thus
Created in my heart a fount of joy.
Then sighing as she spoke, she thus began :
' Dost thou discern in me thy friend, thy guide
Who turned thy footsteps from the common way
While yet with gentle sway I ruled thy heart ? '
And thoughtfully in grave and lowly guise
She made me sit beside her on a bank
O'ershadowed by a laurel and a beech.
' How should I not discern my angel pure ? '
As one cast down with sorrow, I replied.
' In pity of my grief I pray thee say
If yet thou art indeed alive, or dead ? '

" ' I am alive, and thou as yet art dead,
And such thou wilt remain,' she answ'ring said,
' Until at length the solemn hour is struck
In which thou too shalt pass from off this earth.
Brief is our space of time, alas ! not suited
To the extent and length of our discourse ;
Therefore, be wise, restrain thy speech, and cease
Ere the day dawn which is so close at hand.'

---

5 " Trionfo della Morte," cap. ii.

" ' We reach at length the end of this estate
Which we call life,' I trembling said; ' and then,
I do beseech thee tell me, since by proof
Thou knowest it, is there in very truth
Such fearful sharpness in the pangs of death ? '

" ' While yet thou followest the vulgar herd,'
She then replied, ' seeking with all thy might
Its partial favour ever blind and hard,
In vain thou mayest hope for joy or peace.
Death only opens wide the prison gate
To faithful souls, setting them free. To those
Whose hopes and wishes grovel in this clay
Nor rise above it, it is bitter pain.
And now my death which doth thy soul so grieve
Would fill thee with all gladness, couldst thou know
E'en but the thousandth part of my great joy.' "

It seems as if there could scarcely be a better conclusion
to the examination of Petrarch's poetical works, all filled
with the name of Laura and dedicated to her honour, than
the words of consolation which he puts in her mouth
after her death.

Such, then, is the story of the romantic side of
Petrarch's life, however imperfectly sketched; but whatever is wanting in the details should be sought for where
it will best be found, in the "Canzoniere" themselves.

Before, however, bidding a final adieu to Laura, some
few points of comparison suggest themselves between the
character of Petrarch's passion for her and that of Dante
for Beatrice. The great poem in honour of the Florentine
lady still retained the attraction of novelty when her
French rival appeared, to claim in her turn the homage
of another marvellous Italian genius, only second to the
great Alighieri. Both Dante and Petrarch were inspired
with the same fervent wish to immortalize the object of
their devoted love, and, in so doing, both obtained for
themselves also an immortal name.

But Dante laid a broader foundation to support his
homage to Beatrice, and on it he gradually piled all the
science then known, transforming her from a frail being
of mortal clay into a personification of the highest truths.
Thus he placed her on a pedestal from which no womanly
weakness could ever take her down. Laura, on the other
hand, is only a woman—most beautiful, if one may credit

Petrarch, and most perfect; but she is nothing more. Even when, in the passage just quoted, she appears to him, she is still no more than the lady of his passionate love, exercising the same good influence after death which she had maintained over him in life. Perhaps the difference between the lives of the two poets may account for their different modes of celebrating their heroines. There is, it must be admitted, some resemblance between the " Vita Nuova " (that early minor work of Dante's) and the Sonnets of Petrarch, the verses of either poet being often inspired by the trivial incidents of daily life. But Beatrice died in early youth; with her expired, in two senses, the " Vita Nuova" of Dante ; and the great work of his riper years, written when the faculties of his mind were fully developed, is purely visionary, unsustained by any external aid. Again, what a contrast does the life of Dante present to that of Petrarch. Both, it is true, were exiles, but Petrarch was born in exile, and was, moreover, pressed to return with honour to his country. Dante, in the full pride and vigour of manhood, was driven from his native city by his ungrateful countrymen, and never suffered to return under pain of being burnt alive. His whole life was embittered by this treatment: it was also often a hard struggle for him even to exist. He knew well, and his proud nature shrank from it,

> " How salt the savour is of others' bread ;
> How hard the passage to descend and climb
> By others' stairs." [6]

The exile of Petrarch, on the contrary, had every alleviation in the shape of a number of devoted friends and the esteem of most of the European princes, who courted him and desired his favour. We may trace these different circumstances of life in the language, as well as in the ideas of their poetry. Discarding the old trammels of the Latin tongue, Dante had the courage to strike out a new path, and create a language which is, perhaps, the most beautiful and certainly the most melodious of all modern languages. Petrarch completed what Dante had begun. He would not have had force or vigour sufficient to com-

[6] Cary's translation. Par. c. xvii. l. 60.

mence such an undertaking, and many of the most hardy and expressive words and figures of speech would never have existed had it not been for the great genius who gave them his name.

But Petrarch was often superior to Dante in taste, though inferior in depth of thought and creative power. The school of poetry which he formed has left an indelible stamp upon the taste of his country; and while much of the enchanting grace and delicacy of the Italian language is due to him, he also gave it a stability which has caused it to remain almost unchanged for the last five centuries.

PART II.

THE romantic and poetical aspect of Petrarch's character has, for the most part, been alone considered by the generality of readers, but it should be remembered that he was actuated by two other powerful passions—the love of his country and the love of knowledge. With regard to the first, we are not aware of the extent of his political influence until we come to investigate his life. Five hundred years have rolled by since his active mind and eloquent tongue have been at rest from earthly labours ; and yet the struggle between the temporal and the spiritual power of the Papal See, which so troubled his mind, has only ceased, if indeed it has ceased, within the last few years. The other struggle for the liberty and independence of his country, which was represented in his time by Rienzi, has been renewed century after century, in all the various phases through which Italy has passed, till quite recently, when, subsiding into quiet and apparent harmony, she has at last become " Italia una," very different from the " Italia mia " to whom Petrarch cried in vain " Pace, pace, pace." [7]

It is a fact worthy of notice that the " seventy years' captivity," as it is called, during which the Papal See was established at Avignon, should have begun one year after

---

[7] Canzone iv. (sopra vari Argomenti), translated by Lady Dacre.

the birth of Petrarch (1305), and, with the brief interval of Urban the Fifth's three years' sojourn at Rome, should have ended just three years after the poet's death. Seven times the Papal chair at Avignon was destined to be filled in the lifetime of Petrarch. The first Avignonese Pope, Clement V., died in 1314 ; to him succeeded John XXII., and in the last year of his pontificate Petrarch thought his hopes were about to be realized, for he announces in one of his sonnets that—

"Burthened with holy keys and Papal robe,
His steps CHRIST'S earthly Vicar homeward turns." [8]

But these hopes were extinguished by the death of this Pope in the following year.

Petrarch, however, undaunted, at once addressed a Latin Epistle to his successor, Benedict XII., imploring him to return to Rome. But neither the description of her ancient glory nor of her present miserable condition could induce the Pope to return, although he rewarded the author of the learned Epistle by the gift of a canoury in Lombez ; while, at the same time, he ordered a magnificent palace to be built for himself at Avignon. He was succeeded by Clement VI., and to him the Romans applied, as they had done to his predecessor, to restore the sacred seat to Rome. Petrarch, at that time in Rome, having just received the laurel crown, was among the ambassadors chosen by the citizens to present their supplication, and the famous Cola da Rienzi was another member of the embassy.[9] Both pleaded the cause of Rome with much eloquence before Clement VI., and Rienzi elaborately exposed the demands of the citizens :—

1. That the Pope should assume the title and functions of Senator of Rome, in order to extinguish the civil wars kindled by the Roman barons.

2. That he should return to his pontifical chair on the banks of the Tiber.

---

[8] Sonn. vi. :—
      "Il Vicario di Cristo con la soma
        Delle chiavi e del manto al nido torna."
[9] There have been many disputes as to whether Rienzi was companion to Petrarch on this embassy, but sufficient reason for giving credit to the fact is to be found in the new Italian edition of Petrarch's letters by Fracasetti, vol. ii. p. 194.

3. That he should grant permission for the jubilee instituted by Boniface VIII.[1] to be held every fifty years, and not at the end of a century.

Petrarch's eloquence was again rewarded by the gift of the priory of Migliarino, but he complains in his letters that he cannot induce the Pope even to wish to see Italy, although he conceded the point of the jubilee every fifty years. The poet gave vent to his indignation against the Papal Court in his letters " sine titulo," in which he unsparingly condemns, with a courage worthy of Dante, the corruption of the clergy and times. The higher the clerical positions occupied, the more vehemence does he display in exposing and condemning the evil lives of those who held them. It was one of his most earnest desires to reform the discipline of the Church, although, like Dante and Savonarola, he had a firm belief in her doctrines. The system of Church government, which had been bad in Dante's time, became much worse, according to Petrarch, at Avignon, which he compares with the Assyrian Babylon for wickedness and corruption. Innocent VI., a French Pope, succeeded to Clement VI. He had no wish to leave his native country, and was deaf to Petrarch's entreaties. Moreover, he thought the Italian poet a magician, because he could read Virgil![2]

But when Urban V., the next Pope, wrote to offer him the canonry of Carpentras, Petrarch seized the opportunity in his reply to implore him to return to Rome, pointing out with severe frankness the manifold evils resulting from the position of the Papal Court at Avignon. This time his entreaties and remonstrances were not without effect, for at Easter in the following year (1368), the Pope, regardless of the complaints of the King of France and of his own Cardinals, who did not like to leave the rich palaces which they had built, left Avignon, and four months afterwards made a solemn entry into Rome. Petrarch hastened to express his joy in a letter of congratulation to Urban V., who invited him to come to Rome. Petrarch was, however, not allowed to see with his own eyes his darling wish accomplished, for, having

---

[1] See Inf. c. xviii.　　　　　[2] Lettere Senili, L. 3.

set out on his journey, he fell ill and was obliged to return
to Arqua. Shortly afterwards he received the further
shock of hearing that the Pope, regardless of the warning
of Santa Brigitta that he would die if he returned to
Avignon, had set off on his return to France, and had
expired immediately after his arrival at Avignon (1372).

Petrarch lived during only two years of the pontificate
of the successor of Urban V. (Gregory XI.), not long
enough to witness the end of the seventy years' captivity
in 1377. In spite of his hardy remonstrances with the
Papal Court, he was constantly offered, by the various
Popes, offices of the highest importance, such as the post
of Segretario Apostolico, which he refused five times.

It is true that he accepted four ecclesiastical preferments
—the canonry of Lombez, conferred upon him by Benedict
XII. in 1335 ; the priory of San. Niccolò di Migliarino, in
1342 ; the canonry of Coloreto in the church of Parma, in
1346, to which was joined the archidiaconate of that
church in 1350 ; and the canonry of Padua, procured for
him by Jacopo da Carrara, in 1349. But he steadily
refused any cure of souls. In one of his letters he observes :
" I never would, nor will I ever, accept any prelacy,
neither any cure of souls, however richly endowed the
benefice. I have enough to do with the care of my own
soul, if indeed, by God's mercy, I am able to suffice to
that."

His political influence was not confined to the Popes
only. As he shared Dante's views with respect to the
Church, in like manner he entertained his opinions as to
the Emperors of Germany. Distracted from one end to
the other by civil wars between princes, none of whom
were strong enough to keep the peace as arbiter—harassed
by factions, desolated by brigandage, which was encouraged
by the nobles, Petrarch saw no hope for the restoration
of Italy except from without; and he echoes Dante's
passionate cry of " O Alberto tedesco,"[3] in his appeals to
Charles IV., Emperor of Germany,[4] to descend into Italy.

[3] Purg. c. vi.
[4] When before his election Charles IV. came to Avignon to obtain
the favour of the Pope, it is said that on some great festive occasion
he discerned Laura de Sade, and solemnly kissed her forehead in the

It was most strange that a private individual should have dared to make himself not only the counsellor but the admonisher and reprover of a powerful foreign sovereign.[5] But the name of patriotism so kindled the soul of Petrarch that he considered it a crime to remain silent.

"In the midst of the universal silence which prevailed." he says in his letter to Urban V., "my conscience urged me so strongly to appeal to the Emperor of Rome and advise his descent into Italy, that I felt I should be guilty of a crime if I remained silent." The reply of the Emperor, which is to be found verbatim in the letters already quoted (vol. ii. 83), justifies the conduct of Petrarch in writing to him. Far from being displeased, the Emperor expresses an earnest desire to know personally the "privilegiato abitator d'Elicona" who wrote to him, while the effect of Petrarch's remonstrances and entreaties is to be seen in his descent into Italy in the year 1354. In reply to the joyful letter of congratulation addressed to him on this occasion by the poet, Charles IV. summoned him to meet him at Mantua. Petrarch was there eight days, and witnessed his negotiations with the Lords of the Lombard League, at whose head the Emperor was now placed. Charles was very desirous of taking Petrarch with him to Rome to witness his coronation; this, however, the poet firmly declined. But, alas the vanity of all earthly hopes, even when they seem to be realized! Petrarch's two chief projects for the restoration of his country—the return of the Popes to Rome and the descent of the Emperor of Germany into Italy—whereby he hoped to reunite the old factions of Guelph and Ghibelline, were both accomplished only to be immediately undone. Just as Urban V. had fled back to Avignon, leaving Rome in a worse condition than he found it, so with Charles IV., who had solemnly sworn to the Pope that he would not sleep in Rome;[6] no sooner was the ceremony of his coronation accomplished in that city than he hastened to leave it and Italy, upon which he shortly afterwards intended to make war. Petrarch was employed as an ambassador by Galeazzo Visconti, to turn the Emperor

presence of all the guests as a tribute to her beauty and her fame. This event Petrarch commemorates in Sonnet clxxxi.

[5] Lett. Fam. x. 2. [6] Historical fact.

from his purpose, and went to Nuremburg to seek him. The Emperor reassured the ambassador by saying that the affairs of Germany were too pressing to admit of his making war upon Italy. Afterwards, in 1357, he invested the poet with the dignity of Count Palatine in its full glory, with all its rights and privileges. It is also on record that he presented him with a golden cup.

Such, then, was Petrarch's influence over the two great powers of the world at that time—the Pope and the Emperor—the " two Suns," as Dante calls them, " whose several beams cast light on either way, the world's and God's." [7] But he was also connected with many other crowned heads and princes of Europe. Robert, King of Naples, was one of his earliest friends, and Petrarch's connection with him is of a literary, not of a political character. When the laurel crown of the poet was offered to Petrarch by the citizens of Rome, he first went to Naples (1341), to the court " of the great and most learned King Robert, who was distinguished not only for his wise government, but also for his great learning," [8] in order to be examined by the King if he were deserving of the coveted honour. After an examination of three days, he was proclaimed worthy. In further proof of his esteem, the King made him his almoner, and took off his own royal robe, which he put upon him, and sent him with two ambassadors to Rome to be crowned. At the death of King Robert, two years later, Petrarch was sent by Pope Clement VI. as ambassador to Giovanna, Queen of Naples, who had succeeded to her father's throne. The young Queen, who inherited her father's taste for learning, was desirous to become better acquainted with Petrarch, and made him her chaplain.

In 1360 he was sent by Galeazzo Visconti to Paris, to congratulate King John of France upon his deliverance from captivity in England since the battle of Poitiers. He was also employed several times as ambassador in his native country. He was the intimate friend of Andrea

---

[7] Purg. xvi. :—
  Soleva Roma, ch 'l buon mondofeo
  Duo soli, aver che l' una e l' altra strada
  Faceaa vedere, e del mondo e di Deo.

[8] Epist. ad Post.

Dandolo, and negotiated a treaty between the two famous republics of Genoa and Venice. The harangue which he delivered on this occasion is preserved as a marvel of eloquence in the library at Venice. Once again in this year, before his death (1373), he went to Venice to arrange the terms of a peace between that republic and his friends the Carraresi of Padua. It was the last service that he rendered his country, whose civil wars he had striven all his life to appease.

In the life of Petrarch, as in the lives of other great men, there are some strange contradictions, and his conduct with respect to the Roman Tribune Rienzi presents a curious contrast to the rest of his political career. In the nineteenth century, when the universal cry is for liberty and freedom from all restraint, no apology is needed for the enthusiasm which the enterprise of Rienzi awakened in Petrarch's breast, and which poured itself forth in the well-known immortal Canzone, "Spirto gentil." [9]

The mind of Petrarch was imbued with classical studies ; he was the fervent admirer of the ancient heroic deeds of his native country, and his affection for her increased the more she was oppressed and torn asunder by civil discords of which he was both the eye-witness and the victim, being through their means deprived of his patrimony and an exile. Proud, moreover, of the citizenship of Rome, which had been accorded to him on the Campidoglio the same day as his laurel wreath, we cannot wonder if, when he heard proclaimed from the summit of that famous hill the restoration of liberty, the destruction of tyrants, the reign of peace and justice—the "buono stato," as Rienzi himself called his new government—he felt so full of hope as to shut his eyes to the uncertainty and peril of the enterprise, and gave himself up, with all the power of his genius and the influence of his name, to bring about its accomplishment. Such revolutions were then comparatively new to the modern world ; their dangerous character, the fearful jeopardy in which they place the lives of the thousands which they profess to benefit, had not then been experienced, as they have been over and over again since ; a good result being

[9] Canz. ii.

the rare exception, and not the general rule. It is impossible, therefore, to blame Petrarch for believing Rienzi to be as high-minded, as disinterested in the love of his country, as he was himself; for thinking him to be as incapable of abusing as he appeared to be capable of using his power. On the contrary, there is much to admire in the disinterestedness which led Petrarch to risk, by his chivalrous defence of the Roman Tribune, the favours and benefits which he had so long enjoyed from the noble and powerful Roman family of the Colonna, whose political views were diametrically opposite to those entertained by Rienzi. Some biographers aver that Petrarch carried this disinterestedness too far, and, forgetting his obligations to the family who had been his benefactors, he wished them sacrificed, in common with the other great Roman families whom Rienzi attacked, to the general good of the cause. In one of his letters there seems to be some foundation for this statement. He writes :—

"As to the two families who are at the head of the present tumult, the first (the Orsini) are no personal enemies of mine ; the other (the Colonna) are, it is well known, not only my friends, but the objects of my deep affection and veneration ; nor does there exist any princely family in this world more dear to me. Yet the Republic is dearer to me than they are, and dearer still do I hold the peace and future welfare of Rome and Italy."[1]

Petrarch, as has been already mentioned, had formed a friendship with Rienzi, when both, belonging to the same embassy, had used their utmost endeavours to induce the Pope to return to Avignon. When, five years later, the news reached him of what Rienzi had accomplished in Rome—that he had driven out the quarrelling nobles, had re-established liberty, had been given a dictatorship by the Roman people, and was ruling wisely and prudently—he thought his fervent longings for the prosperity and grandeur of Rome were about to be fulfilled. He wrote to Rienzi a letter of congratulation, and defended him, at some personal risk, before the Papal Court. Even when the Tribune, intoxicated with

[1] " Lettere di F. Petrarca," vol. ii. p. 192.

success and power, exhibited failings quite unworthy of
the principles by which he pretended to be guided, and
lost partisans while he gained enemies, Petrarch ignored
his follies and continued to correspond with him, imploring him not to betray the cause of liberty and justice.
After the fall of Rienzi in 1348, when, driven from
Rome, he had wandered about from Court to Court, and
had finally been delivered up to the Pope by the
Emperor, Petrarch again espoused his cause. He be-
sought the Romans to come to the assistance of their
Tribune, and on their refusing to help him he finally
saved the life of Rienzi by spreading the rumour that he
was a poet, as it was then considered sacrilege to take the
life of any one belonging to the "profession sacrée."
Despite the failures of Rienzi and his miserable end,
Petrarch never lost the enthusiasm which he had once
felt for him. The charm, however, of his liberal politics
seems to have been dispelled from Petrarch's mind and
to have been succeeded by totally opposite ideas, which
are shown in his entreaties to the Emperor to descend
into Italy. "A democracy," says Mr. Burke, in his
"Reflections on the French Revolution," "has many
striking points of resemblance with a tyranny."[2]

It now only remains to speak of the literary influence
exercised by Petrarch over his country, and how far he
contributed to the revival of literature. He was, in fact,
the first real restorer of polite letters. His fine taste led
him to appreciate the beauties of Cicero and Virgil, and
his ardent enthusiasm for them inspired his country with
a thirst for classical knowledge. With the exception of
Boccaccio, no one else had so keenly at heart the disin-
terring and bringing to the light the long-neglected Latin
and Greek classics. In order to accomplish this, he
wrote to all the learned men of the day, and sought
among the ancient archives of cities and monasteries.
By these means he discovered, in Venice, some of Cicero's
letters, in Arezzo the oratorical institutions of Quintilian,
in Liège two of Cicero's harangues, which he copied with
his own hand (although he tells us the ink was as yellow

---

[2] Burke on the French Revolution, p. 144.

as saffron)[3] because his indignation was so great against
the *amanuensi* of the time, whose carelessness led them
to commit the grossest errors in transcribing. Had it not
been for Petrarch's unwearied efforts, many manuscripts
would have perished, as several had done no long time
before, forgotten and abandoned to dust and vermin in
the monasteries.

The Greek classics were also destined to revive in the
fourteenth century, and the glory of reawakening in he
minds of men the love of Greek poets and orators fell
also to the lot of Petrarch and Boccaccio. The Greek
friar Barlaam, a Calabrian by birth, but long resident in
Greece, and considered one of the most learned men of
that age, was entrusted by the Greek Emperor Cantacuzene
with a mission to Italy. In the course of his travels,
perhaps in pursuit of the Papal Court, he came to
Avignon, where he met Petrarch, who, having heard of
his fame, begged to be instructed by him in Greek.
Petrarch afterwards pursued the study of the language
with Leonzio Pilato, a disciple of Barlaam; but notwithstanding the assistance of two such great masters, he does
not seem to have made much progress, and it was a source
of some disappointment to him not to be able to read
with ease a copy of Homer, a most rare book in Italy at
that time, which had been presented to him by Nicola
Sigeros, Prætor of Romania. Still, although the attempts of Petrarch and Boccaccio were not attended with
any immediate success, yet they excited a desire for
learning, and prepared the way for the real revival of
Greek literature a few years later. It may be that
Petrarch was hindered from attaining to any perfection
in Greek by the careful and life-long study which he
bestowed upon the Latin classics. Cicero and Virgil
were his models both in prose and in verse, and he strove
to form his style upon them in the folio volume of twelve
hundred pages which contains his Latin works. This
style, although far above the common order of Latin then
employed in the schools, is considered inferior to that of
the scholars of the sixteenth century, and the fastidious

[3] Lett. Sen. xv. 1.
E 2

taste of Erasmus was offended by the incorrectness and harshness of his style. Erasmus complains that Petrarch's writings, although full of thought, are defective in expression, and display the marks of labour without the polish of elegance. Nevertheless, whatever may be their demerits, · there is no doubt that Petrarch rendered an incalculable service to literature in pointing out the road to good Latinity. If the great writers of the sixteenth century surpassed him in Latin prose and verse, still the glory must remain with him of being the first of the moderns who discovered the track of the ancients, and pointed out the road by which it was to be followed. The effect of his influence was like that ascribed by Dante to Virgil, the high moral tone of whose writings prepared men's minds for Christianity.

The principal Latin works of Petrarch (the whole are too numerous to be cited in this paper) may be classed under the following heads :—Philosophical Treatises ; Historical Works ; Dialogues ; his Secret, entitled "De contemptu Mundi"—containing various clues to the events of his life, his tastes and character, and his most secret thoughts, but never intended to be made public ; twelve Eclogues, which are covert satires upon the Court at Avignon ; his Letters. In imitation of Cicero, he formed a habit of writing to his friends upon every subject, and although he burnt chests full of letters, seventeen books remain and have been published, making about three hundred letters in number. In these are to be found the whole mind of Petrarch ; they partake more of the nature of treatises than of letters, and they are full of interesting details.[4] They are also most important as a history of the events and manners of his age ; it is, however, to be hoped that the portraits of the Papal Court are overcharged. But whether he writes to the potentates of Italy, the Colonna family, Rienzi, for an instant master of Rome, the Prelates and Cardinals, the Emperor of Germany, or the Popes who succeeded each

---

[4] These letters have been translated into Italian by Giuseppe Fracassetti. They were published at Florence in 1866, with the addition of many interesting notes relative to Petrarch's life and times.

other upon their thrones at Avignon—he still maintains
a noble candour, and that quiet dignity belonging to
philosophy and literature, the influence of which is felt
and recognized even by the rulers of the earth.

His letters to his intimate friends prove that he was
as steady in friendship as he was constant in love. The
" Lettere delle Cose Familiari," which extended over a
period of thirty-five years, he dedicates to his friend
Luigi di Campinia,[5] because " cominciai col tuo nome," he
says in the last of these letters, " finisco con quello ; " and
his friendship for " Lello," the " Lelio " of his letters,
lasted equally long. Both these friendships were formed
at the same time, at the house of Giacomo Colonna, Bishop
of Lombez, the news of whose death reached Petrarch the
same day as that of Laura, and to whom he paid the high
compliment of coupling the two names together in one
sonnet—

" My Pillar's fallen, my green Laurel dead."[6]

He also addressed to him the beautiful Canzone, " O
aspettata in ciel." [7]

Philip de Cabassoles, Bishop of Cavaillon and Patriarch
of Jerusalem, was another intimate friend. Valchiusa,
where Petrarch spent so many years of his life, was in his
diocese, and not far from it the Bishop had a country-
house. He was distinguished more by his talents and the
variety of his learning than by the careful performance of
his episcopal functions, and Petrarch himself writes to
him as " parvo Episcopo et magno Viro." Passing over
many other friends, who cannot be mentioned for want
of space, in 1349 Petrarch became acquainted with
Boccaccio, who made a visit to Milan on purpose to see
his illustrious fellow-citizen. On this occasion Petrarch
presented him with a copy of his Latin Eclogues written
in his own hand, and Boccaccio in return sent Petrarch
from Florence a copy of the " Divina Commedia," which
he had himself transcribed. The reply of Petrarch to
Boccaccio on the receipt of this present is worth reading.[8]

[5] Luigi di Campinia was the " Socrate " of Petrarch's letters.
[6] " Rotta è l' alta Colonna, e 'l verde Lauro."
[7] Sonn. ii. Seconda Parte.
[8] See Lett. Fam. xxi. 15.

He positively denies the charge of envy imputed to him, and reproves Boccaccio for supposing that to praise Dante would make him jealous ; while he excuses himself for not having read the works of Dante, because he feared such a study would interfere with his own project of writing in the vulgar tongue, and that acquaintance with the "Divina Commedia" would make him either an imitator or a plagiarist. The citizens of Florence, in the year 1351, entrusted Boccaccio with the pleasing task of recalling Petrarch from exile, in letters couched in the most flattering terms, imploring him to return to his native city, and restoring to him his confiscated patrimony. The intimacy between the two friends continued up to the time of Petrarch's death, and some affirm that Petrarch's last hours were spent in translating the "Decamerone," with which he was much delighted, into Latin—the purest Italian into indifferent Latin.

His poem called "Africa" is the last on the list of Petrarch's Latin works, although it was one of his earliest productions. It is a narrative in verse of the exploits of Scipio Africanus. The faults of this poem are said to predominate over its merits, and it is scarcely ever heard of or mentioned now. Petrarch was himself aware of its imperfections ; it was painful to him to hear it spoken of, and in his old age he even wished to destroy it. Yet the fame acquired in the world by the first book (dedicated to King Robert of Naples) of this poem procured for Petrarch that crown of "caduchi allori" of which at one time he was so desirous. In the year 1340, on the same day, he received, in his peaceful retreat at Valchiusa, the simultaneous offer of the poet's wreath, from the Chancellor of the University of Paris and from the citizens of Rome. He gave the preference, not unnaturally, to his native country, and was crowned in the Capitol. The Roman Senate revived the custom for Petrarch after many years' disuse. The ceremony was a curious one : the poet walked, surrounded by six of the principal citizens, and preceded by twelve youths of the noblest families of Rome, clothed in scarlet, to the Capitol.[9] After his

[9] This curious ceremony was revived when the fifth centenary of Petrarch was celebrated at Avignon, July 20th, 1874. The *cortège*

coronation there, accompanied by the same pompous attendance, he proceeded to St. Peter's, where he consecrated his laural wreath, by causing it to be hung up in the dome of the church. But now the poem which obtained for Petrarch this extraordinary mark of honour lies forgotten and unread, while his Italian poetry, which he held in such little esteem that he wrote it on the spare eighty-four pages which remained at the end of his Latin works, has been the delight of Italy and of the scholars of other nations for the last five centuries.

In truth —

> " The noise
> Of worldly fame is but a blast of wind
> That blows from divers points and shifts its name,
> Shifting the point it blows from." [1]

Another contradiction, similar to the political contrast already alluded to, in the life of Petrarch, is to be found in the numerous journeys which he undertook, and which could scarcely have been compatible with his love of quiet and solitude. We read of his peaceful retreats at Valchiusa, at Linterno, and, finally, at Arqua. And yet, according to Tiraboschi,[2] this did not prevent him from being the perfect model of a good traveller—" because, in the descriptions which he has left behind him of the countries which he saw, he shows us what should be the plan and the observations of a learned traveller. He describes all the memorable things which are to be seen in Paris, in Ghent, in Liège, in Aix-la-Chapelle, Cologne, and Lyons, the manners and customs which he observed there, their progress in learning, and all the common traditions in vogue."

He has left behind him a beautiful account of his journey through the kingdom of Naples, and the reflections to which it gave rise.[3]   He intended also to visit the Holy

---

of the crowning of Petrarch was composed of persons representing the principal nobles of the time, and lastly there was the triumphal chariot, splendidly decorated, which was received with enthusiasm.

[1] Cary's trans. *See* Purg. xi.:—
    " Non è il mondan romore altro ch' un fiato.
        Di vento," &c., &c.
[2] Tir. v. p. 128.   [3] Lett. Fam. v. 4.

Land, but was deterred by the perils of a long sea-voyage ; nevertheless, he wrote—for the friend who was going there, and who had asked him to accompany him—the " Itinerarium Syriacum," which describes minutely the places he would pass through on his way, and the things which he ought particularly to observe. It was a book which shed much light on the obscure condition of history and geography of those times. Petrarch even went so far as to make a present of the library of books, which he had collected with so much care, to the Republic of Venice, because he found them such an impediment when he travelled, for they were so numerous that he was obliged to hire several mules to carry them, and he could not bear to leave any behind. In return, the Venetian Senate issued a decree that the public money should be spent in buying and maintaining, with all the necessary expenses, a suitable house for Petrarch's sole use, and this house was " Il Palazzo delle due Torri nel sestiere di Castello."

It has been seen that Petrarch was the father of Italian lyrical poetry ; a zealous and earnest patriot, with his country's best interests always at heart ; the restorer of Latinity, whose finest ancient models he rescued from destruction ; the promoter of the study of Greek ; that he was also a man of science. Some writers even maintain that he believed in the existence of the Antipodes before his countrymen discovered them a century later, founding this assumption upon the sonnet in which he describes —

> " The daylight hastening with winged steps,
> Perchance to gladden the expectant eyes
> Of far-off nations in a world remote." [4]

But his fame is sufficiently established without pausing to consider the probability of this supposition.

His life—long if measured by its incidents, although the number of his years was only threescore and ten— was brought to a close at Arqua on the 18th of July, 1374. He died as he had lived, in the pursuit of knowledge and

---

[4] Canz. iv.:—

> " che 'l dì nostro vola
> A gente, che di là forse l' aspetta."

in the improvement of himself and of mankind; for when his servants entered his room they found him dead sitting in his chair, with his head bent over a book.

His personal character was of a most amiable kind. He neither desired nor despised riches. Without conceit he knew his own worth. He loved fame, but was not eager in the pursuit of it. Liberty and tranquillity were most dear to him, and in order to preserve them he refused many a dignified position, and the chance of still greater wealth and power. His habits and tastes were of a most simple nature. Adversity never disheartened him, and the influence of the court and the world never sullied his character, which was firmly established upon the basis of morality and religion. His patience was exemplary, and his vigorous memory never recalled an injury, while his anger was easily appeased. The error of his life, which he acknowledges with perfect candour in his later poetry, arose from the violence and excess of his passion for Laura, which, although it raised the tone of his moral character, absorbed him too entirely.

" Keep the choicest of thy love for God,"

says Dante (Par. xxvi.); and Petrarch knew that in the early part of his life he had not done this; but what can be more beautiful than the concluding lines of his " Epistle to Posterity " ?—

"And now I make my prayer to Christ, in order that He may sanctify the close of my earthly life, that He may have mercy upon me and pardon the sins of my youth, remembering them not. . . . And with an earnest heart I pray that it may please God, in His own good time, to guide my long erring and unstable thoughts; that as hitherto they have been scattered over many earthly objects, they may now be centred in Him, the One true, unchangeable, certain, and Supreme Good."

ADDENDUM.

Since this essay was first printed, Capponi has published his " Storia della Republica di Firenze," and the following

passage from it is given in a translation as an evidence
of the esteem in which Petrarch is now held in Italy :—

"I consider Petrarch, in so far as regards poetical
expression, a perfect writer in his own language. He
neither errs in artificial ornament nor does he fall into
the opposite extreme of a studied brevity. He is guided
by a wonderful temperance of judgment which withholds
him from ever straining beyond the power of his graceful
poetical genius.; on the other hand he never descends from
that serene elevation of thought inspired by the noble
character of his love, by a disposition naturally virtuous
and an intellectual life fed and nurtured by constant study.

"His writings are a record of affections which, ever
present to his mind, are bidden by his poetical fancy to
overflow thence in a stream as of living water, not with
the impetus of the strong passions which make the utterances of Dante boil, seethe and foam, but, while instinct
with vivid imagination and feeling, they are still restrained by the practised skill which he knew so well how
to summon to his aid in expressing his thoughts.   Hence
it is that the writings of Petrarch have always a peculiar
ease and grace, nor does he ever seek to dive into the
depths of our idiom. . . . In his Rhymes there is never
a word or form of speech which cannot now be used
without affectation.

.   .   .   .   .   .

"Throughout his life no one was less a Florentine or
more an Italian than he was.   He made himself the
citizen of Italy because he would not belong to one particular place.   He was neither Guelph nor Ghibelline,
and in the public events of his country he took no part
except to censure generally the vices by which it was
disturbed.   He fixed his gaze on ancient Rome, whose
literature he strove to revive, and made himself what was
at that time a new discovery, the life of a man of letters,
hence his fame and a tranquil existence, undisturbed by
the hatred and strife which he persistently shunned.
His fame lives by the "Canzoniere," for the great
mass of his compositions in the Latin tongue, including
the letters which he called 'familiari,' are merely exercises
of scholarship.   Yet in his own time these works also were

highly esteemed for the tone of calm judgment which is never absent from his compositions, the noble character of his thoughts, and the love of learning to which the revival of the ancient classical glory of Italy was mainly due." — *Capponi, Storia della Republica di Firenze,* vol. i. lib. iii. c. ix.

TORQUATO TASSO:

His Life and Works.

PART I.

" For I have battled with mine agony,
And made me wings wherewith to overfly
The narrow circus of my dungeon wall,
And freed the Holy Sepulchre from thrall,
And revel'd among men and things divine,
And pour'd my spirit over Palestine,
In honour of the sacred war for Him,
The God who was on earth and is in heaven;
For He hath strengthen'd me in heart and limb.
That through this sufferance I might be forgiven,
I have employed my penance to record
How Salem's shrine was won and how adored."

               Byron, *Lament of Tasso.*

It is a painful reflection that it is almost always a melancholy task to chronicle the lives of the poets. They seem in so many cases, either from outward circumstances or from physical infirmities, to have been selected as the especial victims of " fortune's freaks unkind."

The prince of poets—the " signor dell' altissimo canto, che sovra gli altri com' aquila vola "[1]—affords us the first proof of this melancholy truth ; and, unhappily, many more examples might be found in the lives of those who followed most closely in his path to fame.

But perhaps above all, the subject of this essay has the greatest claim to our compassion ; certainly of all the four classical poets of Italy he was the most unfortunate. He was not made of that stern stuff which enabled Dante with fierce hardihood to endure the rude shocks of

---

[1] " The monarch of sublimest song,
That o'er the others like an eagle soars."
               Inf. iv. 90, 91.

fortune, while his great intellect supplied him with a keen weapon wherewith to take a sharp and everlasting revenge upon his enemies. Alas ! the " gentile cavaliere," the sensitive, chivalrous Tasso, was only too susceptible of the great sorrows in store for him. -

There have been many records of his troubled existence, and great writers both in verse and prose have found it a theme worthy of their best efforts. The following sketch has been compiled from some of these standard works,[2] more in the hope of inducing the reader to pursue, either in them or in Tasso's own beautiful writings, the study of the poet's life, than with any expectation of doing justice in its brief scope to so great a subject. It may, however, acquire some new interest from a recent poem entitled "Torquato Tasso a Sant' Anna,"[3] which adds yet a few more touches of tender feeling to this pathetic episode of Tasso's life.

TORQUATO TASSO was born at Sorrento on the 11th of March, 1544 ; but three other cities of Italy claim a share in the production of so great a genius—Bergamo, the seat of his paternal ancestors for many generations ; Naples, the residence of his mother's family and the scene of his early education ; Ferrara, his home during twenty years of his life.

The parents of Tasso were descended from the most ancient families of Italy. That of his father, Bernardo, may be traced back to the twelfth century, when the family of the Tassi possessed an estate named Almenno, about five miles from Bergamo. Driven thence by the wars to which Italy was a constant prey, they sought refuge among the mountains of the valley of the Brembo. Here they reared a fortress on a rocky eminence called Il Cornello, and became feudal lords of the territory. This mountain was called "La Montagna del Tasso."

[2] Manso, " Vita di Tasso ; " Serassi, " Vita del Tasso ; " Muratori, " Storia della Perfetta Poesia ; " Il Quadrio " Storia e ragione d' ogni Poesia ;" Tiraboschi, " Storia della Letteratura Italiana ; " Maffei, " Orazione in lode di Torquato Tasso " (1596) ; " L' Italia Letteraria Artistica." Ginguéne, " Hist. Littéraire de l'Italie " Milman's " Life of Tasso," &c., &c.

[3] By Riccardo Ceroni, published at Milan, 1874.

It is a disputed point with Italian biographers whether the Tassi, originally a branch of the Torreggiani of Milan, first took their name from this mountain, or whether the family name of Tasso did not exist some two centuries previous to their occupation of the fortress. It is not a matter of great importance; and it is only necessary to observe that the family of the Tassi adopted the former of these two theories.

Their first distinction was due to the re-establishment of the ancient system of posts, the generalship of which in Italy, Germany, Flanders, and Spain was committed to Omodeo de' Tassi in 1290. For many generations this honour was transmitted to his descendants. Hence the family arms of a courier's horn and a badger's skin (Tasso being the Italian for badger), which the post-horses used in former times to carry on their frontlets.

Many branches of the family tree spread as far as Naples, Rome, and Venice; but the most direct shoot of the ancient stock is said to be that from which sprang Bernardo, the father of the poet. Bernardo married, in his forty-eighth year, Porzia dei Rossi, of an ancient family of Pistoia, at that time recently transplanted into Naples, where they had great possessions. Torquato was their only surviving son. One other son they had who died a few days after his birth, and a daughter, Cornelia, born two or three years before Torquato, and to whom he afterwards fled for refuge in the time of his sorest need.

The education of Torquato in his early years was chiefly thrown upon his mother, for at three years old his father was obliged to entrust him to her sole care.

For twenty years Bernardo had been the secretary and faithful follower of Sanseverino, Prince of Salerno. He supported him in his attempt to resist the establishment of the Inquisition in Naples by the viceroy; he accompanied him on his embassy to the Emperor Charles V., the first time when he returned having successfully accomplished his mission; and the second, when, warned of the intended treachery of the Emperor, Sanseverino transferred himself and his services to the French king, Henry II., Bernardo did not hesitate to follow him to

France, sharing the exile and confiscation of property which that step brought upon him.

He little thought, when he left his wife and young son in the Palazzo de' Gambacorti at Naples, that this would be the end of his embassy, and that loyalty to his master would make his return thither for ever impossible.

There was indeed a scheme for another French invasion of Naples, of which Sanseverino was appointed by Henry II. commander-in-chief; and, had it been successful, Bernardo was to have obtained the recovery of his property. But the scheme failed. The French fleet did not arrive in time to effect a combination with the Turkish squadron for the joint attack of both fleets upon Naples. Sanseverino set off in a vain pursuit of his faithless allies to Constantinople, the attention of the King of France was diverted by the war in the Low Countries, and the conquest of Naples was abandoned.

Disheartened and ruined, Bernardo returned from Paris, where he had vainly tried to revive the king's zeal for the Neapolitan enterprise, to Rome, and thither he summoned his wife and children to join him.

Meanwhile Torquato, under the care of D. Giovanni d' Angeluzzo, the master chosen for him by his father before setting out on his hapless expedition, early began to give promise of those rare abilities with which nature had gifted him. These were next developed in the Jesuits' school, one of the first established in Naples, opened in 1551. Torquato was then in his seventh year. His ardour for study was so great, Manso affirms, that he would get up before it was light, so that his mother was to have him conducted with lighted torches to the school. His progress in Latin and Greek was so surprising, that when ten years old he is said to have composed in both these languages, and to have recited his compositions in public. To the same early instructors of his youth may be attributed those deep-seated religious convictions which guided him through life, supported him in his deepest misery, and prompted the poem which won him an immortal name.

From the school where he was thus happily pursuing the paths of learning he was summoned by his father to

Rome ; but the pang of parting with his mother, who had hitherto tenderly watched over him, was very bitter. His grief was poignant, and so indelibly stamped upon his mind, that not even the great troubles of his after-life could ever efface it ; for when these were at their height, after his second flight from prison, not his present suffering, but this early sorrow is recorded in the sonnet which he wrote on that occasion.

Bernardo's wife was prevented from joining him at Rome by the harsh conduct of her brothers, who refused to pay her dower, and would not suffer her to leave Naples. The position of her husband as a declared rebel made it impossible for Porzia to take any steps to recover her fortune ; nor could Bernardo enter the kingdom to rescue his wife. At length, unable, either by tears or entreaties, to move her tormentors, Porzia was obliged to resign herself, and to escape further persecution she took refuge with her daughter Cornelia in a convent. Bernardo was only reconciled to this step by the hope of being able to rescue her at some future time. But this never came to pass. The unhappy lady died of a broken heart two years after her enforced separation from her husband (1556).

Torquato arrived in Rome in 1554. His father, already affectionately proud of his proficiency in learning, now placed him under the direction of Maurizio Cattaneo, one of the first and most learned masters in Italy—a gentleman in manner, and free from pedantry. But Rome did not long continue a safe abode for Bernardo and his son. A fierce war broke out between the Pope, Paul IV., and Philip II. of Spain, and Bernardo, finding it a hopeless task to regain his Neapolitan possessions, retired to the court of the Duke of Urbino. Torquato went with him, and remained at the court two years, sharing the instructions of the young prince Francesco Maria, until his father, who had, during this time, been engaged in completing a poem, the "Amadigi," was invited by the great Venetian academy "Della Fama" to have it printed at the Aldine Press, then under the direction of Paolo Manuzio. Bernardo repaired to Venice with all speed, and was appointed secretary to the "Accademia." He did not hold this office long, the duties being of a tedious and laborious character; and he quitted his post just in time to save himself from the ruin brought on the whole academy by the fraudulent conduct of its founder, Federigo Badoaro. This catastrophe prevented the printing of the "Amadigi" by the Aldine Press; it was confided instead to the hands of Gabrieli Giolito, and published, in 1561, with a dedication to the "Invittissimo e Cattolico Re Filippo II.," as a last hope of inducing the Spanish court to restore to the author his forfeited estates. The "Amadigi," though tedious, is supposed to have some merits; and Bernardo might have been considered a poet, if his son had not written the "Gerusalemme Liberata."

Torquato had been with his father during his sojourn at Venice, and had specially devoted himself to the perusal of his native classics—Dante, Petrarca, and Boccaccio; and the fruit of these studies appears in the polished and masterly style of his great poem. He was next sent to study the law in Padua, under the guidance of Scipione Gonzaga. These legal studies were pursued with such conscientious diligence, that in his seventeenth year he took his degree in civil and canon law. Nevertheless, they were as distasteful to the young Torquato as they had been to Boccaccio, Petrarca, and Ariosto. In his case, as in theirs, the stern study of the law was powerless to quench the inextinguishable spark of poetic fire. That same year (1562) the "Rinaldo" appeared, which created an extraordinary sensation in Italy, and covered "Il Tassino" (as he was called to distinguish him from his father) with distinction. But in a short space of time it was so entirely eclipsed by the "Gerusalemme Liberata," that Tasso himself scarcely counted it among his works. Serassi, quoting Menage, observes "that the "Rinaldo" is the work of a youthful poet, but that poet is Tasso; just as Longinus said the "Odyssey" was the work of an old man, but that old man was Homer."[4] The chief professors of the University of Padua thought so highly of this poem, that they pressed Bernardo to allow his son to publish it immediately. The learned members of the various literary academies which at that time

4 "Vita del Tasso," lib. i. 117.

abounded in Italy expressed their approval, either in letters or sonnets, to the young poet, who, stimulated by their approval, could no longer resist his natural inclination, and resolved to detach himself henceforth from legal studies, and give his undivided attention to the pursuit of poetry and philosophy.

The fame of his " Rinaldo " procured Tasso an invitation to the University of Bologna from the president, Pier Donato Cesi, who was trying to revive the ancient glory of the university, and, by the offer of large stipends, induced the distinguished professors of the day to give lectures to the pupils, while he undertook the charge of the colleges and schools, which had fallen into decay. Tasso attained ` to much distinction, disputing and lecturing in the public schools, especially on the subject of poetry. He laid down those rules and principles of an heroic poem which afterwards guided him in the composition of the " Gerusalemme Liberata." He likewise attended Sigonio's public lectures on the "Poetics" of Aristotle, and the private instructions, in philosophy, of Sperone, Piccolomini, and Perlasio.

His sojourn at Bologna was cut suddenly short by a disturbance of which he was unjustly the victim, and which appears to foreshadow, in some sort, the kind of persecution which pursued him all his life. The dangerous weapon of satire, frequently employed by the students of the university in attacking either each other or the professors, or sometimes the great noblemen of Bologna, had, as yet, never brought any retaliation upon those who employed it. Tasso, for no apparent reason, was selected as the first victim of a severer rule. A playful satire upon some gentleman of Bologna, in which he included himself (the ridicule, in reality, centring on his own head), ex- . posed him to a visit from the police, who searched among his papers for the offending squib; and this not being forthcoming, his other papers were seized and laid before the magistrates. The high spirit of Tasso could not brook this insult, and after justifying himself against the harsh and ill-founded accusation, in an indignant letter to his father, he turned his back on Bologna, and returned to his former friends at Padua. The Paduan Academy of the " Eterei " (Ethereals), of which he was a member, welcomed him with joy, and he, after the fashion of the academicians, who each took some nickname or other, chose that of " Il Pentito " (The Penitent), to denote his sorrow at having ever forsaken their society, and pursued with renewed vigour his favourite researches after poetry.

He had already conceived the scheme of the " Gerusalemme," and on this all his studies were made to centre, gathering as it were from each science the choicest flowers wherewith to adorn and enrich his poem.

At length his studies at Padua were completed, and Tasso hastened to join his father at Mantua, to whom he communicated the scheme of his new poem, and showed him at the same time the three discourses on the art of poetry, which he had prepared to help him in the treatment of his subject. Bernardo generously admitted the probable superiority of his son's poem to his own, inasmuch as he had ministered to the popular taste by a series of romances, while Torquato had followed the footsteps of Homer and Virgil in limiting his poem to a single action. Meanwhile the hopes placed by Bernardo in the King of Spain had proved fruitless, and it behoved him, though with sore reluctance, to endeavour to secure a place at some one of the courts for his son Torquato, as his only means of subsistence. Had it not been for his own bitter experience of the unsatisfactory and precarious life of a courtier-poet, Bernardo might have been tempted by the brilliant spectacle presented by the courts of Italy in the sixteenth century. It seemed as if each and all of these had one common object in view—the protection and encouragement of all branches of art, literature, and science ; in short, that their chief aim was to encourage and stimulate the young genius of Italy.

It was the age of art, poetry, painting, and architecture, combined to illustrate all that was beautiful in men's eyes. Titian, Tintoretto, and Paolo Veronese, had succeeded Michael Angelo and Raffaello ; Palladio was beginning to erect the stately architecture which has ever since borne his name ; while the new poem of the " Rinaldo " gave promise that another name would soon be added to the classical poets of Italy.

It was the age of science. Sarpi had recently composed his admirable " History of the Council of Trent," which had occupied theologians for many years. Music, mathematics, philosophy, and astronomy, were being developed by the Galilei, both father and son, Doni, the musician and mathematician, Sigonio and Robertello, and many others.

Such was the scene upon which the young Tasso was destined to play no insignificant part. He had already proved himself worthy to claim a place in that brilliant assembly of genius and intellect, and had given a pledge that he would shine as a star in any one of those gay courts which should be fortunate enough to secure him.

But Bernardo knew that the Italian princes were as capricious in withdrawing as they were magnificent in bestowing their favours, that their courts were full of unscrupulous courtiers and petty intriguers. He had hoped that his son's legal studies would have placed him in a position of honourable independence ; but Tasso refused to enter the law, and his father did not know how to maintain his son otherwise than by placing him at the court of one of the Italian princes. Already there was a rivalry between the two brothers, the Cardinal Luigi d Este and Alfonso II., the reigning Duke of Ferrara, which should claim the young poet. On the one hand, the cardinal urged the first right of possession in the poem of " Rinaldo," already dedicated to him ; on the other hand, the duke wished, by offering Tasso a place at his court, to claim a right in the forthcoming greater poem.

For some time Tasso declined to enroll himself among the gentlemen of either prince, professing equal service and duty to both the duke and the cardinal. At length, in 1565, he was invited to Ferrara by both brothers, with the intimation that he would for the present belong to the. cardinal's household, and that he was to meet his patron at Ferrara in December, to be present at the marriage of the duke with Barbara, Archduchess of Austria.

Tasso was in his twenty-first year when he arrived at Ferrara, in October, 1565. Look at him now—for in a

few short years we shall have a more painful picture to
contemplate. If we study the account of him by his
friend and contemporary biographer, Manso, we shall find
that his face bore the stamp of great intellectual power in
the high, noble forehead, the grey, thoughtful eyes and
their melancholy beauty of expression. His features were
regular and well cut, his hair of a light brown. He was
above the average height, well-built, with strong agile
limbs, that yielded to none in fencing, riding, and all
manly exercises; and his presence was such as might
grace any court.

The first years of his life at Ferrara were peaceful and
happy; he looked back upon them with longing eyes, and
could not be persuaded, until he had learned it from
bitter experience, that misery and danger awaited him
there. The city was gay with the festivities of the
approaching wedding when he first entered it; the preparations for the tournament and all the accessories of the
brilliant scene charmed the poet's fresh youthful fancy.
He was courteously received, and apartments were assigned
to him in the house of his patron, where he could finish
his great poem, of which the first six cantos were already
complete.

The court of Ferrara was at that time a splendid
specimen of Italian magnificence, and the Este, without
tracing back their genealogy to the fabulous origin
assigned to them by Tasso and Ariosto, were among the
most ancient families in Italy. The sisters of the duke—
Lucrezia, who afterwards married the Duke of Urbino,
and Leonora—were the chief ornaments of this court.
The reputation of their beauty had already reached
Tasso, and in his " Rinaldo "⁵ he had celebrated the " crin
d' oro," and the "chiare luci " of Lucrezia d' Estense. At
the time of his introduction at court, the one sister was in
her thirtieth, the other in her thirty-first year. They were
ladies 'of cultivated minds, and Tasso's great abilities
were already known to them. They admired the poetry
which he had already written, and greatly encouraged
him to finish his "Gerusalemme Liberata," while they
shared the high expectations which the promise of this

⁵ Canto viii. 14.

poem had already excited in Italy. It was surely no
wonder if one so gifted soon became the favourite companion of their leisure hours. He read to them portions
of his poem, asking their opinion on different points, and
wrote sonnets in praise of their beauty and various gifts.
'They unite," he says in one of his letters, "discernment
with intellect, majesty with courtesy, so that it is difficult
to determine for which of these qualities they are most
to be admired." His was not a nature to be insensible to
their courtesies, or to the pleasures of an existence which
in every way commended itself to his refined taste.

This pleasant stream of life might have flowed on in an
uninterrupted course, had it not been impeded by his
fatal passion for the Princess Leonora. Unhappily he
was early captivated by her rare beauty and many at-
tractions, and she became the object of the devotion and
admiration natural to a person of his eager enthusiastic
disposition. He commemorated in a canzone the first
occasion on which he saw her, and there is no doubt that
the episode of Olinda and Sofronia, in the "Gerusalemme,"
is intended to represent her and himself.

> " She fair, he full of bashfulness and truth,
> Loved much, hoped little, and desired nought;
> He durst not speak, by suit to purchase ruth,
> She saw not, mark'd not, wist not what he sought;
> Thus loved, thus served he long, but not regarded,
> Unseen, unmark'd, unpitied, unrewarded. ' [6]

In vain did the friends of Tasso endeavour to make
him withdraw this episode, pronouncing it to be disconnected with the rest of the poem. He always steadily
refused to do so. His letters, his canzone, his treatises,
all bear witness to the truth of this hopeless and ill-fated
attachment, and are full of the praises of Leonora, whose
name he thus masks under a play of words :—

> " E le mie rime,
> Che son vili e neglette se non quanto
> Costei *le-onora* col bel nome santo,"

just as Petrarch would play upon the name of Laura,
presenting her under various images, now as the emblem
of fame, and now as the fresh breeze (l' aura).

[6] " Gerusalemme Liberata," Fairfax's translation, book ii. c. 16.

Tasso, aware of the danger to which this passion exposed him from the proud house of Este, feigned an attachment for a lady of the court, Lucrezia Bendidtio, to mask the real state of his feelings. In so doing he became the rival of Pigna, the duke's private secretary; and thus in avoiding one peril fell into another. He is also supposed, in his early youth, to have had another attachment to a young lady of Mantua, Laura Peperara, whose name is often mentioned in his sonnets; but it appears from incontestable evidence, as will be seen later on, that his passion for the Princess Leonora was never absent from his mind, that, in fact, it was the rock on which his life made shipwreck.

For many years he succeeded in concealing from everybody the real state of his mind, discussing in the Academy of Ferrara with calm philosophy the abstract questions, which had revived the old "Corti d'Amore" of Provence, and holding the lists for three days against every comer, in his "Fifty Conclusions on Points of Love." Twenty years afterwards he rearranged his "Conclusions" in a dialogue, called "Il Cataneo,"[7] which is considered a masterpiece among his prose writings.

The first seven years of his life at Ferrara, the happiest of Tasso's existence, were passed chiefly in the city, except when, on the occasion of the duke's absence, he paid visits to his literary friends at Padua, Milan, and Pavia, or to Mantua to visit his father.

Bernardo Tasso was subsequently appointed, by the Duke of Mantua, governor of Ostia, whither Tasso was summoned to attend him on his death-bed, September 4, 1569. Bernardo was happy in his death, for he lived long enough to see the first dawn of his son's fame, while he was spared the knowledge of the misery in store for him. The affection between father and son is a very touching trait in the lives of both. Bernardo never hesitated to admit the superiority of his son's poetical genius; and Torquato, on the other hand, never forgot this generosity, and held his father's opinion in the highest esteem.

In 1572 Tasso was called upon to attend his patron,

7 Vol. viii. 321.

the Cardinal d' Este, to France. Previous to his departure he made his will, "because," he said, "life is uncertain, and it might please God that I should never return from France." He bequeathed the completed portions of his "Gottifredo," as he called the "Gerusalemme Liberata," to the care of his three friends, Scipio Gonzaga, Domenico Veniero, and Battista Guarini, to be revised, corrected, and published. The rest of his unpublished poetical works, the "Canzoni" and "Madrigali," he directed to be buried with him ; and all his goods to be sold, that the profits might be employed in putting up a monument to his father in the church of San Egidio at Mantua, with a Latin inscription which he had himself prepared, as a last act of filial love and duty.

Tasso was presented by the Cardinal d' Este at the French court, as the bard who was about to celebrate the feats of arms of Godfrey de Bouillon, and the other French heroes of the first Crusade. His fame had already preceded him, and he was received with every mark of favour and distinction. Charles IX., the reigning monarch, with all his faults, was a patron of literature, and had some pretensions to being himself a poet ; he was therefore quick to appreciate the privilege of receiving at his court the first poetical genius of Italy. During his sojourn of a year at Paris, Tasso was introduced to all the eminent *litterati* of the day, and made the acquaintance of Ronsard, of whose poetry he had long entertained a high opinion.

France was at that time distracted by the Huguenot wars, and the crisis of "St. Barthélemi" (1572) was approaching. Tasso, whose early education had implanted in his mind a horror of schism, and an unquestioning belief in the doctrines of the Roman Church, wrote a treatise expressing his opinion that the heresy of the Huguenots should be uprooted with unflinching severity ; but the massacre of St. Barthélemi did not take place till some months after his departure from Paris. He also wrote a description of French manners and customs, comparing Paris with Milan and Venice, to the disadvantage of the former of these two cities, while as far as regards the latter he declares it to be difficult to decide whether of the two, Paris or Venice, is the most rich and prosperous.[8]

On his return from Italy Tasso quitted the service of the Cardinal d' Este. Some writers aver that the cardinal was jealous of the favours heaped upon the poet by the French king. But this is not proved; we only know that for some reason or other Tasso abandoned the court of his former patron, and lived for a short time at Rome, in a state of great poverty. The cardinal does not appear to have been very liberal to the gentlemen of his court. The goods which Tasso mentioned in his will, to be disposed of after his death, were in pawn at the time, and there is reason to fear that when he was in Paris he was often in great destitution, though he steadily refused the royal gifts repeatedly pressed upon him by Charles IX.

PART II.

FROM Rome Tasso was summoned by Alfonso II. d' Este, the brother of his late patron, to the ducal court of Ferrara. The duke, as we have already seen, desired, in the first instance, to retain him as one of the gentlemen of his court; on the other hand, it had long been the object of Tasso's ambition to be admitted into his service. He had endeavoured to obtain his wish through the influence of various powerful friends, and he attributed his success to the influence of the Princess Lucrezia, now Duchess of Urbino, and to her sister Leonora.

The gratitude which he felt on this occasion—alas, how soon to be cancelled !—is recorded in his letter to his friend Scipio Gonzaga : " He (that is, Alfonso) took me out of a state of misery and obscurity, and set me in the light and splendour of his court. Raising me from poverty, he placed me in a position of ease and comfort, declaring me to be worthy of every distinction, inviting me to sit at his table, and admitting me into the intimacy of his private life. Nor was any favour that I asked of him ever denied me."[9]

[8] " Opere del Tasso," vol. ix. ; Lettera al Conte Ercole de' Contrari.
[9] Maffei, " Storia della Lett. Ital." vol. i. p. 300.

Again, the passage in the "Aminta" is meant as another
graceful acknowledgment of his gratitude. The "Uom
d' aspetto magnanimo e robusto," who stood on the threshold of the "felice albergo," and with "real cortesia"
invited Tirsi to enter, is doubtless intended for Alfonso,
while Tirsi, who cannot decide whether the title of "Duce
or Cavaliero" best befits his courteous host, is meant to
represent himself. "Ei grande e'n pregio, me negletto e
basso." [1]

But there is also another passage (act i. sc. 2) which
tells us a different tale, picturing the evils of a court life,
and the persecutions to which he was subject.

Tasso was admitted into the duke's household in 1573.
In 1579 the calamity overtook him which darkened the
rest of his life—which precipitated him from the height
of happiness to the depth of misery, and has ever since
made him an object of the tenderest compassion. It is
by no means an easy task to trace the beginning of his
misfortunes. Many of his early biographers, in their
anxiety to shield the house of Este, give a purposely confused account of their origin. But later accounts tear
away this flimsy veil, and reveal the treacherous cruelty
which lurks behind it. During the first three years his
life was peaceful and happy. He wrote his "Aminta," a
pastoral drama composed in two months' time, so perfect,
says Muratori, that it left no chance to posterity of ever
surpassing it. All the former Pastorali—the "Sacrifizio"
of Beccari, the "Aretusa" of Lollio, the "Sfortunato" of
Argenti—appeared as the roughest sketches of that
species of composition beside the polished beauties of the
"Aminta," which will always remain as a gem in the Italian
language for graceful elegance of diction and purity of
style. Parini considered that in it Tasso had succeeded
in engrafting the choicest specimens of Italian ideas and
language on the ancient beauties of the Grecian stock.
He is especially happy in his "cori," which are masterpieces of vigorous style, and each individual specimen in
itself a perfect piece of poetry. Take for example the
one at the end of the second act, beginning—

[1] "Aminta," act i. scene 2.

"Amore, in quale scuola,
Da qual mastro s' apprende,
La tua si lunga e dubbia arte d' amare ? "

Yet Tasso himself never thought very highly of the "eclogue," as he called the "Aminta," nor did he take any steps to have it published. It was not printed until after the control of his works had passed out of his hands during his imprisonment. At that time (1580) it was printed at the Aldine Press, with a preface by Aldo il Giovane, in which he laments with much feeling the sad condition of "Il Signor Torquato." [2]

The "Aminta" was represented with great splendour at the court of Ferrara in 1573 ; again a few years later at Mantua, when the artist and architect Buontalenti painted the scenery, and the Duchess of Urbino summoned Tasso to her court that she might hear the famous "Pastorale" from the lips of the author.

Tasso made a happy sojourn there of a few months, and during that time he wrote a sonnet (one of his most finished productions), "Negli anni acerbi tuoi, purpurea Rosa," to the duchess, now in her fortieth year. Lucrezia rewarded his graceful compliments with a collar of gold and a valuable ruby, presents which afterwards, in his great poverty, he was obliged to barter for money.

Tasso's next care was to finish his great epic poem, which was eagerly looked for throughout Italy. In his anxiety to give to his country as perfect a production as possible, he consulted all his friends upon various passages of the poem, making journeys to Padua, Bologna, Rome, Sienna, and Florence, omitting no opportunity of gaining assistance in his task from all the learned men he knew. Thus portions of the poem would pass from hand to hand, till the printers somehow or other gained possession of them and surreptitiously printed them, to the great annoyance of Tasso, before the whole work was complete. In this manner, now two cantos, now four at a time, appeared in various cities of Italy, but even in this imperfect state they were received with enthusiastic applause.

At length, in 1575, the first complete edition of the poem was published, and throughout the literary "Acca-

[2] Tasso, "Opere," vol. ii. p. 10.

demic" and circles of Italy nothing else was discussed, while comparisons were immediately instituted between the "Gerusalemme" of Tasso and the "Orlando Furioso" of Ariosto. A greater mistake could hardly have been made, for it is obvious that there is an essential difference between the two poems. Tiraboschi observes that you might as well compare the "Æneid" of Virgil with Ovid's "Metamorphoses;" but of this a few more words will be said at the end of the paper. It is only mentioned here because it was the first cause of the fierce attacks of the Accademia della Crusca, which so vexed and wounded the sensitive spirit of Tasso, the first cloud which announced the storm of trouble about to burst over his devoted head.

On his return to Ferrara in 1576 the duke appointed him biographer of the house of Este, in place of his former secretary Pigna, who from that time forward became his bitter enemy, and stirred up the jealousy and malice of the other courtiers to show itself in open persecution. Tasso's letters were opened and intercepted, and his papers stolen.

Notwithstanding their petty intrigues and jealousies, they had not as yet succeeded in poisoning the duke's ear against him, and he stood as high as ever in the favour of the court. The princesses continued to show him every mark of esteem. Leonora, in order to distract him from these harassing vexations and troubles, invited him to her villa at Consandoli, on the borders of the Po, about eighteen miles from Ferrara. Soothed by her kindness, and happy in her presence, he put the finishing touches to the episode of Erminia,[3] one of the favourite passages of his poem. He was never tired of polishing and re-polishing this cherished work of his genius, and, far from having sanctioned the edition published in 1575, he complained bitterly that the poem had been fraudulently snatched from his hands before it was complete, and persuaded the duke to write to the Pope, to the Republic of Genoa, the Duke of Parma, and many other Italian princes, to prohibit the publication of the poem without his sanction. Up to this period he seems to have succeeded in concealing

---

[3] "Gerusalemme Liberata," c. vii.

from every one his passion for Leonora, although, to those who are now aware of his secret, the thought of her seems to pervade all his writings, and appears under some form or another in all the varied productions of his poetical genius.[4]

But on his return from Consandoli, in an unguarded moment he confided the first hint of his secret to one of the courtiers—Maddalò by name—whom he trusted and believed to be his friend. Maddalò proved himself instead to be a traitor of the blackest dye. Tasso became aware of his treachery—a quarrel and a duel ensued. The cowardly traitor brought his two brothers with him, and all three set simultaneously upon Tasso.

But Tasso, not unlike one of the brave heroes of his poem, proved himself more than a match for all his three enemies, so that they fled before him, and the streets of Ferrara resounded with the saying—

> "Colla penna e colla spada
> Nessun val quanto Torquato."

> ("Wield he the sword, or wield he the pen,
> Torquato is greater than other men.")

This skirmish had unhappily the effect of increasing his suspicions, and he sank into a state of melancholy from which nothing could divert him. He mistrusted everybody; he even began to doubt himself. He thought himself guilty of heresy—he feared his faith was not so firm as it ought to be—that his philosophical speculations had led him into error respecting the great truths of religion. Tormented and perplexed, he volunteered to go twice before the Inquisition at Bologna and Ferrara, and, although somewhat reassured, he was not satisfied, because absolution had not formally been administered to him. Then another apprehension assailed him, lest his enemies should take away his life either by poison or the sword. One of the attendants aroused his suspicion to such an extent that he forgot himself so far as to draw his dagger upon him in the apartments of the Duchess of Urbino. For this action the duke caused him to be arrested, but more

---

[4] The whole question has been ably treated by Professor Rosini in an essay upon the " Amore " del Tasso, "Opere dei Tasso," vol. xxxiii.

out of regard to his own safety than in punishment for
the offence.

Up to this time the duke seems to have had patience
with eccentricities and suspicions which might have
aroused harsher feelings, for he soon set Tasso at liberty,
and invited him to his villa at Belriguardo. It is here
that Goethe lays the scene of his drama of "Tasso." But
here, whether weary of the poet's importunities, or whether
his malicious enemies first awakened in the duke's mind a
suspicion of Tasso's passion for the princess, is not known;
but Alfonso, as the only way of disposing of the unheard-
of presumption that a gentleman of his court should dare
to raise his eyes to one of the princesses of the house of
Este, caused it to be intimated to Tasso that he should
feign himself mad.

It was, indeed, no wonder that Tasso left Ferrara in
indignation, recording the insult in the never-to-be-for-
gotten lines—

"Tor mi potevi, alto Signor, la vita,
Chè de' Sovrani è l' usurpato diritto,
Ma tormi quel, che la bontà infinita
Senno mi diè, perchè d' amore ho scritto
(D' amore, a cui natura e il ciel m' invita),
E delitto maggior d' ogni delitto.
Perdon chiedei, tu mel negasti: addio:
Mi pento ognor del pentimento mio."

He fled away poor, footsore, wayworn, to his sister at
Sorrento, to whom he first showed himself in the disguise
of a shepherd, and, to try her affections, told her that her
brother was far-off in peril of his life. When reassured,
by her unfeigned grief, of her affection, he told her the
truth, and she affectionately received him, striving by
every means in her power to soothe his troubled mind.

While at Sorrento, Manso tells us that he received a
twice-repeated summons back to Ferrara from "Madama
Leonora." But it appears from Tasso's own letter to the
Duca d' Urbino that the duke never invited him to return.
Happier far would it have been for Tasso had he resisted
the invitation; for although on his arrival at Ferrara he
was received at court, Alfonso had not forgiven him. The
poet's enemies continued to pour their malicious tales into
his patron's ear. Tasso was never allowed a personal

interview with the duke, and very soon the princesses were forbidden to receive him.

Again he fled from Ferrara to Mantua, to Urbino, to Torino, where, under the name of "Omero Fuggiguerra," he arrived in such a sad plight, that the keepers of the gates of the city would not have admitted him had not Ingegneri, the Venetian printer, who had printed sixteen cantos of the "Gerusalemme," recognized him, and announced who he was.

In vain did the Marchese Filippo d'Este and the Prince Carlo Immanuele implore him to stay at their court. His unlucky steps took him back to Ferrara for the third time. He arrived there in February, 1579, just before the entry of the duke's third bride.

He presented himself at the threshold of the palace. The duke, intent on the wedding preparations, would not receive him; the princesses were not allowed to do so; the courtiers jeered at him. Tasso's bruised and wounded spirit could endure no more insults. He broke out into fierce invectives against the duke and the whole house of Este, retracted his praises, cursed his past life, abused the vile race of courtiers. Alas! there were too many evil tongues ready to carry these reproaches to the ear of the duke, and Tasso was shut up as insane in the hospital of Sant' Anna in Ferrara.

It is not the intention of this essay to dwell on the piteous spectacle presented by Tasso in the asylum of Sant' Anna, nor to recall the painful circumstances connected with it—details of physical and mental anguish so terrible that the pen of his contemporary historians refused to fill them in, and left the passages blank. Moreover, a subject so pathetic has naturally furnished a theme for great writers in poetry and prose.

Byron caused himself to be locked for an hour in the poet's cell, whose narrow limits contained

> "Scarce twice the space they must accord my bier,"

before he wrote the poem which records his sufferings.[5]

Shelley brought away with him a piece of the very door "which, for seven years and three months, divided this

---

[5] "Lament of Tasso." Byron's Works, vol. iii. p. 113.

glorious being from the air and the light which had
nourished in him those influences which he has communicated through his poetry to thousands." Montaigne
visited him, and writes compassionately of his "piteux
estat." And two modern poets,[6] his countrymen, once
more relate to free Italian ears the story of a prince's
tyranny and a poet's fame.

Whatever may be the surmise as to the motive which
prompted the iniquitous conduct of the duke, the real
reason has remained wrapped in that impenetrable mystery
with which it pleased the Italian princes to shroud their
crimes. It is hardly necessary to remind the reader that
records of similar cruelties stain the history of almost every
State and Republic of Italy. The rippling waves of the
Venetian lagune yet hide the witness of many a deed of
darkness, and the treacherous instruments still preserved
in the arsenal remain as tangible proofs that no law of
friendship, chivalry, or honour, was allowed to stand
between a tyrant and the object of his revenge.

It suited the purposes of Alfonso that Tasso should be
considered a madman, therefore he was imprisoned in the
foul precincts of Sant' Anna. The biographers of the
house of Este use every endeavour to prove that the poet
was really out of his senses, in order to excuse the conduct
of the duke. Admitting, for the sake of argument, this
to be true, would it justify him in condemning the great
genius of the age to languish among the common herd of
lunatics, stunned by their perpetual meaningless clamour,
shocked by the sight of their sufferings, placed, in short,
in circumstances revolting to every one of his refined and
delicate senses? Had his affliction been of the nature
which the duke pretended it to be, he should have been
treated with every mark of consideration and respect, and
not exposed to treatment which, far from curing it, was
calculated to aggravate it in the highest degree. But such
was not the case. Indeed, the perfect sanity of the poet's
mind only added to the horror of his situation, enabling
him to sound with fearful accuracy the depths of the abyss
into which he had fallen. What higher proof of his

---

[6] Riccardo Ceroni, and Aleardo Aleardi.

sanity could be urged than that it withstood shocks sufficient to shake the reason of most men from its seat.

Let any one read his Dialoghi[7]—treatises composed during his imprisonment—models of calm, dispassionate reasoning, or his poetry, full of the deepest and tenderest pathos, and then judge if Tasso's reason was not entirely within his control. Would they not rather wonder that, in the midst of the fearful circumstances in which he found himself, he was able to retain a poet's keen imagination, a philosopher's serenity of thought?

The original of one of his treatises ("Il Malpiglio Secondo") written throughout in his own hand, is still to be seen in the British Museum,[8] and as we reverently turn its yellow parchment pages, what a train of compassionate recollections do they awake! Copies can also be seen in the same place of his letters to the Duke of Urbino, imploring him to procure his release from captivity.

But we must pass over the recital of his numerous entreaties, addressed either directly or indirectly to his inexorable tyrant; the palpable contradiction presented by his being called upon to write from a lunatic asylum the defence of his poem against the attacks of the Accademia della Crusca—" a handful," says Monti, of " insolent sophists, who, like a pack of yelping curs round a sick lion, have made it their business to insult the great genius of the age ;"[9] and the alternations of hope and fear which must have often made his heart sick, to notice the effect produced by his sufferings upon his character.

Despite the cruel nature of his imprisonment, no abuse of his tormentor ever passed his lips, nor did he ever turn against him the weapon he had once used in his cause ; for it should always be remembered that the words, " Tu Magnanimo Alfonso," still stand, unerased from the first page of the " Gerusalemme Liberata."

No dark thought of putting an end to his almost unendurable misery by suicide seems ever to have pre-

[7] 1. Il Messaggiero. 2. Il Gonzaga. 3. Il Padre di Famiglia. 4. Il Malpiglio Secondo, &c., vols. vii. viii. "Opere del Tasso."
[8] Manuscripts. Additions to the department of MSS. in the British Museum, 1841—1845, folio 12,045, p. 29.
[9] Maffei, " Storia della Lett. Ital." vol. i. p. 31.

sented itself to his mind. The following passage in the
" Torrismondo " gives us a clue to his thoughts on this
awful subject. In it he blames him who—

> " Against himself
> Would arm his impious and reckless hand,
> Scare from its sacred tenement the soul
> Which o'er the body keeps a holy ward,
> Placed there by GOD, yielding alone to Him
> The trust He gave. Who, when the task is o'er,
> Will call it back to heaven whence it came." [1]

He held fast to those earnest religious convictions which
had early sunk deep into his mind, and now in the midst
of the wreck of his hopes he fixed his thoughts steadfastly
upon GOD, " Who," he says, in one of his letters, written
from Sant' Anna, " never abandons those that firmly
believe in Him." And nothing ever shook this trust, not
even when in the lonely hours of the night, worn with
illness, and unable to rest, his fevered fancy would people
his cell with strange forms and phantoms tempting him
to despair.

But the years of patient endurance were not to remain
unrewarded; the pale, haggard face was not always to
gaze piteously through the iron bars of his prison, for
the long-desired release came at last. We must again
have recourse to surmise to account for the motive which
suddenly induced Alfonso to set his victim free.

During the confinement of Tasso in the asylum, Leonora d' Este died, in the forty-fifth year of her age. Up
to this period Alfonso gave no hope of ever releasing
Tasso from imprisonment, but after that time he was
gradually brought to relent. First a change of apartment was provided for the unfortunate poet. Later he
was allowed to pay a visit to the Duchess Marfisa d' Este,
who was so enraptured with his poem that she implored her
cousin (Alfonso) as a personal favour to allow her to invite

---

[1] " Torrismondo," act i. scene 2.—So Spenser (who died one year
after Tasso) writes :—

> " The term of life is limited,
> Ne may a man prolong nor shorten it ;
> The souldier may not move from watchful sted,
> Nor leave his stand until his Captain bed."
>
> *Faery Queene*, Book I. c. ix.

the author to her villa at Maddaler for one day. This was granted, provided that he was conveyed there and back to Sant' Anna in a close carriage. After this, by degrees, the rigour of his imprisonment was relaxed; and at length, but not till he was so ill that it was hardly possible for him to recover, in compliance with the supplications of the whole city of Bergamo, the united prayers of Vincenzo Gonzaga, Cesare d' Este and Virginia de' Medici, whose marriage was about to be solemnized, on the 5th of July, 1586, Tasso was set free.

Free once more to breathe the pure air of heaven, to drink in those beauties of nature which he has so eloquently described, to listen to the song of the birds, to enjoy the sweet smell of the flowers and all the summer glory of his enchanting country—to him these must in truth have seemed "an opening paradise."

Before closing this painful chapter of his life, we must call attention to one of the worst traits in Alfonso's character—his refusal to allow Tasso to kiss his hand before leaving Ferrara—a last favour which, in token of his free forgiveness, the injured poet asked of his former patron.

Tasso lived nine years after his release from captivity. At first he was courteously entertained in the palace of the Duke of Mantua, the father of his deliverer, Vincenzo Gonzaga. "I am in Mantua," he writes to his friend Licino, "the guest of his Excellency the duke. I have been allowed to choose my own attendants out of his household. I am treated with deference and courtesy. I have good food, delicious fruit, excellent bread, and choice wines like those my father used to delight in."[2]

This state of ease and tranquillity was unhappily of short duration. Duke Guglielmo of Mantua died. Vincenzo, his son, was too much taken up with the cares of his new dignity to bestow much thought or care upon Tasso, who again set out on his wanderings. The poverty and misfortune which had clung to him all his life still attended him; and it is sad to see him roaming restlessly from city to city, from place to place—he, the author of the

---

[2] Manso, "Vita di Tasso," p. 187.

great poem of the age, forced to implore the loan of ten
scudi to pay his expenses to Rome.

At first also he was tormented by fears lest Alfonso
should even now drag him back to the cell whence he had
escaped with such difficulty. A modern poet [3] describes
his situation in very pathetic language, which can hardly
be done justice to in a translation:—

> " O'er fields and plains he roams,
> Pale, soiled, a mendicant from door to door,
> His mind distraught with anguish. Can this be
> The gentle poet knight? Ever behind,
> Nearer and nearer still, there seems to come
> Fast in pursuit the gallop of a horse ;
> Perchance some officer to drag him back
> To foul Sant' Anna's narrow prison walls !
> Were there in azuth around forms with weird hands
> Outstretched to snatch from him his cherished lays,
> The polished work, the ceaseless toil of years,
> And cast them to the winds? Strewing the sheets
> Along the way-worn track, or on the banks
> Which line the desert way! He almost doubts
> In sheer perplexity his very self.
> Was his poetic genius but a dream,
> A futile fancy his immortal work ?
> Tancred, Clorinda, all the noble forms
> And bright creations of his poet's muse,
> But vain imaginations ? "

Half tempted by the offer of the Ethical and Poetical
Chair of the Academy "Degli Addormentati," at Genoa,
he felt obliged to decline it because of the impaired
powers of his memory; and once again he returned to
Mantua, to dedicate his recently-finished tragedy of
"Torrismondo" to the new duke. A long course of
insult and injury had rendered the unhappy poet sensitive to an almost morbid degree. Dissatisfied with his
reception, fancying that his new dignity had changed the
countenance of his former friend towards him, he left
Mantua for Rome, with the especial intention of making
a pilgrimage to Loretto. Footsore, poverty-stricken, and
well-nigh exhausted, he accomplished his vow, and then
pushed on towards Rome. But fresh disappointment
awaited him there. He had neither strength nor spirit
left to struggle and strive among the crowd of place-

---

[3] Alcardo Aleardi, p. 113.

seekers in the court of the Papal palace to obtain the reward which ought freely to have been bestowed upon the greatest poet of the day.

Again he turned away and fled to Naples, cherishing, as a last hope, the thought of recovering his forfeited paternal inheritance. In this, as in every other matter connected with worldly prosperity, he was unsuccessful. Nevertheless, in that peaceful and beautiful sojourn his mind was able to rest content. The soft, delicious climate was like balm to his shattered health; his eye rested with pleasure upon the bay which has no rival in Europe, the deep blue of the glorious sea, the stately buildings, the fresh fountains, the abundance of fruits, and the ever-blowing flowers; and his interest was daily awakened by the scene of animation before him in the concourse of strangers from all parts of the world, the splendour of their equipages, and all the gay throng of chivalry which had had such charms for him in former days.

In order to escape from the courteous invitations which were showered upon him, he retired for a short time to the quiet monastery of Monte Oliveto. Many went thither to pay their respects to him; among others Manso, Marchese della Villa, his great friend, and the writer of the biography often quoted in this paper. We next hear of Tasso paying a visit to Bisaccio, the villa of the Marchese; and we read with pleasure the report of Manso, that " Il Tasso is now become so keen a huntsman, that he despises all inclemencies of weather. In the evening we spend many pleasant hours listening to music and singing. He especially delights in the *improvvisatori*, admiring their readiness in versification, in which he always considered himself to be deficient." [4]

But again his love of wandering carried him back to Rome, to be again received with coldness by his former friend, Scipio Gonzaga, and to throw himself once more upon the hospitality of the monks of Monte Oliveto, whence also he fled away, and was afterwards discovered in circumstances of the greatest poverty in the hospital of the Bergamaschi. However, his troubled life was not destined to endure much longer

[4] Maffei, " Storia della Lett. Ital." vol. i. p. 316.

" The slings and arrows of outrageous fortune."

He had patiently borne each and all of the

" whips and scorns of time,
The oppressor's wrong, the proud man's contumely,
The pangs of despised love, the law's delay,
The insolence of office, and the spurns
That patient merit of the unworthy takes."

But a tardy justice was at last to be paid to his genius ; and like a flame for a brief instant before it expires was the earthly glory of the unfortunate Tasso. The Duke of Mantua pressed him to return to his court. The Grand Duke of Tuscany invited him to Florence, and there all the academies and the literary world, with the exception of the envious Cruscans, poured out to welcome him and do him honour. In Rome, through the good offices of Cinzio Aldobrandini, the nephew of Pope Clement VIII., he was given an apartment in the Vatican, with an annual income of 200 scudi. Here he completed the "Gerusalemme Conquistata," an unfortunate result produced by the harsh criticisms showered upon the "Gerusalemme Liberata." Lastly, the wreath of poet's laurel which had crowned Petrarch was now destined to adorn Tasso's head.

It is a fact worthy of note that in both cases this distinction was obtained by an inferior production of either poet: the "Scipio Africanus" of Petrarch, and the "Gerusalemme Conquistata" of Tasso. And this coveted honour, which Tasso had deservedly won in the first flower of his youth, now came too late. The ceremony was delayed that it might be performed with more solemnity ; and his health, long undermined by disease, hardships, and sorrow, at length gave way. His wanderings were over for ever when his weary steps halted at last at the threshold of the quiet monastery of San Onofrio, on the summit of the Janiculum. "I come," he said to the monks, who received him with pitying glances, " to die among you." Here he spent the last weeks of his life sitting under the shade of the oak, whose boughs stretched out over the garden, looking on the beautiful prospect before him of the ancient capital of the world. Surely those mighty ruins, on whose dim outlines his thoughtful gaze loved to rest, must have added one more example to the long, stern lesson of his life as to the vanity of human greatness, the futility of earthly desires.

But further teaching was scarcely needed now. His spirit, long ago chastened by suffering, and firmly fixed on another and brighter world, was only waiting the last summons to flee away and be at rest. It was not long delayed. On the 10th of April, 1595, he was told by the Papal physician, sent on purpose to attend him, that there was but little hope of his recovery, and from that day till the 25th, when he died, he turned his thoughts heavenward.

There is a touching simplicity in the contemporary narrative of the last days of his life. "Father," he said to his confessor, who was attending him, "write, that I give my spirit back to God who gave it, my body to the earth whence it was taken, to be laid in this church of San Onofrio. My goods I leave to the Lord Cardinal Cinzio, and I pray him to restore to Il Signor Giambattista Manso the little portrait of me painted by his wish, and only lent to me for life. To this monastery I bequeath this Sacred Image of our dear Lord,"—and, as he spoke, he clasped the crucifix of singularly beautiful workmanship which hung beside his bed. A few days afterwards he received the last sacraments of the Church, and died peacefully with the unfinished ejaculation on his lips, "Into Thy hands, O Lord——."

That same evening his body, according to his wish, found a last resting-place in the church of San Onofrio.

The simple inscription "Hic jacet Torquatus Tassus," graven in the stone, still marks the place of his repose,—

> "And nought remains to mark thy last abode
> But the bright waters of a sparkling well,
> A simple stone, and the eternal smile
> Of the Campagna. Suffer us once more
> To wake thy golden lyre, that we may touch
> With trembling hand the chord which tells thy fame."[5]

When we remember that the pen of Tasso never rested

[5] Aleardo Aleardi, p. 115.

from the time when, at seventeen, it produced the "Rinaldo" up to the very last days of his life, and that he died in his fifty-first year, we cannot wonder that twenty-five volumes remain to us of his writings. It would not only be presumptious, but impossible, to attempt to do more than attempt to give a passing notice of them in these pages.

His prose compositions may be divided into "Dialoghi," "Discorsi," and "Lettere." His "Discorsi," Ginguéne [6] tells us, especially the one which relates to heroic poetry, prove how much he had meditated on the poetics of Aristotle; the "Dialoghi" how deeply he had studied Plato. Any one of these Dialoghi, the "Messaggiero," for instance, is well worth reading as a sample of the clear reasoning and pellucid style which characterize his prose as well as his poetic writings. Of these last the "Rinaldo" and "Aminta" have already been mentioned; of the "Torrismondo," begun before and finished after his imprisonment, Tasso himself had not a high opinion. The dialogue is reckoned dull and heavy, but the "cori," like those in the "Aminta," are full of fire and spirit, and the concluding one pictures forth his recent sufferings with great pathos. The whole manuscript, in his own handwriting and the original vellum binding has been recently added to the collection in the British Museum. [7]

The poem on the Creation ("Il Mondo Creato") was the last work of Tasso's life, but only the two first books were ever finished, the five last being merely sketched out. In the completed portions there are some fine passages—the creation of light on the first day, [8] that of the firmament on the second day, and a remarkable protest against the presumptuous folly of astrologers and

[6] Vol. v. p. 30.
[7] Catalogue of Additional Manuscripts, 1860. Add. 23778. This autograph manuscript of Tasso, filled with numerous alterations and corrections, was given by Licino (the friend who announced to Tasso his release from Sant' Anna) to Abbioso the poet (1588); it subsequently fell into the hands of the Minorite Ottaviano Cameriani of Ravenna, and was presented by him to Cardinal Cybo (1650), whose arms it still bears on the cover.
[8] "Mondo Creato," p. 19.

star-gazers. Milton is supposed to have borrowed many of his ideas for "Paradise Lost" from this poem.

But all these minor works sink into comparative insignificance beside the great production of his genius, the "Gerusalemme Liberata;" and here again the discussions and controversies which occupied for years the attention of the literary Italian world can scarcely be reduced into a few paragraphs.

It is necessary, however, to point out as briefly as possible the cause which first raised the storm of criticism.

When the "Gerusalemme" first appeared, the poem of Ariosto was at the zenith of its fame, and it was imitated with servility by all the inferior poets. But the genius of Tasso early taught him that, if he was to rival Ariosto, it could not be by following in his steps, that he could not surpass the "Orlando Furioso" as an achievement of romantic poetry. An epic poem, however, like those of Homer and Virgil, had as yet been untried by an Italian poet, and this was the path which Tasso resolved to follow in pursuit of fame. This appears in his reply to the letter full of eulogy addressed to him by Orazio Ariosto, the nephew of Ariosto: "The crown you would honour me with," writes Tasso, " already adorns the head of the poet to whom you are related, from whence it would be as easy to snatch it as to wrest the club from the hand of Hercules. I would no more receive it from your hand than I would snatch it myself. I honour him (Ariosto); I pay him every mark of respect. I publicly declare him to be my father in the art of poetry, my master, my prince," &c.

But despite these protestations, despite the pains Tasso had taken to follow a completely different route from Ariosto, his enemies would insist upon accusing Tasso of the presumption of contending with Ariosto; and the ill-advised but well-meant treatise of Camillo Pellegrino [9] only confirmed them in this idea.

We will not attempt to deal with the pedantic criticisms and wholesale vituperations by which the recently

[9] "Opere di Tasso," vol. xviii. 20.

founded "Accademia della Crusca"[1] hoped to attain
an early celebrity. To these Tasso replied with calm
dignity,—

> " With a glory round his furrow'd brow,
> Which emanated then, and dazzles now,
> In face of all his foes, the Cruscan quire,
> And Boileau, whose rash envy could allow
> No strain which shamed his country's creaking lyre,
> That whetstone of the teeth—monotony in wire."[2]

It is a more pleasing task to quote the opinion of Metastasio. "If Apollo," he says, "were to take a fancy to
endow me with a great poetical genius, and commanded
me to declare which of these great poems ('Orlando
Furioso' and 'Gerusalemme Liberata') I should wish
the production of my genius to resemble, I should
certainly make my choice with great hesitation, but I
think my natural inclination to order, exactitude, and
method would decide me in favour of the 'Gerusalemme.'"
"Thus he writes," says Tiraboschi, whose comment on
this opinion is still more interesting, "with the modesty
of a really great man ; but I should reply with more
courage to Apollo, and my answer would be different.
Were he to ask me to write an epic poem, I should beg
him to make me resemble Tasso ; were I to undertake a
romantic poem, I should desire to imitate Ariosto ; but if
I were to choose which of these poets I should most wish
to resemble in their natural gift for poetry, I should first
of all beg Tasso's pardon, but I should pray Apollo to
bestow on me the natural gift of Ariosto."[3]

It is certainly a truth not to be denied, that Tasso was
apt to overlay with too refined and artificial ornament
scenes of natural pathos which would have been more
vigorously painted by the bolder hand of Ariosto. But
this trivial failing does not justify the harsh opinion
expressed in the spiteful lines of Boileau :—

> " Tous les jours à la cour un sot de qualité
> Peut juger de travers avec impunité,
> A Malherbe, à Racan, préférer Théophile,
> Et le clinquant du Tasse à tout l'or de Virgile "—

---

[1] 1583.
[2] "Childe Harold," canto IV. xxxviii.
[3] Tir. vii. 1267, 1268.

which, eagerly caught up and repeated, have done more than any other criticism to damage Tasso's reputation as a poet. Ginguéne tries to explain away the lines. Boileau, he says, never meant to imply that because Tasso's poetry contained some alloy it was not also full of precious metal. He only blamed those who prefer the artificial portions of " Gerusalemme " to all the solid gold of Virgil, and, afterwards, in another passage of his " Art Poétique," the French satirist considerably modified his opinion of Tasso. It may be doubted, by the way, whether he was aware that Tasso's happiest imitation, the famous verse on the sick child, was taken from Lucretius. Unhappily, Boileau's partial recantation is forgotten, while the former lines are remembered ; and it is difficult not to think, with Byron, that these were inspired by an envious motive.

Let us now turn from refuting the criticisms of the " Gerusalemme Liberata," to point out some of the great intrinsic merits of the poem. In the choice of his subject Tasso was especially fortunate. At all times calculated to enlist the earnest sympathy of the Christian reader the circumstances of the age give it a still more marked and definite interest. The peaceful condition of Europe had left the Christian States free to turn their arms against the Turks, and it seemed probable that they would shortly be compelled to render their " grande ingiusta preda," [4] for just at the moment when Tasso, in his twenty-seventh year, was still engaged on his poem, the Christian forces had won the famous victory of Lepanto (1571). This war against the Turks naturally diverted the stream of European thought back into the old channel of the Crusades, and many warriors entertained the hope that another crusade would shortly be organized.

The oration pronounced in honour of Tasso before the Academy at Ferrara, the year after his death (1596), concludes with a passionate entreaty to all the princes of Europe to avenge the depredations of the Turks, and not to cease from warfare till, like new Godfreys, they had

---

[4] " Gerusalemme Liberata," c. i. 5.

hung up their victorious arms as trophies before the Holy Sepulchre.

In the military plan and operations of his poem, Tasso is considered unrivalled by any other poet, and this success is considered, in some measure, to be due to the instructions of Alfonso.   During the happier days of his court favour at Ferrara, Tasso would consult the duke, who piqued himself on his generalship, as to the march of the troops, their plan of attack, the positions of vantage, the method of conducting the siege, and all the military features of the enterprise.

Again, Godfrey de Bouillon is a model general, while he is also an example of calm, faultless virtue. The other knights, Tancred and Rinaldo, despite their courage and chivalry, are not so attractive as heroes as the bright, captivating Clorinda, or the modest, gentle Erminia as heroines.   Each of the detached episodes in which they appear is in itself a perfect picture, while they do not hinder the unity of purpose which gives such a distinct coherence to the action of the poem, causing it to march in an undeviating course to its conclusion.

These are some of the main features of the " Gerusa-· lemme," but every Italian scholar will rather turn to the poem itself, and recall some of the favourite passages which it contains—the grand opening stanzas, the soul-stirring description of the Crusaders' first sight of Jerusalem, the pathetic beauty of Dudone's death, the flight of Erminia, Tancred, and Clorinda, their battle and her death, which can hardly be read with dry eyes.   In the description of nature, Tasso is peculiarly happy, whether he describes the gradual coming on of night with her " stellato velo " (vi. 103), or the sea with her "cerulei campi spumanti" (xvi. 4), or the cool waters of a spring which "mormorando sen va gelida e bruna " (xv. 56), or when he seizes upon the slightest circumstance, such as the varied hue of the feathers,

" Che di gentile
Amorosa colomba il collo cinge " (xv. 5),

and interweaves it as a bright ornament in his chain of description, or, as a last example, when he rises to the sublime in his account of the ruins of Carthage (xv. 20).

It was, in truth, no wonder that the polished stanzas found a responsive chord in every Italian heart from the first moment of their publication. The princes caused them to be read aloud in their courts, the priests murmured them in the shade of the cloisture, the people loved them, the gondolier would recite them in soft melancholy cadence as he steered himself through the water-streets of Venice or launched out towards the Lido ; the brigand of the Abruzzi, with their sound still in his ears, would not hurt a hair of the poet's head when he journeyed alone and unfriended towards Rome ; even the galley-slaves of Livorno, as, chained together, they dragged their weary steps along the shore, would chant fragments of the Crusader's Litany in the "Gerusalemme Liberata."

In the space of six months after its first publication it was reprinted seven times—six times in Italy and once in France,[5] and two thousand copies of Ingegneri's edition were sold in two days.

As the "Rinaldo" marked the dawn of Tasso's poetical genius, and the "Gerusalemme Liberata" its meridian splendour, so the "Gerusalemme Conquistata" may be considered as its sunset. The expiring rays still shine on such passages as the "Dream of Godfrey" (c. x.), or the attack on Jerusalem ; but whereas the "Gerusalemme Liberata" will be considered one of the classics of Italy so long as her language remains, the "Conquistata," pared and tamed down in deference to the opinion of his merciless critics, and filled with elaborate allegories, is scarcely if at all read, and then only to compare with its predecessor, and lament over the omission of the finest passages of the first poem.

Space forbids the mention of his numerous Canzone and Madrigali in every varied form of poetical beauty ; but however brief and imperfect this notice may have been, enough has perhaps been said to prove that his works were indeed the faithful mirror of his mind and character.

In his philosophical essays—and it should be remem-

⁵ Milman's "Life of Tasso," vol. ii. p. 29.

bered in what fearful circumstances many of these were written—we notice a calm, patient reasoning, a well-balanced order of thought, unmoved by passion, unshaken by misfortune. Nor can we render full justice to this gravity and sobriety of mind till we have learnt from his enthusiastic poetry that, far from being cold and reserved, his nature was sensitive and passionate in the highest degree, his tender love of everything that was beautiful or noble speaking in every line of every poem, and awakening a kindred feeling in the heart of his reader.

Of gentle birth, he was also a gentleman in the truest sense of the word. Courage, chivalry, loyalty, were among the brightest ornaments of his character, and to these may be added that essentially Christian virtue, forgiveness of injuries. How perfectly he fulfilled this last duty let each who reads his life judge for himself.

Lastly, the "Gerusalemme Liberata" gives us the true clue to that deep piety which sustained him throughout his troubled, storm-tossed life, and guided him safely into the haven of peace and rest. It is true that the earthly crown of glory slipped from his dying grasp, but we cannot grieve on this account when we remember the words which he puts in the mouth of his favourite hero, and which are now so applicable to himself—

> " Già non si deve a te doglia nè pianto;
> Chè, se morì nel mondo, in ciel rinasei ;
> E qui, dove ti spogli il mortal manto,
> Di gloria impresse alte vestigia lasci.
> Vivesti qual guerrier cristiano e santo,
> E come tal sei morto : or godi, e pasci
> In Dio gli occhi bramosi, o felice alma,
> Ed hai del ben oprar corona e palma."
> *Gerusalemme Liberata*, canto iii. 68.

> " We need not mourn for thee, here laid to rest ;
> Earth is thy bed, and not thy grave; the skies
> Are for thy soul the cradle and the nest ;
> There live, for here thy glory never dies;
> For like a Christian knight and champion blest,
> Thou didst both live and die ; new feed thine eyes
> With thy Redeemer's sight, where, crown'd with bliss,
> Thy faith, zeal, merit, well-deserving is."
> *Fairfax's translation.*

THE PRINCE PRINTERS OF ITALY.

PART I.

THE rivalries and jealousies of the Italian States, their struggles for liberty, and their individual feuds, have been a common theme with historians of the Middle Ages.

But however deplorable may have been the effect of such a continual state of civil war upon the general welfare of the country, it has not been altogether barren of good results.

The rulers of the various Italian States were indeed always striving to outshine each other in the splendour and magnificence of their courts, but they cherished at the same time a far nobler emulation. They soon perceived that genius of any kind was the brightest ornament which they could obtain for their respective courts, and that, by the protection which they vied with one another in affording to literature and art, they secured celebrity at the time, and a lasting renown for the future. They were, therefore, at all times careful to cherish and kindle the smouldering fire of that native genius which was the special heritage of Italy, and which she preserved through all the rude vicissitudes of external conquest and internal warfare.

In Italy first appeared that dawn of light, destined in its meridian splendour to dissipate the dense ignorance into which Europe generally was plunged. The earliest efforts of her language, half a century before Dante wrote the poem which so largely contributed to form it, were protected and fostered at the court of Frederick II., King of Sicily. To touch only upon great examples :— In 1316 we find Dante entertained at the court of the Scaligeri at Verona, and the princely hospitality of his host is immortalized in that portion of the " Divina

Commedia" which, as a further proof of Dante's gratitude, was dedicated to Can Grande della Scala—"Il
Gran Lombardo," as the poet calls him.

Similar hospitality was shown to Dante during the last
years of his life by Guido da Polenta, Lord of Ravenna ;
and Petrarch, following closely upon the footsteps of
Dante, was sought after and honoured by all the princes
of Italy, as we have recently shown in these pages. Nor
did the princes only extend their favour to what may be
called the creative genius of the thirteenth century ; they
were also foremost in promoting that research among the
long-lost classics which was the distinguishing mark of
the next century.

This research, first begun by Petrarch and Boccaccio,
and pursued with infinite labour in circumstances of great
difficulty, received in the fourteenth and fifteenth centuries very general encouragement. The Pontiffs in
Rome, the Medici in Florence, the Visconti, afterwards
succeeded by the Sforza, at Milan, the Arragon kings of
Naples, the Houses of Gonzaga in Mantua, and of Este
in Ferrara, the Dukes of Urbino—all promoted this revival of learning. They sent emissaries to all parts of
the world for the purpose of collecting manuscripts, and
no journey was accounted too dangerous or too protracted
to obtain them. Pre-eminently, Lorenzo de' Medici
spared neither trouble nor expense in his researches. He
sent to explore both Europe and Asia for Greek and Latin
manuscripts, which, when brought to him, he purchased
at any price ; and twice, with a magnificence worthy of
his name, did he despatch the celebrated Giovanni Lascari
to the Sultan Bajazet, in order that under the Imperial
protection he might carry his researches through Greece.
Two hundred manuscripts, of which eighty were new
discoveries, were the result of these journeys.[1]

On the discovery of the twelve comedies of Plautus in
1429,—for up till that time only eight were supposed to
exist—copies of the manuscript had immediately to be
made for the several houses of Visconti, of Este, and of
the Medici. It is further related as a proof of the esteem

---

[1] Tiraboschi, "Storia della Letteratura Italiana," vol. vi. p. 137.

in which these treasures of classical learning were held
by the princes, that a manuscript of Livy's Annals, sent
by Cosmo de' Medici to Alfonso, King of Naples, sufficed
to appease a quarrel between them ; though the king was
counselled by his physicians to examine it carefully
lest Cosmo should have introduced poison between the
leaves.[2]

But none of the princes of this time deserve so much
praise as an encourager of learning as Nicholas V.
(Thomas Sarzana), who became Pope in 1447. He
founded the Vatican Library, and left·it at his death
enriched with 5000 volumes, a treasure far exceeding
that of any other collection in Europe. Every scholar
who needed maintenance, found it at the court of Rome,
and several Greek authors were translated into Latin, by
order of Pope Nicholas V.[3]

Almost all the works of the classical authors were
either found in Italy or elsewhere by Italians, and the
enthusiasm which had been shown in collecting manuscripts next took the form of bestowing them in those
magnificent libraries which are among the great wonders
of Italy. Niccolò Niccoli, a Florentine of eminent learning, first conceived the idea, and founded the first public
library in the convent of the S. Spirito at Florence, of
which Boccaccio's private collection of books was the
germ, he having left them as a legacy to that convent.
From this eventually sprang the famous Medicean library,
only one among many of the princely libraries of Italy.

The fall of the Eastern Empire towards the middle of
this century compelled the Greeks in considerable numbers to seek a refuge in Italy, when they further disclosed
those immortal monuments of their language which the
Crusades had been the first means of revealing to the
European mind. Thus a new and still more powerful
stimulus was given to the general desire for information.

This thirst was very partially relieved while the fountain of learning continued to trickle out, drop by drop,
through the difficult and costly channels of copies and
transcriptions. But the wonderful discovery of Guten-

---

[2] Tiraboschi, "Storia della Letteratura Italiana," vol. vi. p. 126.
[3] Hallam, "Lit. of Europe," vol. i. p. 143.

H

berg suddenly opened the spring, and diffused the long-pent-up waters of learning over the civilized world.

Printing could not have been invented at a more propitious moment for the perfecting of this wondrous art. The especial circumstances of the age caused it to be universally appreciated, and it seemed to crown the joint labours of the princes and learned men with a success which, in their wildest dreams, they could not have expected to attain.

Although Germany must fairly claim the honour of this great invention, it has never been questioned that Italy was the first to follow in her footsteps; and it is worthy of notice how quickly she adopted and succeeded in appropriating to herself the invention of another country. This was only natural. Abundantly rich in her own talents, she had no cause to envy a foreign discovery, and at that moment of supreme activity of mind she did not hesitate to adopt the new invention, although it did not originate with her. On the contrary, nursed and cherished in the centre of art and learning, printing soon reached its highest perfection.

The rude wooden movable characters, Gutenberg's great discovery and improvement on the still ruder engraved blocks of wood, from which the so-called "block-books" were printed, and which was the earliest form of the art [4]—were now discarded for types cut by the artist-hand of a Francia; men of profound erudition and cultivated talents were employed to select and revise the manuscripts about to be printed; while princes were willing to devote much of their wealth, and even to sacrifice a portion of their territories, to this new and wonderful method for the diffusion of knowledge.

Thus when Aldo Manuzio, who may be rightly called the father of Italian typography, first set up his printing-press in Venice, it was Alberto Pio, Prince of Carpi, who defrayed the cost,—whose family name of "Pio" Aldo was permitted to bear, on account of the great affection and intimacy which existed between them, and by it the

---

[4] Hallam, "Lit. of Europe," vol. i. p. 150. "This mode of printing from blocks of wood has been practised in China from time immemorial."

princes of Italy will always be associated with the first great printer of their country.

Before proceeding to speak of Aldo, whose life and works are more generally known, some few words should be said about his patron, whose remarkable talents and singular excellence, while they deserved a better fate in his lifetime, have been allowed to remain too long in obscurity after his death. Tiraboschi,[5] the great historian of Italian literature, first brought them to the light. Till that time no one had ever written any account of the life of the Alberto Pio. He was the son of Leonello, Prince of Carpi, a small principality, now only a town in the present Duchy of Modena. His mother was the sister of Pico della Mirandola, the accomplished friend of Lorenzo de' Medici. It had been arranged that Alberto Pio, and his brother Leonello, should divide the principality with Giberto and his brothers, the descendants of another branch of the same family. This division of authority, especially when the estate to be governed was of small dimensions, caused, as may easily be imagined, fierce and continual dissensions, and the estates of the Pio family were the scene of perpetual warfare. As usual, the Emperor of Germany was appealed to, and, as usual, no good result ensued. The neighbouring Dukes of Ferrara also strove more than once to appease the quarrel in Carpi. But the truces were always of short duration, until in the year 1500, Giberto, in order to revenge himself on his cousin Alberto, sold his rights over the principality of Carpi to the Duke of Ferrara, receiving in exchange a few towns belonging to the dukedom.

Thus did Ercole, Duke of Ferrara, first obtain a hold over the principality of Carpi, and his successor, Alfonso, was not slow to avail himself of this semblance of a right. By the payment of 100,000 florins to the Emperor Charles V., he obtained from him in 1552 the investiture of the principality, in defiance of a former decree of the Emperor Maximilian, which upheld the rights of Alberto Pio and annulled the cession made by Giberto to the Dukes of Ferrara. The Prince of Carpi, when thus

---

[5] "Storia," vol. vii. pp. 236, 283, *et seq.*

robbed of his dominions, retired to the Court of Francis I., and found his best consolation in those literary pursuits which in his brighter days he had so liberally protected.

Passing by the further political vicissitudes of Carpi before its final absorption into the Duchy of Ferrara, which have but a remote bearing on the subject of this paper, we will now look upon her prince from a literary point of view. Our admiration for the eminence which he obtained, both in the cultivated use of his own mind and in his endeavours to promote it in others, is increased by the consideration of the perpetual state troubles by which he was harassed. From his earliest years, at the age of four, he was the pupil of Aldo Manuzio,[6] and for nine years he enjoyed the advantage of so distinguished a tutor, whereby he acquired a permanent taste for literature. The gratitude which the young prince felt on this account to Aldo, lasted through life, and showed itself on every occasion. Aldo, on the other hand, had the highest esteem for his young pupil, and paid a striking tribute to his zeal for learning in dedicating to him the first volume of his magnificent edition of Aristotle of 1495, called "Editio Princeps."[7] In this dedication, Manuzio addresses Alberto Pio as the patron of all learned men, his own patron more especially; adverts to his enthusiasm for collecting Greek books, thus following in the footsteps of his learned uncle, Pico della Mirandola; and dwells upon the fair promise of his early years, so admirably spent in the improvement of his own mind and in endeavouring to promote the revival of learning, since he had for many years been indefatigable in collecting Latin, Greek, and Hebrew manuscripts, while he entertained with a princely magnificence the most learned men he could find, to correct and explain them.[8]

Of a similar nature is the eulogium of Federigo Asolano, who also dedicated to the Prince of Carpi the second volume of the works of Galen. But Aldo Manuzio was

---

[6] Manni, "Vita di Aldo Pio Manuzio," p. 9.
[7] This edition of Aristotle was in five vols., the first bearing date 1495, the last 1498.— Hallam, "Lit. of Europe," vol. i. pp. 224, 225.
[8] Tiraboschi, vii. p. 291.

more especially bound to express his sense of obligation to Alberto Pio, for, together with his uncle, Pico della Mirandola, this prince had formed a design which may well entitle them to be called the "Prince Printers of Italy." Their scheme was to publish an entire set of new and correct editions of Latin and Greek authors, in order the better to promote the study of the two languages.

The greatest printer of the age, Aldo Manuzio, was chosen to execute their project, which Erasmus, in his "Proverbs," afterwards printed by Aldo, rightly terms one of princely magnificence: for it included the restoration of literature fast falling to decay; the disinterment of that which had lain concealed for ages; the supply of what was deficient; the correction, by careful comparison, of manuscripts which appeared erroneous.[9]

For this purpose Alberto Pio, although according to Rénouard he was then only twelve years old, and his uncle, Pico della Mirandola, resolved to set up a magnificent printing-press in Carpi for Aldo Manuzio, giving him absolute possession of one of his castles in which to carry on the work, and even as a further mark of honour investing him with the government of a part of his territory. An Academy of Arts and Sciences was to be included in the scheme, in order that these might flourish in his dominions, and Carpi be the centre whence the Aldine editions should emanate. Unhappily, so splendid a design was frustrated by the political disturbances already alluded to, and Aldo had to betake himself to Venice; where he set up, in 1488,[1] his famous printing-press, the cost of which was defrayed by the two princes, Alberto Pio and Pico della Mirandola, who by no means abandoned that part of the project because they could not have the glory of executing it in their own dominions. On the contrary, they gave large sums of money for this purpose, and throughout the various vicissitudes of the life of Aldo these two princes, despite their own political troubles,

9 Maffei, "Storia della Lett. Ital.," vol. i. p. 242.

1 Manni, "Vita di Aldo Pio Manuzio," p. 12. There have been various opinions as to the exact date of this event, but Manni founds his assertion on Aldo's Preface to Aristotle, dated 1495, in which Aldo affirms that he has been seven years engaged in the "difficult and costly undertaking of printing."

continued to befriend him. The printing-press thus
established at Venice had a marvellous success. Before
twenty years elapsed there was scarcely a Greek or Latin
author whose works had not issued from it in one of those
beautiful editions now so rare and so eagerly coveted.

The full merit of these editions can only be rightly
appreciated when we consider that the manuscripts from
which they were printed were often imperfect, mutilated,
and half effaced; the copies of the same author not
always agreeing together, and demanding as much patience,
wisdom, and sagacity on the part of the critic as manual
dexterity on the part of the printer.

Hitherto books had been usually printed in folio, but
Manuzio was first inspired with the idea of publishing
them in a smaller and more convenient form.

In order to compress the contents of these folios into
the 8vo size which he invented, and which has since
become so common a form of volume, he caused to be
engraved that peculiar kind of type, which for a long
time bore the name of the "Aldine Type," and which we
now term "Italic."

It was originally copied from the handwriting of
Petrarch in the manuscript of the "Canzoniere," and the
characters to which Aldo owes so much of his fame, and
which may justly claim our admiration for the grace and
taste of their forms, are supposed, with good reason, to
have been cut by no less a hand than that of the great
artist Francesco Raibolini, or "Il Francia."

From the beginning of the invention of printing, the
types were for the most part engraved by either gold-
smiths, coiners, or engravers of some kind or another,
and the chief masters in the art were always chosen for
this purpose. It is well known that "Francia" was unrivalled in his goldsmith work; that the medals and
money stamped with coins of his engraving were equal to
those of the famous "Caradosso" of Milan, and that
when employed to paint the Altar-piece of the Bentivoglio Chapel, he signed his work "Franciscus Francia,
Aurifex," as if to denote that he was by profession a
goldsmith, and not an artist.[2]

[2] Lanzi, "Storia Pittorica dell' Italia," vol. v. p. 20.

The first time that this type was employed was in the edition of Virgil published by Aldo in 1501, and he is careful to acknowledge his obligation to the great artist in the following inscription :—

> " In Grammatoglyptæ Laudem
> Qui graiis dedit Aldus, in latinis
> Dat nunc Grammata sculpta dædaleis
> Francisci manibus Bononiensis." [3]

It is only much to be lamented that Aldo did not continue to act in accordance with this acknowledgment. Far from doing so, he obtained from the Government of Venice a monopoly for the use of these types during a period of ten years, and three successive Popes—Alexander VI., Julius II., and Leo X.—laboured to secure Aldo this monopoly, while it was forbidden to Francia to cut types for any one else, and to all, save Aldo, was their use forbidden. In all the history of monopolies and privileges one more odious than this could hardly be found. Even admitting, as it is commonly urged, that Aldo first invented the characters to which he gave his name, the mere fact of their having been executed by another hand ought to have restrained him from demanding, and the Government from according, so unjust and so exclusive a monopoly. In the rare and beautiful edition of Petrarch which Francia published at Bologna, where he set up his printing-press after his separation from Aldo, is to be found, on the title-page, his lament that he had lost both the glory and the profit which he would have derived from the characters cut by his own hand, had not both fallen to the share of Aldo Manuzio. The rival printers of Soncino, near Cremona, who first printed the Hebrew characters, and who, although they afterwards set up their printing-presses throughout Italy, always preserved the name of their native town till it

---

[3] Rénouard, "Annales des Alde," vol. i. p. 165. There has been some doubt as to whether this Francisci was the same person as the famous Francia, but Sir Antonio Panizzi, in a beautiful little treatise (from whence this information has been drawn) entitled " Chi era Francesco da Bologna," and privately printed in 1856, proves this point to the satisfaction of all his readers. See also Blade, " Life of Caxton," vol. ii. p. 24.

became a family name, declared also, without hesitation, that Aldo had usurped from Francesco da Bologna the honour of the invention and the design of the running characters.[4] They further added that no one was to be compared with Francia for skill in engraving, not only Latin and Greek, but also Hebrew characters.

It must, however, also in fairness be stated that Renouard does his best to justify Aldo from this accusation, by asserting that the inscription in the Virgil is an all-sufficient acknowledgment of the artist's share in the invention of the running characters.[5] Be this as it may, it would still seem much to be regretted that even the semblance of so great a blot should rest on the character of a man who, like Aldo Manuzio, spent his whole life in efforts to contribute to the progress of the human mind and the advancement of civilization.

It is indeed difficult to form an idea of the enthusiasm with which Aldo laboured to place once more before mankind those grand productions of ancient classical literature which had so long been allowed to remain in obscurity. If he discovered a manuscript which had not yet been printed, he never ceased in his efforts till he had gained possession of it, regardless of trouble and expense. While he thus promoted the interests of learned men, they in return gave him their best assistance. From all sides contributions of manuscripts flowed in, some for sale, and some sent gratuitously as gifts.

From 1501 to 1505 this Aldine Press was in the fullest activity, publishing all the principal classical and Italian authors in that smaller form of which the Virgil of 1501 had been the first sample. The transition from the cumbersome and expensive folios to these cheap and portable editions was so great a step in the progress of printing, that it appeared only second in importance to the discovery of the art itself.

Nor does the reputation of Aldo rest only on his printing, or even on his editorial labours, the Greek and Latin dissertations, prefaces, and criticisms with which he illustrated the books which issued from the press; he

---

[4] Familiarly called "caratteri corsivi."
[5] "Annales des Alde," vol. iii. p. 22.

left behind him also some original works, chiefly of an instructive kind, of considerable merit. His first work was a Latin Grammar written to take the place of the old scholastic "Doctrinale" of "Alexandri da Villa Dei," written in barbarous and meaningless rhymes, which had been the torment of his youth. This was followed by a Greek Grammar, a Greek and Latin Dictionary, and other works, whose names cannot be inserted in this paper for want of space.

PART II.

SOME writers have affirmed that Aldo Manuzio first invented the Greek types. This, however, Rénouard declares to be only so far true that up to the time of Aldo, whenever a Greek passage occurred in a book, it was left blank to be filled up with the pen, because few of the printing establishments were furnished with Greek types. But Greek books, many of them of importance, were known to be printed before that time, such as the Grammar of Lascaris at Milan in 1476, a Homer at Florence in 1488, and others besides. Nevertheless, there is no doubt that Aldo was the first to introduce a great improvement in the existing Greek types, which were badly shaped and rudely cut, whereas he had new ones formed after the pattern of the best manuscripts. Moreover, Greek books, which had been printed slowly and at rare intervals, now issued from the great Venetian Press with astonishing speed. When Aldo had amply furnished himself with Greek and Latin types,[6] his next step was to adopt a peculiar device whereby his books might be distinguished all over the world. He chose

[6] A contemporary writer affirms that Aldo had silver types cast for his favourite editions. Another declares that the Pope promised Paolo Manuzio a set of types in the same precious metal, "argentei typi;" but Rénouard casts doubt upon this, declaring that the expense of casting types in silver would have been too great. Nor would they have been sufficiently durable. On the same account he refuses to believe that silver types were employed to print a Bible at Cambridge, by Field, in 1656.—"Ann. des Alde," iii. p. 85.

with singular sagacity the mark of the Dolphin and
Anchor well known to all, and which, adopted by English
printers[7] and publishers, is still employed to adorn many
of the choicest editions of our books.

The Dolphin was chosen because of the speed with
which the fish is said almost to leap through the waves,
while the Anchor, on the contrary, represents stability
and repose. By these emblems Aldo meant to imply that,
in order to labour to any purpose, the scheme of work
must be carefully and maturely weighed, and then be
executed with rapidity.[8]   It is said that two Emperors,
Titus and Domitian, made use of the same emblem, and
that Aldo was presented by a member of his Academy
(Il Bembo), with a silver medal of the time of Titus,
bearing the stamp of the Dolphin and Anchor.   Although
he had for some time entertained the idea of employing
this device, it was only used for the first time in 1502,
for a small 8vo Dante, and all the books which subsequently issued from his press bear this celebrated
emblem.   As might have been expected, there were many
counterfeit dolphins and anchors employed by printers,
who, disregarding the monopolies granted to Aldo, sought
by the aid of this stamp, and by imitating his types, to
pass off their books as productions of the celebrated
Aldine Press.   Among these were the Giunti of Florence,
of whom Francesco d' Asola, a partner and relation of
Aldo, bitterly complains in his Preface to the Titus
Livius of 1518.   He discovered their fraud by the fact
of the dolphin's mouth being turned to the left, and not
to the right, as in the Aldine stamp.   Theodoric Martens,
a Belgian printer, who died at Alost in 1534, stamped his
editions with a double anchor ; to which Erasmus, many

---

[7] As, for example, William Pickering, of London, with the inscription " Aldi Discip. Anglvs."   His edition of the British Poets
is in the small 8vo form which Aldo had invented.   The mark
which he adopted for his books was the later and more finished impression of the Dolphin and Anchor, struck in the time of Paolo
Manuzio, and technically termed " L' Ancora grassa."   The original
stamp of the Aldine Press, as employed by the great Aldo, appears
in the books of Mr. Basil Montagu Pickering, the present publisher.

[8] " Annales des Alde," vol. lii. p. 97.

of whose works he printed, makes allusion in his epitaph
upon the printer :—

"Here I lie, Theodoric of Alost.

.   .   .   .   .   .

The sacred anchor remains, emblem dearest to my youth.
Be Thou, O Christ, I pray, my sacred anchor now." [9]

The dolphin and anchor were indeed more or less
imitated by many printers of this century at Paris, Basle,
Cologne, Rome, Parma, &c., &c. John Crespin, of Geneva,
placed them at the foot of a Greek Testament, with the
initials J. C. and the following lines :—

"Les agités en mer, Christ, seule anchre sacrée
Asseure, et en tout temps seule sauve et recrée."

These printers, for the most part, adopted the device after
the death of Aldo, but during his lifetime he suffered
most annoyance from the printers at Lyons, who imitated his editions without scruple, and even copied his
prefaces.

These frequent piracies at last compelled Manuzio to
draw up a formal remonstance, in which he pointed out
the typographical errors and general incorrectness of the
fraudulent editions. But even this the Lyonese printers
turned to account, for they quickly extracted the erroneous
sheets, which they replaced with new ones, corrected
according to Aldo's remonstrance, and thus their fraud
was doubly secured.

It is now time to speak of the Academy, the " Aldi
Neacademia," formed by Aldo in Venice for the especial
purpose of presiding over the editions of the classics, and
ensuring their excellence and correctness. All the learned
men of Italy of that time esteemed it an honour to belong
to this Academy.[1] The name of Erasmus is also enrolled
among the list of members. His " Adagia," as has been
already stated, were printed at the Aldine Press, and
Aldo announces, in the preface, that he had purposely

[9] " Hic Theodoricus jaceo prognatus Alosto

.   .   .   .   .   .

Anchora sacra manet, notæ gratissima pubi
Christe, precor, nunc sis anchora sacra mihi."
[1] For a list of members see Rénouard, " Ann. des Alde," vol. iii.
pp. 36—38..

delayed the printing of many classical additions in order to publish immediately this most excellent work. Erasmus, on the other hand, observes, in the same book, that "If some tutelary deity had promoted the views of Aldo, the learned would shortly have been in possession not only of all the Greek and Latin authors, but even of the Hebrew and Chaldee, insomuch that nothing could have been wanting in this respect to their wishes." [1]

It is sad, however, to relate that this friendship between Aldo and Erasmus, which had been founded on mutual esteem, did not last. It was even exchanged for a dislike almost approaching to hatred, and difficult to account for. Whereas it had been the pride of Erasmus to assist in the correction of the great Venetian Press, he afterwards indignantly disclaimed having undertaken the correction of any but his own works, and is careful to explain that he never received from Aldo the wages of a corrector of the press. Some affirm that the Italian manner of living appeared to Erasmus frugal and parsimonious when compared with the good cheer of Germany or of his native country, and that he left Venice on that account. But a more probable solution would seem to be that as his opinions inclined towards those of Luther and his party, they became distasteful to Aldo, who had every reason to attach himself to the cause of the Popes, to whom he owed three successive monopolies. It is certain that, after the quarrel, whenever Aldo or his successors printed a book for Erasmus, they inserted the contemptuous designation of "Transalpinus quidam homo" in the title, instead of the name of the author, as if to signify his complete disgrace at the court of Rome. Moreover, the Prince of Carpi, who had supplied the funds for establishing the Aldine Press, was strongly opposed to the views of Erasmus, and even went so far as to refute them in a work of much erudition. When Luther first began to declare his opinions, the eyes of the world were fastened on Erasmus as one of the most learned men of the age, to see which side he would embrace. While the Lutherans, in spite of the protesta-

[1] Roscoe's "Life of Leo X.," vol. i. p. 168.

tions of Erasmus, declared that he held their opinion, he
was an object of interest to two parties in the Church of
Rome : the one headed by Leo X., Clement VIII., and
Cardinal Sadoleto, who tried by praise and flattery to
keep him within the pale of the faith and to induce him
to lay down those opinions which led him to be suspected ;
and on the other hand, those who thought it their duty to
protest openly against him, to point out his errors and
mistakes, in order that others might not make shipwreck
of their faith upon the same rocks which had wrought
his ruin.   Foremost among these was Alberto Pio, Prince
of Carpi.   Erasmus, to whom the character and learning
of this prince were well known, and who had besides
seen him often in Venice, remonstrated with him for the
harshness of his language, to which Alberto replied in a
learned treatise, dated May 12, 1526, pointing out to
Erasmus the dangerous nature of his opinions, so little
removed from those of Luther, at the same time praising
both his genius and learning.
· Erasmus defended himself against this attack, and the
controversy continued.   Theology had always been the
favourite study of the literary prince of Carpi, and he now
undertook an elaborate work, singularly free from the
scholasticism of the age, eloquent in style, and full of
erudition, in which he examines and compares the works
of Erasmus and of Luther.   This work he printed at
Paris, where he had taken refuge after the sack of Rome
by the troops of Charles V.   It was in the press when he
died (1531), and was published in Paris that same
year.[3]
   These few fragments are all that can be collected of
the history of a prince who has perhaps literally, the most
right to be called a Prince Printer of Italy, his name
appearing in conjunction with that of the first Venetian
Printer on the title-page of each one of those splendid
volumes of Venetian typography as they issued from his

[3] " Alberti Pii Carporum Comitis Illustrissimi et Viri longe doc-
tissimi præter præfationem et operis conclusionem, tres et Viginti
libri in locos lucubrationum variarum D. Erasmi Roterodami quos
censet ab eo recognoscendos et retractandos."—Tir. "Storia,"
vii. p. 295.

press. His tutor and friend, the great Manuzio, whom he had been the means of so largely benefiting, and who in return, had spent his whole life in executing the vast literary designs of the prince, had pre-deceased him by some years. Aldo died in 1515, at the age of sixty-six, before he could accomplish his cherished project of printing a Bible in three languages,—Hebrew, Greek, and Latin. One page only was executed of this great undertaking, but the beauty of the characters of all three languages, in each of which Aldo was an equally good scholar, is sufficient to show what a noble work the first Polyglot Bible would have been had he lived to execute his design.[4]

Aldo was by his own especial wish buried at Carpi, in the Church of San Paterniano.

But the reputation of the Aldine Press, which he had founded, was not destined to expire with him, nor was the patronage of the princes of Italy only exercised in Carpi.

Paolo Manuzio, the third son of Aldo il vecchio, and the only one who followed the profession which his father had rendered so famous, was but three years old at the death of Aldo. The work of the Aldine Press was not, however, suspended on that account, but, still bearing the name of its illustrious founder, was maintained by Andrea Torresano d'Asola, the father-in-law of Aldo il vecchio, with whom he had entered into partnership on marrying his daughter, and who had assisted him in his pecuniary difficulties. Andrea was himself an adept in the art of printing, and, some years previous to his entering into this partnership, had purchased the printing establishment of Nicholas Jenson, another Venetian printer of some reputation, which thus became incorporated into the Aldine Printing House. The operations of this great firm were thereby still further extended, and were carried on by Andrea d'Asola and his two sons, Francesco and Federigo, during the minority of Paolo Manuzio.

The books printed during this period are marked

"In ædibus Aldi et Andreæ soceri."

---

[4] For fac-simile of page see Rénouard, "Annales," iii. p. 44.

The stamp of the Press was preserved unchanged, with the addition of the peculiar mark of the Torresani—a tower with the letters A. T.—till the death of Andrea in 1529, when the establishment ceased to work for a few years.

It was reopened in 1533, by the young Paolo Manuzio, who, although only twenty-one, inspired confidence both by his name and the diligence with which he had applied himself to his studies. In 1540 the partnership with his uncles, the Torresani, was dissolved. They went to Paris, where they set up, a few years later, a printing establishment, while Paolo, with the advice and assistance of his father's learned friends, conducted the Aldine firm at Venice. The books which now issued from this press bore either the inscription " Apud Aldi Filios " or " In ædibus Pauli Manutii." A new and more careful stamp of the dolphin and anchor was struck, which is termed by Italian booksellers " L' Ancora grassa," to distinguish it from that of Aldo il vecchio. In 1546 the stamp underwent a still greater change, the anchor having, to use an heraldic term, two cherubs for " supporters " on either side, and the words " Aldi Filii " substituted for the single name, which, divided in two, " Al-Dvs," was formerly placed on either side the anchor.[5]

In the year 1571, the Emperor Maximilian II. conferred upon Paolo a patent of nobility, with the right to add the Eagle of the Empire to his coat-of-arms, which was the same as the mark of his press. But Paolo died before he could make use of this new device, and the only books which bear it were printed after his death by his son.

Paolo Manuzio, being now sole proprietor of the firm, applied himself diligently to follow his father's footsteps, and gave himself up entirely to literary and typographical labours. The editions which he issued from his press were universally famed for their beauty and correctness, and for the erudition of their notes and prefaces. His edition of Cicero of 1540 was considered the best and

[5] For these various forms, see Rénouard, " Annales," iii. pp. 98— 101.

most important of any classical author yet published.[6] The "Aldi Neacademia," which his father had founded, and which had existed but a few years, was replaced in Paolo's time by a great "Accademia Veneziana," also called "Della Fama," from its emblem—a representation of Fame with the motto : " Io volo al ciel per riposarmi in Dio." It was founded in 1556 at the cost of Federigo Badoaro, a Venetian senator, and about a hundred of the most distinguished literary and scientific men of Italy belonged to it, with Bernardo Tasso, father of the poet, as president. It was intended for the general encourage- ment of the arts and sciences, with the special objects of correcting the numerous mistakes of the old books on philosophy and theology, adding annotations and disserta- tions, and translating them into various languages. The printing was entrusted to the Aldine firm, and Paolo Manuzio was chosen as corrector of the press. He was, besides, appointed to fill the chair of eloquence in the Academy. In a short time many books were issued, which, for the beauty of their type, the quality of their paper, and the accuracy of their corrections, obtained a great reputation for this Academy. But, unhappily, the brilliant expectations to which this institution had given rise, were dashed to the ground by the bankruptcy of its founder, and the " Accademia della Fama " was as short- lived as the " Aldi Neacademia " had been. It struggled on for a few months after this catastrophe, until its com- plete collapse, after an existence of but four years, and thirty years went by before another Venetian Academy could be established.

Still, the manner in which Paolo Manuzio, during his brief connection with this institution, had discharged his functions, won for him a great reputation, so that when after its collapse he travelled through Italy for the pur- pose of visiting the fine libraries which it was the pride and glory of the princes to collect, it was the endeavour of each and all to retain him in their principality. The Senate of Bologna offered him a large sum to carry on his printing in their city, and the Cardinal Ippolito d' Este tried in the same way to retain him in Ferrara, but the

6 Hallam, " Lit. of Europe," vol. i. p. 325.

honour of an Aldine establishment was reserved for the Imperial city. In the year 1539, the Cardinal Marcello Cervini and Alessandro Farnese had formed the design of setting up a printing-press in Rome for the purpose of printing the manuscripts of the Vatican. Antonio Blado Asolano, the printer selected to execute the design, previous to going to Rome, went to Venice to implore the assistance of the Aldine Press in the preparation of types, paper, and other requisites for the undertaking. The Venetian firm gladly lent their powerful assistance, and beautiful editions of Greek and Latin authors soon issued from the Blado Press, of which the most remarkable was a Homer with the commentaries of Eustathius, published in 1542.

But it was the age of Luther, and the presses of the Holy See were required for other purposes than for that of reproducing ancient classical authors. Pius IV. therefore summoned no less a person than the great Venetian printer to establish a branch of the Aldine Press at Rome, for the purpose of printing the works of the Fathers of the Church, and other ecclesiastical writers, in order to oppose some barrier to the flood of new opinions which was rapidly overspreading the world. At the cost of Pius IV., who, besides an annual salary of five hundred scudi, paid in advance the whole expense of the transfer of himself and family, Il Manuzio opened his printing-house in the Campidoglio, the very palace of the Roman people, and the books printed there bear the stamp of "Apud Paulum Manutium in ædibus Populi Romani, 1561."

It would seem as if so classical a residence and so important an employment must have fixed Paolo Manuzio for ever in Rome. But nevertheless, from various reasons (and no satisfactory one has yet been discovered), either because his gains were not in proportion to his labours, or because the climate was not suited to his health, after the lapse of nine years he left Rome and returned to Venice.

Yet he was never able, after his sojourn in Rome, to settle again. He went both to Genoa and Milan, and in 1573 once more to Rome, for the purpose of visiting a daughter whom he had left in a convent there.

I

Gregory XIII. then occupied the Papal chair, but like
his predecessor, he knew too well the value of a man
of so great a literary reputation as Paolo to let him
escape out of his hands. Gregory offered him an annual
stipend, with entire liberty to attend to his own pursuits,
if he would once more conduct the Aldine Press at Rome
Paolo agreed, but his second sojourn in Rome was
shorter even than the first; not, however, this time from
any inconstancy on his part, but because death overtook
him early in the following year (1574). Although
Paolo Manuzio was inferior to his father, in that he only
maintained what Aldo had created, he was equal to
him as a printer and editor. Some writers say that his
taste as a critic was not so faultless as that of Aldo il
vecchio, but his works place him among the most polished
writers, both in Latin and Italian, of his age. His
most famous Latin treatises are the two upon the Roman
Laws and Polity.[7] In his letters Manuzio carefully
copied the style of Cicero, whose letters he also commented on. The literary men of his time even went so
far as to say that it was difficult to decide whether
Manuzio owed most to Cicero or Cicero to Manuzio. But
while Hallam places him among those writers of the
latter part of the sixteenth century who were conspicuous for their purity of style, he blames him for too
close an imitation of Cicero, which causes the reader soon
to weary of his writings, however correct and polished
they may be. Paolo Manuzio also wrote and published
various small treatises in elegant and beautiful Italian.
He made a careful study of Roman antiquities, and was
the first to discover on an ancient marble the Roman
Calendar which he published in 1555, with an explanation, and a short treatise on the ancient manner of
counting the days. Like all eminent men he had his
detractors, such as Gabriello Barri, who accused him of
being a plagiarist, but the accusation was entirely without
foundation.[8]

At the same time Tiraboschi blames Paolo for his dis-

---

[7] "De Legibus Romanorum," and "De Civitate." Hallam,
"Lit. of Europe," i. 523.
[8] See Tiraboschi, vii. 211.

content, and for his repeated complaints of the indifference
shown by the princes of his time to the progress of
literature. The short sketch of the life of Manuzio just
given is sufficient to prove the injustice of these complaints, and Tiraboschi shows that at the time when
they were made (1595) there was not a province in Italy
without a prince whose pride and glory it was to cherish
and protect literature and learning, and who has not left
behind him the recollection of his munificent protection
of science and art. But Manuzio was often hindered in his
great labours by ill-health and the weakness of his eyes ;
and this may perhaps account for that peevish and
querulous disposition which led him to find fault with the
times in which he lived.

He left four children, but only one son—called Aldo,
after his illustrious grandfather—was destined to maintain
the family reputation.

Aldo "il giovane," so called to distinguish him from
the founder of the family, seemed destined to fulfil the
brilliant expectations suggested by his name, by publishing, at the age of eleven, a small collection of choice
Latin and Italian authors, together with a treatise upon
the two languages ;[9] and this was followed, in three
years' time, by a more learned and more considerable
treatise upon Latin orthography.[1]

That his father must largely have assisted him in these
two works can admit of little doubt; indeed, Rénouard[2]
suggests that it was probably the work of Paolo himself,
with some few contributions from his son, and that the
father published the book in the name of Aldo in order
to give him a brilliant start on his literary career.

His after reputation did not at any rate keep pace with
so remarkable a beginning, and the success which he did
achieve was due more to his name than to his individual
efforts. He profited by his residence at Rome during his
father's lifetime to augment his collection of ancient inscriptions, by studying the monuments themselves instead

---

[9] Eleganze insieme con la copia della lingua Toscana e Romana,
scelte da Aldo Manuzio, 1558.
[1] Orthographiæ Ratio ab Aldo Manuzio.
[2] " Ann. des Alde," vol. iii. p. 176.

of the accounts of them in books. He was thus able considerably to improve his work on Latin orthography, of which he published a new edition in 1566. This work, the fruit of great research, is even now consulted by those who wish to write or reprint Latin books.[3]

Paolo Manuzio entrusted his son with the management of the Aldine Press at Venice, himself conducting the branch which he had transferred to Rome.

The Venetian Press, under the superintendence of Aldo il giovane, did not so much produce new works as reprints of those editions on which its reputation was already founded. From 1540 to 1575 it was chiefly occupied upon the works of Cicero; and the most celebrated work of Aldo il giovane was his commentary upon the works of this author, in ten volumes. Five of these it must, however, be stated, were the work of Paolo, and only the latter five were added by his son.

In 1572 the young Aldo married Francesca Lucrezia, a daughter of a branch of that same Giunti family of printers who had been the early rivals of the Aldine Press. His career at Venice does not seem to have been very distinguished, although, perhaps more as a tribute to his name than his merits, he was made Secretary to the Venetian Senate, and other marks of distinction were conferred upon him. Yet he was not loyal to a city which had honoured himself and his family, or to an institution which had immortalized his name. In the hope of greater gains and a more extended reputation, he accepted the post of Professor of Latin Eloquence at Bologna, in the room of the learned Sigonius; and he left Venice (1585) never to return, having previously made over the famous press which bore his name to Niccolo Manassi.

Aldo il giovane had a full share of that princely favour which his father and grandfather had enjoyed. His " Life of Cosimo de' Medici " procured him the favour of Francesco, his descendant, the then reigning duke, who placed him in the chair of *belles lettres* at Pisa, through which he became a member of the Florentine Academy.

---

[3] " Ann. des Alde," vol. iii. p. 178.

At the same time he was offered a similar position at
Rome, vacant by the death of the famous Latin scholar
Muretus. This he at first refused, but it was kept open
in the hope that he would one day accept it, which at
last he determined to do. Yielding to the entreaties of
Pope Sixtus V., he transferred himself and his vast
library—the result of the united labours of his father and
grandfather—to Rome in the year 1588. He fulfilled
the duties of the Professor's chair during the lifetime of
this Pope, and at his death in 1590, his successor,
Clement VIII., gave Aldo, in addition to this post of
honour, the more lucrative position of superintendent of
the Vatican Printing Press. This responsible office he
only held during five years, dying—it is commonly supposed, of a surfeit—in 1597. Such was the unsatisfactory
life, which by no means fulfilled the brilliant promise of
its early years. Dazzled by the glory of a premature
reputation, Aldo neglected the profession which his father
and grandfather had raised to so much honour ; and instead of being, like them, the first printer of his age,
filled an inferior place among literary men. It would
seem also that he possessed more learning than taste in
employing his knowledge, and that, while gifted with a
retentive memory, he was by no means in other respects
a genius. His works are those of a learned man, well
acquainted with his subjects, but written in a dry, repulsive style. One of those supposed to be the most
interesting is the " Life of Castruccio Castracani," the
usurper who became Lord of Lucca. The life of this
singular individual had already been written by Macchiavelli in Italian, and by Tegrimi in Latin ; but Aldo,
dissatisfied with both these biographies, made a journey
to Lucca for the purpose of consulting the public archives
and family documents. With their assistance he published at Rome a new life of this extraordinary soldier of
fortune, entitled, " Le Attioni di Castruccio Castracani
degli Antelminelli, Signore di Lucca." It is praised by
De Thou, and a new edition was published at Pisa as
lately as 1820.

Aldo il giovane left no surviving children, and with
him the family became extinct ; while the Press which

will for ever bear their name, passed into other hands.
He died, moreover, without a will, and the splendid
library of 80,000 volumes, which it had taken three
generations to collect, was divided among his creditors.
Angelo Rocca wrote an epitaph upon the three Manuzii,
in which, however, he shows an undue partiality for
Aldo il giovane.[4]

The annals of the Aldine family have been given a
prominent position in this paper, and pursued as closely
as its brief limit will allow, because they illustrate not
only the progress and perfecting of the typographical art
in Italy in the fifteenth and sixteenth centuries, but also
the princely favour and patronage to which that art was
in its infancy so much indebted. The circumstances also
in which the Manuzii were placed, and the nature of their
labours, give their history an interest which does not
perhaps belong to that of any other printer. Nor are
similar circumstances likely to occur again. Never again,
as in the case of Aldo il vecchio, will it fall to the lot of
any printer to exhume and rescue from destruction the
ancient classics ; nor will it again be the privilege of any
prince to lend his countenance and supply the funds
requisite for so arduous and so glorious a task.

"Reddo Diem" is the apt motto placed by Manni on
the title-page of his life of Aldo Pio Manuzio, and it is
not easy to determine whether the Venetian printer
deserves most the gratitude of posterity for the light of
knowledge which his discoveries shed upon the world, or
for the preservation of that knowledge by an art which
he brought to perfection and which seems to render a
future dark era impossible. But although these two
achievements may fairly give him the claim to be considered the chief printer of Italy, it must be admitted
that in point of time others had preceded him. It is

---

[4] "Aldus Manutius senior, moritura Latina
Græcuique restituit mortua ferme typis.
Paulus restituit calamo monumenta Quiritum
Utque alter Cicero scripta diserta dedit.
Aldus dum juvenis miratur avumque patremque
Filius atque nepos, est avus atque Pater."
RÉNOUARD, *Ann. des Alde*, vol. iii. p. 208.

commonly supposed that the first Italian press was set
up by two Germans, Sweinheim and Pannartz, in the
monastery of Subiaco, then inhabited by German monks
in the Roman Campagna. They first printed the works
of Donatus, followed by those of Lactantius and the " De
Civitate Dei " of St. Augustine.

From Subiaco the monastery was transferred to Rome,
where it was under the patronage of the Popes, Paul II.
and Sixtus V., who conferred the Episcopate of Aleria, in
Corsica, on the corrector of their press, Giannandrea dei
Bussi, a man of great learning, but at that time in the
very depths of poverty. Another bishop, Giannantonio
Campino, Bishop of Terramo, corrected the proofs of a
rival printing-house. that of Udalrico Gallo at Rome.[5]

Before the time of Aldo, Venice had her printing-presses,
one set up in 1469 by Giovanni da Spira and Vendelino
his brother, another that of Niccolo Jenson, which, as has
been already seen, was purchased by Andrea d' Asola, the
father-in-law of Aldo.

In this same year books were also printed in Milan,
which may boast of having printed the first Greek book,
the Grammar of Lascaris, of Constantinople, in 1476, by
Dionigi da Paravisino.

Florence was celebrated for the family of the Giunti,
who attained a great reputation in their own city, and
also established branches of their firm at Venice and
Lyons. Luc Antonio Giunta and Filippo his brother were
the first printers in this family, and like the Manuzii, of
whom they were often the not very scrupulous rivals, they
published a great number of editions of the classics. Of
these, the most celebrated was an edition of Plutarch's
Lives in Greek, first published in that language by Filippo
Giunta ; while Bernardo, his son, published the celebrated
edition of Boccaccio's " Decamerone."[6] The Giunti maintained their printing reputation through several generations, and their rivalries with the Aldine firm were finally
extinguished by the marriage of the grand-daughter of
Luc Antonio Giunta with the grandson of Aldo il vecchio,

---

[5] Tiraboschi, " Storia." vi. pp. 162, 166, 168.
[6] Rénouard, " Annales," iii. p. 341.

in 1572. The family did not become extinct till the middle of the next century.

The art of printing spread in Italy with surprising rapidity, not only in the large cities, among which it was soon the exception to find one without a press, but also in the smaller towns, and even villages. Books were printed in St. Orso, near Vincenza; Polliano, near Verona; Pieve di Sacco, Nonantola, and Scandiano, in the duchies of Modena and Reggio; so that it may fairly be said that if Italy did not invent the art, she did her utmost to propagate it with rapidity.

Moreover, the influence of printing was not confined to the field, however vast and fruitful, of classical learning. It also penetrated into the wide and comparatively untried area of Oriental literature, and the restoration of the Greek and Roman languages was speedily followed by the study of the Eastern tongues, which, although necessary to the better knowledge of the sacred writings, had been for a long time neglected. The first Hebrew book ever printed is supposed to have been the Pentateuch, printed at Bologna in 1482, prior even to those issued by the famous Hebrew press at Soncino, already alluded to, which was established in 1484. In the next century the Hebrew language was studied to a considerable extent for controversial purposes, on the one side by the German Protestants, and on the other by the champions of the Roman faith. It was the favourite language of the great Bellarmine, himself a considerable Hebrew scholar.

The Syriac and Chaldee, closely related to Hebrew, were studied for the same theological purposes, also the Arabic, by far the most fertile in books. The first Arabic press was set up at Fano by the Venetian Giorgio, at the cost of Pope Julius II. It was the first press with Oriental types established in Europe, and although no book was issued from it during the lifetime of that Pope, one year after his death (in 1516) there appeared the first attempts at a polyglot Bible in a Psalter printed in four languages, Hebrew, Greek, Arabic, and Chaldee, of which a Dominican, Agostino Giustiniani, was the editor.[7]

This instance of good-will, which in the midst of his devouring ambition Pope Julius II. manifested to literature and art, would have been more highly esteemed, had not his immediate successor, Leo X., the worthy son of Il Magnifico, opened another Augustan age for literature and learning in Italy. And yet an eminent literary historian observes, "that although these times are generally distinguished as the age of Leo the Tenth, I cannot perceive why the Italians have agreed to restrict to the court of this Pontiff that literary glory which was common to all Italy. It is not my intention to detract a single particle from the praises due to Leo X. for the services rendered by him to the cause of literature. I shall only remark that the greater part of the Italian princes of this period might with equal right pretend to the same honour; so that there is no particular reason for conferring on Leo the superiority over all the rest."[8] Still, the patronage of the Holy See, which was accorded to the earliest beginnings of printing in Italy, was exercised with a continual munificence worthy of especial consideration. The Popes lost no opportunity of protecting and furthering the progress of an art whose manifold importance to the Holy See became daily more apparent.

Leo X. has been blamed, and not without reason, for cultivating the classics to the neglect of sacred literature. The two opposite historians of the Council of Trent (Fra Paolo Sarpi, and Pallavicino) seem to agree upon this point.[9]

A further witness to the devotion of this Pope to classical study and literature appears in his edition of the first five books of Tacitus, purchased for five hundred scudi from the Abbey of Corvey, in Westphalia, and printed and published at Rome in a new and costly edition at his own private expense, with the monopoly secured for ten years under pain of excommunication. The edition of Plato dedicated to him by Aldo Manuzio

---

[8] Roscoe's "Leo the Tenth" (from Andres, "Dell' origine d' ogni Letteratura"), i. p. 380.
[9] See their judgments—Sarpi, "Storia," i. pp. 11, 12; Pallavicino, "Conc. di Trento," lib. i. cap. ii. p. 51.

was also secured to the Venetian printer in a similar manner.

On the other hand, instances may be urged of the encouragement afforded by him to many learned men who devoted themselves to the study of the sacred writings. On being informed that Pagnini, a learned ecclesiastic then in Rome, had undertaken to translate the Bible from the original Hebrew, Leo requested to be allowed the inspection of this work. He also ordered that the whole should be transcribed at his own expense, and gave directions that it should be immediately printed.[1] Tesco Ambrogio of Pavia, who is said to have understood no less than eighteen different languages, was employed by this Pope to translate the liturgy of the Eastern clergy from the Chaldee into Latin, and was also appointed by him to a chair at the University of Bologna, where he delivered instruction in the Syriac and Chaldee languages. Moreover, the great Cardinal Ximenes dedicated his Complutensian Polyglot Bible to Leo, as an acknowledgment of the encouragement which he had afforded to Oriental learning. Leo the Tenth died in 1582. It was during the brief Pontificate of his immediate successors, nine of whom filled the Papal chair in an interval of sixty-three years, that the Manuzii (Paolo and his son Aldo) were summoned to establish a branch of their printing-press in Rome.

It was the glory of Sixtus V., elected Pope in 1585, to securely establish the Vatican printing-press. This press was principally intended for early Christian literature, and the dedication to him of the works of Gregory the Great, by Pietro da Tossignano, sets forth that infinite praise is due to Sixtus V., both for the idea and the execution of so magnificent a scheme as the publication of the Holy Fathers of the Church, whereby a great and solid advantage is obtained for the Catholic Faith. The splendid editions of the Vulgate and of the Septuagint, and many other works of great value, were the fruit of this last scheme of Sixtus V.

After the death of Aldo il giovane, the regulation of

---

[1] Roscoe's "Life of Leo X.," vol. ii. p. 401.

this press, which had been placed under his charge by Clement VIII., and upon which 40,000 scudi had been already expended, was confided to Domenico Borso. This expense does not appear so extraordinary when it is remembered that this press was furnished not only with Greek and Latin, but also with Hebrew and other Oriental characters, with paper of great value, and every other requisite for the perfection of this art. Above all, the most learned men of the age were paid high salaries to supervise and correct the editions which issued from it.

Many of the Cardinals imitated the example of the Popes. Even before Sixtus V. had conceived or executed his vast scheme, another, almost equally magnificent, had been carried into effect by Cardinal Ferdinando de' Medici. In 1580 he opened a printing-press in Rome, with Oriental types, to be entirely devoted to the publication of books in Eastern languages, for the purpose of propagating the Roman Faith among the people of the East, and bringing them into the fold of the Roman Church. Gregory XIII. placed under his care the two Patriarchates of Alexandria and Antioch, and declared him also Protector of Ethiopia, thus committing the salvation of those far-off countries to his charge.

The Cardinal did not neglect his trust, but despatched learned and expert travellers throughout Syria, Persia, Ethiopia, and other Oriental provinces, in search of manuscripts, which they brought to Rome to be printed. First there issued from his Oriental press an Arabic and Chaldaic Grammar, the works of Avicenna and Euclid, then the four Gospels, first in Hebrew, and afterwards in a Latin version, of which 3000 copies were printed. He had also intended to print the Bible in six of the principal Eastern languages, in order that these, joined to the four already printed, Latin, Greek, Hebrew, and Chaldee, might make altogether a Bible in ten languages, the grammar and dictionary of each tongue also forming part of the work. But the simultaneous death of Pope Gregory XIII., and of his own brother Francesco de' Medici, whom he succeeded as Grand Duke of Tuscany, prevented the accomplishment of this design. His Oriental press, however, continued to work for many years. In fact, most of the books in Oriental types published at Rome in the beginning of the seventeenth century contain the imprint—"Ex Typographia Medicea linguarum externarum." These types were afterwards transported to Florence, and are still preserved in the Palazzo Vecchio.

Thus it may be said that both the Pontiffs and Cardinals of the sixteenth and seventeenth centuries made use of their power no less than of their treasure in furthering the interests of science. Indeed, the dedications of the infinite number of books printed in this century, the letters of the learned men of the age, and all the various monuments of Papal magnificence which still exist in Rome, bear witness to this fact.

The two other princely houses which vied the most with Rome in munificence were those of Este and of the Medici. It would be difficult to decide which of these two carried off the palm in the opinion of contemporary writers. To Cosimo de' Medici, Florence and all Tuscany, of which he was the Grand Duke, are indebted for the enthusiasm with which during his reign the arts were cultivated, and the perfection to which they were brought. The favour of this prince was also extended to printing, and at his own cost he sent for Arnaldo Arlenio, a German printer, established him in Florence, and associated him with Torrentino, whose beautiful editions date from 1548.

Torrentino's editions cease with the year 1563, and it is supposed that the wars in which Tuscany was then involved caused him and his associate to seek a more peaceful retreat in Mondovi, where the Duke Emmanuel Philibert is said to have entered into partnership with them. He at any rate assigned them a provision of twenty scudi a month for three years, a fact of which Arlenio reminds him in a petition for the maintenance of his partnership with the heirs of Il Torrentino, and the payment of the promised provision, which, by some mistake, they had as yet not received. The duke acceded to their request in a decree issued at Turin, March 15th, 1571.[2]

The Duke of Ferrara did not suffer himself to be

[2] Note to Tiraboschi, vii. p. 218.

eclipsed by the magnificent patronage of the Grand Duke
of Tuscany.   Alfonso II. d' Este also opened a printing-
press in Ferrara for the special purpose of printing works
hitherto unedited, and manuscripts which he had acquired
by diligent search.

So many famous printing-houses, established in every
part of Italy, contributed to the general cultivation
of literature.   The multiplication of good copies of books
rendered them accessible, not only to the princes themselves, but also to private individuals; while numberless
new libraries were formed, and the famous old ones increased.

It would have been impossible in these few pages to do
more than indicate how powerful was the assistance
accorded by the princes to the art of printing during
the first two centuries after its introduction into Italy.
But enough has perhaps been said to prove that her
potentates were fully aware of the great advantages to
be derived from so wonderful an invention ; more especially as it seemed to come as a reward for their incessant
labours to promote the interests of literature, science,
and art.   Not only did the stores of classical learning
thereby revealed to them repay their efforts, but the
Pontiffs found also a return for their liberality in the
spiritual weapons with which printing supplied them,
out of the armoury of the early Fathers.

Such were some of the first effects produced in Italy
by an art whose influence was scarcely less great over
the other countries of Europe, although productive of
different results.   Printing reached its highest perfection
shortly after its introduction into Italy.   In point of
rapidity of execution no doubt the quantity of printed
matter issued in the present time is immeasurably greater.
But, on the other hand, as to the quality of typography,
there can be no comparison between the ephemeral
productions of these days and those marvellous works, of
which one alone would suffice to establish the reputation
both of printer and editor.

The early Italian editions are not only sought for and
prized on account of their rarity, but also on account of
their unrivalled beauty, the excellent quality of their

paper, the brilliancy of their types, the largeness of their
margins, and the careful attention bestowed on every
typographical detail.   Nor then, as now, were some ex-
travagantly-luxurious editions issued side by side with
others of startling inferiority, with bad paper and worse
ink.   The great printers of those days—the Aldi of Italy,
the Elzevirs of Leyden, the Estiennes of Paris—printed
for the general benefit of all readers.   It is true that their
publications were often dearer than the common productions of some inferior contemporary printer, but then
these great printing-houses issued no bad editions—all
were good, carefully executed, correct, and in good taste.
So much for the manual labour which belongs to the
printer ; but if we turn to the intellectual share of the
work which fell to the lot of the editor, there is still more
to excite our admiration in the sagacity and erudition
displayed in selecting the works most fitted for publication, and in arranging for their issue in the best possible
manner.   Looking back on those early days of printing,
on the reverence with which the new discovery was employed, and the grand end which it subserved, we experience a feeling of regret that familiarity with its use
should have placed in unworthy hands, and diverted often
to unworthy purposes, perhaps the greatest discovery man
was ever permitted to make.

   " It is a very striking circumstance," says Mr. Hallam,·
" that the high-minded inventors of this great art tried, at
the very outset, so bold a flight as the printing of an entire
Bible,[3] and executed it with astonishing success.   It was
Minerva leaping on earth in her divine strength and
radiant armour, ready at the moment of her nativity to
subdue and destroy her enemies. . . .   We may see in
imagination this venerable and splendid volume leading
up the crowded myriads of its followers, and imploring, as
it were, a blessing on the new art by dedicating its first-
fruits to the service of heaven."

   In Italy, also, as we have seen, printing was never

   [3] Commonly called the "Mazarin Bible," the edition being
unknown until found about the middle of the last century in
Cardinal Mazarin's library at Paris.— Hallam, " Lit. of Europe,"·
i. p. 153.

employed except in the service of erudition, or, higher still, in that of Divine revelation.

Thus contemplated, the art of printing seems raised above the ordinary level and bustle of common life, and surrounded by the same kind of dignified repose which especially belongs to the great libraries of Italy—those store-houses of accumulated science, the result of years of labour on the part of her learned men, and costly expenditure on the part of her princes.

There may have been many political and social evils' connected with the division of Italy into a variety of States, each more or less despotically governed, but it must be owned that the emulation caused by that very fact stimulated a number of individual efforts whereby the treasures of classical learning were secured to the world, literature and the arts were cherished and protected, and the graver sciences promoted in the same manner. To the same source may also be traced the rise and rapid progress of typography in the country. Italy has long sighed for unity and liberty, and within the last few years both these wishes have been accomplished. Great things are also expected from a form of government which seems to realize the wishes of her greatest sons. No longer does Rome

" Vedova, sola, e dì e notte chiama :
Cesare mio, perchè non m' accompagna ? " 4

Cæsar, in the person of a native monarch, sits firmly in the no longer empty saddle, and upon a free country now devolves the duty of cherishing the genius which may spring out of her inexhaustible soil ; yet must she never forget the debt which she owes to those princes by whose fostering care the great art of printing was upheld during its early struggles for existence in Italy, nor yet the noble purposes which, under their direction, it was made to serve.

4 Purg. c. vi.

THE ITALIAN DRAMA.

PART I.

THE "LUDI" OR EARLY MYSTERY PLAYS—THE "CAR-NASCIALESCHI" OF LORENZO DE' MEDICI—THE "ORFEO" OF POLIZIANO

A.D. 900—1500.

> " Ce qu'on ne doit point voir, qu'un récit nous l'expose —
> Les yeux en le voyant saisiroient mieux la chose.
> Mais il est des objets que l'art judicieux
> Doit offrir à l'oreille et réculer des yeux."
>   BOILEAU, *L'Art Poétique.*

In choosing the title of the *Italian* Drama, the writer wishes to imply that the slight sketch contained in these papers will only date from the revival of dramatic art in Italy. The classical fame of the Roman theatre, closely connected as it is with the immortal productions of the land where the drama first burst into life, remains in far abler hands.

It will, however, be seen that the rules and forms of the ancient drama had taken such deep root in Italy that they sprang up again, after centuries of devastation, to give life and shape to the first efforts of her modern tragedians. Even at the time of the fall of the empire, the theatres which had witnessed the classic scenes of the Roman drama were not entirely destroyed. They still served for the scenic representations of the "Mimi" as they were called, who were supposed to be directly descended from the ancient "Mimi" of the Attellanian "Fabulæ."[1] Most of the Italian writers on the drama agree in saying

---

[1] A kind of play or farce, which took its name from "Attella," a town belonging to the Osci in Italy. These farces were a sort of rude game played by the Roman youth, who represented the characters of ancient mythology.

that those which were called *Commedie dell' Arte*, were
the only comedies represented in Italy during the tenth,
eleventh, and twelfth centuries. In these dramas the
author's business was confined to arranging a skeleton plot
called a *scenario*, leaving with the actors the option of
filling it up with speeches according to their fancy, just
as in the present day, each actor chooses his own gestures
and actions to represent his conception of the part he has
to play. It was, however, understood that a certain
standard dress, and certain fixed jests belonged to each
part, and these were adhered to so strictly, that they have
descended even to our times in the familiar forms of
Harlequin and Punch (Puncinello). The dress of the
former (Arlecchino), originally called *Centona* or *Centunedo*,
being one garment made of numberless pieces, still preserves its character.

By degrees the *dramatis personæ* of the "Mimi"
became enlarged by Pantaleone·(a Venetian merchant);
Dottore, a Bolognese physician; Spaviento, a Neapolitan
Braggadocio, and other representatives of the various States
of Italy. Each spoke the dialect, and each wore the
costume of his native city. Far from being discouraged
by the ecclesiastical authorities, they received the decided
support of such grave Fathers of the Church as St. Thomas
Aquinas and St. Anthony; the latter only adding a
proviso that Harlequin should not be represented by a
clergyman, nor Punch be exhibited in church.

The scenic representations of the "Mimi" were after all
only relics of former times, but like the ancient classical
drama,—not to speak of the rude attempts of many a
barbarian nation, Scandinavian, Peruvian, and Chinese,—
the real efforts of the resuscitated Italian drama took a
religious form. The pilgrims, on their return from the
Holy Land, or S. Giacomo di Galizia, or the Madonna del
Puy, first began the custom of reciting publicly with a
certain amount of gesture and action the sacred story of
the Passion of our Lord, the life of the Blessed Virgin,
the Acts of the Apostles, and other passages either from
the Scriptures or from the legends of the saints.

At first these recitations, which rapidly became very
popular, were performed in the open air, either in the

churchyards, the public piazze, or the fields and highways.
But soon these places were discarded as unworthy of the
sacred character of the mystery plays, and they were
represented in churches where stages were erected ex-
pressly for the purpose. These sacred dramas resemble
the Greek plays in having both for their authors and per-
formers persons dedicated to the service of religion. If
the first Grecian poets were also priests, and, up to the
time of Sophocles, recited in person their dramatic compositions to the people, the mystery plays were also composed and performed by the ecclesiastical, and not the lay
members of the Church. We learn from reliable authority
that six sacred dramas were written by the nun Rosvita
of Gandersheim between the years 980 and 1000; and
Muratori quotes a decretal of Gregory IX. specially en-
joining that the priests, deacons, and subdeacons shall,
under the authority of the bishop, represent these dramas
with fitting masks and dresses, for the diversion of the
people.

But if the drama was reawakened to life by the same
motive which prompted its birth, and if we may trace
several points of resemblance between its origin and its
revival, many obvious reasons interfered to prevent these
representations, in their religious form, from approaching
in the smallest degree to the excellence of the ancient
Greek theatre. Among the Greeks there was no office of
higher importance in the State than that of the poet.
Hence few were chosen for it but such as could unite to
their natural poetical gift a perfect acquaintance with the
politics and opinion which it was necessary to instil into
the people. They knew how to turn the theatre to
account in moulding the popular mind to the ends which
the government had in view—how to find in it the most
powerful stimulus to their patriotic zeal, and their eager
desire for liberty. But priests of the Middle Ages, who
were the authors and directors of the sacred dramas, had
no such object in view, and, being scarcely less ignorant
than the people they professed to teach, their influence, far
from raising the popular tone, could only serve to increase
the ignorance and superstition which so generally prevailed.

Then, if for a moment we consider the nature of
Pagan worship, absurd in principle, defective in means,
partial and inconsistent in result, we shall see that
out of these very errors the fine arts which combined
to illustrate the Greek drama drew their greatest advantages. Where the religious teaching was wholly bent
on fomenting human passions, instead of reproving
them, where the gods, leaving the instruction of mankind to philosophers, appeared only as gods of pleasure
—pleasure which, though inspired by poetry, eloquence,
and music, was still pleasure—it is evident why these
fine arts came to be considered as celestial gifts to be
gained at whatever cost, and to be worthy of the highest
esteem.

Again, when the people considered the manifold weak-
nesses, not to say vices, attributed to the objects of their
public veneration, it must have been obvious that there
was no such vast and appalling difference between gods
and men, as to render the former unfit to be represented
on the stage for the amusement of the latter. Further,
their patriotic feelings were appealed to by each representation of those mythological legends from which it was
their proudest boast to derive history. Thus while every
circumstance combined to exalt the Grecian drama to its
lofty summit of perfection it had also a political importance
which rendered it one of the most dearly-prized institutions of the State.

But when, after the lapse of centuries of darkness and
ignorance, the drama began to revive in the land of its
adoption, all the auspices which had been so favourable to
its origin were changed. We need no words to prove
that the sacred mysteries of Christianity are at once too
awful and too incomprehensible to be presented on the
stage as a spectacle for men. Human understanding being
incapable of attaining to the full conception of these
sacred subjects, they must be brought down from their
infinite height to come within the range of so limited a
vision, when, by a natural consequence, that which is
human and material must fall miserably short in an effort
to represent what is spiritual and divine.

A very few examples will perhaps show better than

K 2

any argument how rapidly these sacred dramas, originally pious in their intention, degenerated into abuse.

As early as the year 1264 we find that certain statutes *della Compagnia del Gonfalone* in Rome provided that these " Ludi," as the mystery plays were termed, because they were an essential part of the games and festivities held at Easter and Pentecost, should be represented twice in the year.

The feast of the " Pazzi " (maniacs) is the most conspicuous example of the profanity of these ceremonies. Under the presidence of a mock archbishop, called the " Arcivescovo dei Pazzi," the offices of the Church were turned into elaborate ridicule; but the details are too repulsive to be put forward here, and the reader can form a very fair idea of the whole ceremony from Walter Scott's description of the form it took in Scotland under the lordship of the " Abbot of Unreason."[2]

Another example may be found in the "Ludo Pascale della Venuta e Morte dell' Anticristo," annually performed by injunction of the Roman statutes. It was a sort of confused drama, in which the Pope and the Emperor, with other sovereigns of Europe, appeared on the scene, with the Antichrist, accompanied by personifications of Heresy, Hypocrisy, and Heathenism. In 1304, we read of the "Inferno" being represented at Florence, on the river Arno, which was covered with every sort of boat, steered by demons and filled with condemned souls, amid loud cries and flames and every other horrible notion that the subject could suggest. The concourse on the Ponte alla Carraia to see this extraordinary spectacle was so great that the bridge gave way and thousands were precipitated into the river beneath.

These are some specimens of the sacred dramas, which lasted for centuries, not only in Italy but all over Europe, till at last they were prohibited on account of their shocking profanity. They may be looked upon as the first efforts of the revived Italian drama. Still as they were played sometimes as *sceni mute*, without any words, sometimes with speeches invented on the spur of the

---

[2] See "The Abbot," p. 108.

moment, no pains were taken to preserve their forms or their dialogues, so that up to the fourteenth century we have no real specimens of Italian dramatic poetry.

But as ignorance declined, and the study of classic lore began to revive, it became evident that these "Ludi" could never reach the level of the ancient drama. Fearing at first to venture in the untried path of the new language, as yet unformed by the "Divina Commedia," the dramatic writers kept closely to the track of the old Latin tongue in their aim after a more exalted kind of drama. The first of these, Albertino Mussato, a learned Paduan, born in 1261, carefully modelled his Latin plays upon the pattern of Seneca. One of his tragedies called "Eccesinis," treating of a modern subject, the death of Ezzelino, tyrant of Padua, won so great a reputation at the time that, like Petrarch, Mussato was honoured by a laurel crown, presented to him by the Paduan university in 1313. The Bishop of Padua further issued an edict that on every Christmas Day the doctors, regents, and professors of the two Paduan colleges should go to his house in solemn procession to renew annually the offer of the crown.

Although Mussato is supposed to have written his tragedy in strict imitation of Seneca, he has not always attended to the unities of time and place. Tiraboschi truly observes that, in any case, "una cattiva originale non potea fare che una cattiva copia." Still, although pronounced by critics to be full of defects, they also admit that the passions are drawn with some force, and that a real interest runs through the play.

Albertino Mussato died at Chiozza in the year 1329, at the age of seventy. He was so close a contemporary of Dante that it is curious there should be no mention of him in the "Divina Commedia." It appears from Petrarch's letters, that in his early youth he also attempted to write a Latin comedy *per sollevar l' animo*.[3] He called it "Philologia," but was so convinced of its worthlessness that he took no pains to preserve it, and it never saw the light. It is a question, which some affirm and some

[3] Vol. i., lib. ii., lett. vii., p. 361.

deny, whether he was the author of two other dramatic compositions, one on the siege of Cesena, in 1357, by Cardinal Albanoz, the other upon the fate of Medea, which are still preserved in the Libreria Laurenziana at Florence.

Many other plays in modern Latin succeeded these first attempts, but they do not seem to have been ever represented. The earliest prose Italian dramatic composition is said to have been translated from the Latin play "De Captivitate Ducis Jacobi," by Secco Polentone, and to contain a remote reference to the arrest of General Jacopo Piccinino in 1464.

But soon throwing off the stiff bonds of translation, the vernacular began to assert itself with decided freedom and vigour in the "Maggiolate," "Ballate," and "Intuonate," for which it was so eminently adapted. The "Maggiolate," as their name would show, were the May-day festivities, of which a feeble remnant has descended to our own day; the May-pole being represented in those times by a living shrub, which, adorned with festoons and flowers, was planted opposite the window of the Queen of Love and Beauty, with every festive accompaniment of poetry, music, and the dance. The "Ballate" and "Intuonate" were merely sonnets, usually selected from the "Vita Nuova," set to music and sung to a kind of dance, as if the same instinct which prompted the inflections of the voice to express the feelings of the soul guided the movements of the body to the same end.

Although this kind of poetry can hardly be said to partake of the dramatic character, it prepared the way for the "Carnascialeschi." These were originally Carnival festivities, but, under the skilful treatment of Lorenzo de' Medici, they developed into a species of consecutive drama. Up to his time the "Carnascialeschi" were carried on in dumb show, with figures of wax or wood dressed in grotesque characters. The "Trionfi" of Petrarch were frequently chosen for these representations, and Lorenzo was the first to suggest that the words should be used also, set to a musical accompaniment.

On one occasion the "Trionfo della Morte" was elaborately prepared by the Florentine painter Piero di

Cosimo, nothing being omitted to strike terror into the hearts of the people. The funeral car, invested with every emblem of mortality, paraded the city, accompanied by troops of citizens singing the following lines :—

> " Morti siam come vedete
> Così morti vedrem voi;
> Fummo gia come voi siete,
> Voi sarete come noi."

Lorenzo himself composed many of these " Carnascia-leschi." His great desire was to wean the people by degrees from the sacred dramas which had so long occu-pied the stage ; but aware of the jealousy and suspicion with which any such reform would be received, he pre-pared the way by himself writing a sacred drama, only of a far higher order than any of those hitherto repre-sented. It was called " SS. Giovanni e Paolo "—not, however, the great Apostles, but two servants of the daughter of Constantine, who were put to death for the faith in the time of Julian the Apostate. It is written with a simple grace worthy of the ancient classical dramas, and the moral is carefully drawn. " L' Abramo e l' Isaaco " of Feo Belcari and Pulci's " Barlaam e Josafat" were contemporary productions of the same improved nature.[4] Lorenzo's next attempt was a drama called " Il Trionfo di Bacco e d' Arianne," full of vigour and grace. He had soon many imitators eager to follow in the new path which he had struck out. The " Virginia " of Bernardo Accolto, founded on one of the novels of Boccaccio, was quickly succeeded by the " Cefalo " of Niccolo da Correggio, a man of no ordinary ability, famous as a soldier, but more famous for his poetry. He was held in such high esteem by his contemporaries, that Ariosto dedicates two lines to him in the " Orlando Furioso :"—

> " Un Signor di Correggio . . .
> Con alto stil par che cantando scriva."
> *Orlando Furioso*, cxlii. s. 92.

Pre-eminent among the successful followers of Lorenzo was his friend and contemporary Angelo Poliziano. His

---

[4] Two interesting volumes of these " Rappresentazioni," as they were called, may still be seen in the British Museum.

talents first declared themselves in his "Stanze per la Giostra di Giuliano de' Medici," from the rich treasures of which neither Ariosto nor Tasso disdained to borrow. Thus, while the theatres at Rome, under Pomponio Leto, were representing with laborious pains translations of the plays of Plautus and Terence, Poliziano, the youthful poet of Florence, produced the first real Italian drama. His "Orfeo," written in a highly-polished style, with regularity of plot and unity of intention, marks a distinct era in the dramatic history of Italy. Poliziano was only eighteen when he wrote this drama at the special request of Cardinal Francesco Gonzaga. Moreover, it was completed in two days' time, in the midst of all the tumult and rejoicings of a great festivity.

The first editions of the "Orfeo" were so mangled and confused as to give no idea of its real beauty and elegance. But, fortunately for Poliziano's fame, the learned Padre Affo discovered an ancient and perfect manuscript in the convent of the Santo Spirito at Reggio, which has enabled him to give us a correct edition of the play. It is styled a tragedy, and is divided into five acts, which division is announced at the end of the prologue, in the lines :—

> "On stia ciascuno a tutti gli atti intento,
> Che cinque sono ; e questo è l' argomento."

The dialogue is regular, the style clear and correct, and there is a beautiful chorus at the beginning of the second act, in which the Dryads bewail the death of Eurydice. The speech of Orfeo as he stands before the gate of the Inferno (act iv., scene 1) is so fine that we feel it might indeed draw.

> " Iron tears down Pluto's cheek,"

and have

> " Made hell grant what love did seek."

There follows a spirited dialogue between Pluto and Proserpine :—

> "Chi è costui che con l' aurata Cetra,
> Mossa ha l' immobil porta."

> " Who is he, who with his golden lyre,
> Hath moved the gate immutable ? "

Then Orpheus makes his pathetic supplication in the rolling stanzas of the *ottava rima*, so difficult to render with any justice in a translation :—

> " Hear me, ye rulers of that hapless race,
> For ever banished from the light of day,
> To whom the creatures of all time and place
> And nature's works their mournful tribute pay :
> Hear my lament, and show some pitying grace,
> Love ever leads me onward on my way—
> I come not cruel Cerberus to bind,
> But still my love, my only love to find.

> " A serpent hidden 'neath the flow'ry mead,
> Hath ta'en from me the jewel of my life,
> So doth my heart in constant anguish bleed,
> And nought can still its grief and bitter strife ;
> But if, of the time thou didst in triumph lead,
> Trophy of famous love, a captive wife,
> Still any trace within thy mem'ry live,
> Once more to me my lost and lov'd one give.

> " All earthly things at last must enter here,
> Each mortal life to thy domain must fall,
> And all that moves beneath the lunar sphere
> Sooner or later must obey thy call.
> Brief be our span above, or long and drear,
> Thy dismal shores must claim us each and all ;
> Here is the utmost limit of our way,
> Here must we yield us to thy endless sway.

> " Thus must my fairest Nymph, one day, be thine,
> O'erpassed the term of nature's earthly life ;
> But thou the creeping tendrils of the vine,
> And grapes unripe hast shorn, with ruthless knife,
> To reap, while green, the harvest's promise fine,
> Oh who would work such grievous havoc rife—
> Give then, give back my dearest hope to me,
> No gift I ask, only a loan of thee.

> " Then by those waters, turbid and forlorn,
> Of Stygian marsh and Acheron's sad waves ;
> And by that chaos whence the world was born,
> By Phlegethon, whose burning torrent raves ;
> And by that fruit, O Queen, which pleased thee well,
> When first thou cam'st within these shades to dwell.
> If still injurious fate my prayer deny,
> Then will I ne'er return, but here will die."
> *Orfeo*, act iv.

Pluto is moved to grant Orfeo's request with the one fatal condition attached to it.

Resuming for an instant the old classical fetters, Poliziano makes Orfeo exult, in Latin, over his "half-regained Eurydice," but immediately afterwards returns to the vernacular, so exactly adapted for the beautiful and plaintive lament of the unhappy bride :—

> "Ahimè che troppo amore
>   Ci ha disfatti ambidun!
> Ecco che ti son tolta a gran furore
> E non son or più tua—
> Ben tendo a te le braccie, ma non vale
> Che indietro son tirata—Orfeo mio, vale !"

Although the play is written in five acts, each act being very short, it is comprised in brief compass.

Whatever disputes may occupy the Italian *letterati* as to whether the "Orfeo" was the first representation in the vernacular—and many are of opinion that it did really precede the "Cefalo" by a few years—in regard to merit they are unanimous in giving it the first place on account of its immense superiority to any of the Italian dramas hitherto produced.

Poliziano was the brightest ornament of Lorenzo de' Medici's brilliant court, and that discerning patron of literature and art thought no favours or distinctions too great for his young favourite. But in spite of Lorenzo's patronage, in spite of his learning and rare gifts, Poliziano was far from happy. He was the victim of a morbid discontent, arising partly out of the extreme deformity of his personal appearance, which is said to have preyed upon his mind, partly from his unpopularity, for he had many enemies jealous both of his court favour and rare talents. He died in 1494, surviving only two years the death of his friend and patron Lorenzo, to whom he was deeply attached. He has been accused of sharing the infidel opinions in his time so rampant in Florence ; but, on the other hand, it is urged that he translated from the Greek the work of St. Athanasius upon the Psalms of David, and that he made a careful study of Hebrew in order to arrive at a better understanding of the sacred writings. A contemporary writer assures us that he died in the Christian faith, being attended on his death-bed by Fra Domenico da Pescia, one of the two Dominican friars who shared Savonarola's martyrdom. It is also stated that, by order of the great preacher himself, Poliziano was vested after death in the garb of St. Dominic and buried in the church of San Marco.

His remains were afterwards removed into the church, and laid beside those of Pico della Mirandola, his contemporary and friend.

PART II.

"IL TEATRO ITALIANO ANTICO."

A.D. 1500—1600.

> "Sometime let gorgeous tragedy
> In sceptred pall come sweeping by,
> Presenting Thebes, or Pelops' line,
> Or the tale of Troy divine;
> Or what (though rare) of later age
> Ennobled hath the buskined stage."
>
> *Il Penseroso.*

WE have seen how Poliziano, with one vigorous effort of his genius, struck off from the Italian drama the fetters of a dead language; and sent it forth into the world in the freedom of its own beautiful speech.

But nearly a century elapsed before the dramatists of Italy knew how to make a real use of their liberty. They had been so long accustomed to the stiff rules and forms as well as to the language of the ancient drama, that they continued to follow in its track with leaden footsteps, content to sacrifice to a servile imitation much of their inventive genius and all confidence in their own powers.

Gian-Giorgio Trissino, commonly called the "Father of Italian Tragedy," framed his "Sophonisba" in strict obedience to the rules of Greek art. His natural gifts were sufficiently remarkable to make this voluntary bondage the more unfortunate, while his tragedy being founded on a Latin argument, there seemed the less need to subject it so rigidly to the rules of Greece. Many passages of real pathos, which occur in the " Sophonisba," show to what a far greater height of excellence the author might have reached had he left his genius to take its natural course.

Still, on the other hand, the claim of the " Sophonisba " to the first place in Italian tragedy may be due, in some measure, to the regularity of its plot, the preservation of the unities of time and place, and a strict adherence to the other canons enforced by the rigid rules of dramatic art. In fact its claim to precedence rests chiefly upon superior merit, for in point of time it might be disputed by two other tragedies in the vernacular.

Even if we consent to look upon the " Orfeo " more as a *pastorale* than a tragedy, there was a rival " Sophonisba " written in 1502, by the Marchese Galeotto del Carretto, dedicated to Isabella d' Este, Duchess of Mantua ; and this was succeeded by another tragedy—the " Pamphila " of Antonio da Pistoia—represented on a wooden theatre in the palace of Ercole II., Duke of Ferrara. But these tragedies scarcely obtained any reputation at the time, and are now considered by critics more in the light of confused allegorical dialogues than regular dramas.

The " Sophonisba " of Trissino, on the contrary, created a great sensation when it was represented at Rome in 1515, before Leo X., and its merits and defects have been ever since freely discussed by the great writers on Italian literature. Scipione Maffei gives it the first place among the early tragedies of the Renaissance. Voltaire considers it the first tragedy worthy of the name "que l'Europe ait vu après tant de siècles de barbarie." He finds many points to praise, though lamenting its stiff adherence to classical rule, which criticism he points with all the happiness of French illustration : " Il s'appuie sur Homère pour marcher, et tombe en voulant le suivre : il cueille les fleurs du poëte grec, mais elles se flétrissent dans les mains de l'imitateur."

Notwithstanding these defects, Trissino has no rival to dispute his claim to the first place among the tragedians of the " Teatro Italiano Antico." Even now the tragedy may be read with interest :—the character of Sophonisba is' sustained throughout with dignity and pathos combined—

> " With her th' Italian scene first learned to glow,
> And the first tears for her were taught to flow—"

and it cannot be denied that some of her speeches are full of tender feeling. The scene before her death, where she takes leave of her maidens, contains passages which have been especially admired. The appeal to her absent mother—

> " Oh my mother! and art thou far away!
> Might I but once have seen thy face again,
> And in thine arms have laid me down to die!" [5]

and the farewell to her son—

> " O figlio mio tu non avrai piu madre!"

The chorus in the third act, the poetical figure which paints our life—

> " as some treasure rare
> Not to be squandered in occasions base,
> Nor yet withheld from service of renown :
> For that a noble death throws back its light
> O'er the forgotten life that's passed away—" [6]

and many similar passages of the kind would repay the reader for a patient study of the drama.

The popularity of the " Sophonisba " was not confined to Italy. It rapidly found its way into France, and Voltaire is not ashamed to admit that the French dramatists gained the first ideas of the rules of their art from the Italian tragedian.

Gian-Giorgio Trissino was descended from an ancient family of Vicenza. His father was a Captain in the service of the Republic of Venice. His mother belonged to the Veronese family of Bevilacqua. He was born in

---

[5] " O madre mia quanto lontana siete,
Almen potuto avessi una sol volta
Vedervi ed abbracciar nella mia morte."

[6] " La nostra vita è come un bel tesoro,
Che spender non si devi in cosa vile
Nè risparmiar nell.' onorate imprese ;
Perchè una bella e gloriosa morte
Illustra tutta la passata vita."

Sophonisba, p. 79.

1478 and died in 1550. His idolatry of the classics, which perhaps hampered his natural genius, he derived from the instruction of his Athenian master, Demetrio Calcondila. The "Sophonisba" was composed at Rome, where the talents of the author early recommended him to the notice of Leo X., to whom in return for his consistent patronage Trissino dedicated his "Sophonisba." In this dedication the author apologizes for employing the Italian instead of the Latin language, and for having chosen to express himself in blank verse, which he considers more adapted for moving the passions than rhyme. He was often employed by the Pope as an ambassador to various States, and it is said that he refused a Cardinal's hat. He never accepted any ecclesiastical dignity, and Voltaire is inaccurate in prefixing the title of "Le Prélat" to his name.

Giovanni Ruccellai (born 1475, died 1526), the nephew of Lorenzo de' Medici and the friend of Trissino, followed closely in the footsteps of the first Italian tragedian. But if, stimulated by the modern plot, there is more originality in his tragedy of "Rosmunda," he falls back again into the character of a humble imitator in his next drama, the "Oreste."

The story of the "Rosmunda" is sufficiently interesting to make it worth while to look at the play, and some lines of really remarkable beauty are to be found in the "cori." Yet the "Oreste," in spite of its being only an imitation, is praised by Scipione Maffei as superior to "Rosmunda," and is considered worthy of claiming a distinct position among the old tragedies of Italy.

After the attempts of which we have spoken, a few years passed without being marked by any dramatic effort worthy of notice, till the "Canace" of Sperone Speroni (born 1500, died 1588) excited general interest and some controversy. This tragedy, which was much applauded by the author's fellow-academicians of the "Infiammati" at Padua, aroused a storm of criticism from the general literary world, a just retribution perhaps for the author's malignant attack upon Tasso, whose "Gerusalemme Liberata" Speroni had condemned unread. However much he pretended to defy the criticisms which now

assailed him in his turn, they induced him to alter and
amend his tragedy in many points; and despite all the
tempest of invective and criticism showered upon it at the
time of its publication, the "Canace" is now looked upon
as one of the landmarks of the Italian drama. Its variety
of versification and its florid style were among the many
points to which exception was taken, as being unsuitable
to the gravity and dignity of the tragedy. Nevertheless
there were many who praised the style for a certain grace
and delicacy which had hitherto been foreign to the
drama, and who imagined that Speroni's style had served
as a guide both to Tasso and Guarini in their respective *pastorali* of the "Aminta" and the "Pastor
Fido."

It would make a wearisome catalogue to cite even the
names of all the tragedies which followed in the wake of
those already mentioned, nor would the recital of names
of dramatists who were not great ornaments to the Italian
theatre repay the reader.

Some few exceptions ought to be made, in favour of
(1) the "Orbecche," the best of the nine tragedies produced
by the fertile genius of Giambattista Giraldi (born 1504,
died 1569), who first recommended the division of the
drama into acts and scenes. It was represented in 1541,
with splendid scenery, before Ercole II., Duke of Ferrara,
with so much truth and passion that the audience were in
tears.

The "Orbecche," so called from the name of the
daughter of the King of Persia, is founded on an Eastern
plot so full of horrors that the prologue finds it necessary
to prepare the minds of the august spectators at some
length for what they are about to witness. They are
warned that they are no longer in Ferrara, the happiest
and most peaceful of cities; but in Susa, the *crudo
albergo* of every disaster and crime they can imagine.
Yet the interest of the piece does not wholly depend on
the horrors which it contains, and, as in most of these old
tragedies, many gems of poetry are to be found in the
"cori."

(2) The "Œdipo" of Anguillara, represented in 1565 at
Vicenza, on a wooden stage, constructed by Palladio for

the occasion, in which Luigi Groto,[7] commonly called "Il ciéco d' Adria" on account of his infirmity, played the part of Œdipus. This man, although blind from his birth, became not only an actor of some merit, but also wrote two tragedies considered worthy of a place in the "Teatro Antico"—"L' Adriana," and "La Dalida.' The plot of the first of these is said, like Shakespeare's "Romeo and Juliet"—to which it bears a close affinity—to be founded on the novella "La Giulietta" of Luigi da Porto ; and those who have the patience to read it through will observe several points which resemble the favourite English play.

(3) The "Antigone" of Luigi Alamanni, which was honoured by a theatre constructed by Palladio, and further adorned for its representation at Venice by twelve great pictures for scenes, painted by Zuccaro himself.

(4) The "Soldato" of Angelo Leone (published 1550) is mentioned not so much on account of any intrinsic merit, as because it is supposed to have first suggested the idea of a "tragedia cittadina," or domestic tragedy, a pleasing variety from the "sceptred pall" with which the Italians had hitherto invested the tragic muse.

(5) The "Acripanda," by Antonio Decio da Horte, represented at Florence (1592), is again a departure from the mythological track, but is none the less full of the horrors and cruelties which an Egyptian plot can so well suggest to the imagination ; yet the first scene of act iv., where the murdered children appear as ghosts to comfort their bereaved mother, is so pathetic that it almost compensates for the horrors which lead up to it. We subjoin a few stanzas selected from Mr. Walker's admirable translation of this beautiful scene.

ACRIPANDA, CHORUS, GHOSTS OF THE TWINS.

Ghosts.

"Thou to whom our birth we owe,
Loved in life and in the tomb,
Turn and hear a tale of woe,
Turn and mark thy children's doom.

.   .   .   .   .

---

[7] Born at Adria 1541, died at Venice 1585.

" Why lament to see us soar,
Where the tides of transport flow,
Gifted from the heavenly store
Far beyond our loss below ?

" Would you wish to lure us down,
Here to wander with the dead ?
Tho' the bright imperial crown
Sparkled on each youthful head.

· · · · ·

" Fickle chance no longer here
Runs her ever-changing round,
Sad misfortune's frown severe,
Never clouds the hallowed bound.

· · · · ·

" Banish sorrow, banish fears,
Taint not thus our pure delight,
Nor will unavailing tears
Deprecate our heavenward flight.

" May the fates benignant join
To thy life's allotted space,
All the long revolving line,
Severed from our hapless days."

Acripanda.

" Whither, denizens of air,
Whither do you flit away,
Your allotment to prepare,
In the realms of endless day ? "

Chorus.

" See ! they mount, and now they go,
Like an arrow from the bow ;
Now they skim the starry bound !
Now they pierce the blue profound !
Melting now like vapours grey,
See the phantoms flit away,
Where their forms they seem to shroud
Deep in yon disparting cloud !
High the heavenly portal glows ;
Angels open—angels close."

WALKER'S *Historical Memoir on Ital.
Tragedy, p.* 123.

(6) The " Merope " of Torelli-Torelli, who was the last
to make use of the " Coro Fisso." This ancient institution, which the Italians had copied from the Greeks, was
destined to give place to the new and popular invention

L

of the "recitative." It is still undetermined where the chorus was placed on the stage, but it was always accompanied by music of a solemn character, in the style of the choral church music of the period, sometimes even with the addition of a dance to a slow measure, like the early "Maggiolate" and "Carnascialeschi."

(7) The "Torrismondo" of Tasso, written during his imprisonment at Bergamo (1587), sheds its lustre upon this period of Italian tragedy. This has already been mentioned in a former paper,[8] so we will not reconsider it here, only pausing to observe that although an inferior production of that great author, it is considered by Italian critics far superior to the other dramas of the age. Although many of the tragedies of this century obtained high laurels at the time, few, if any, would now elicit applause if they were once more put upon the stage. The admiration then so universal for the ancient classical theatre caused every effort to resemble it to be looked upon with favourable eyes, nor did the dramatists remember that the difference of language, manners, and times demanded a different kind of action and expression to that chosen by the ancient writers, or that the rivers of blood with which they chose to inundate the stage were any drawback to the enjoyment of the spectators. It is obvious that the long narratives which are to be found in the Greek tragedies were ill-adapted for reproduction by modern imitators, and that the use of the chorus had little to recommend it to modern ideas.

It was however perhaps natural that the Italians should begin by copying the Greek drama in order to prepare the way for those great dramatic compositions which, while they preserved the best features in the writings of the ancient dramatists, would avoid the defects peculiar to the customs and genius of their nation and times.

While the early tragedians of Italy, strictly bound by classical rule, continued for nearly a century servile followers and imitators of Sophocles and Euripides, in their efforts to revive the tragic drama, the comedians were no less victims to the same bondage.

---

[8] See page 88.

We have already seen how Ercole I. had caused the plays of Terence and Plautus to be represented in the theatre at Ferrara, first in their original language, and afterwards in the literal translations of those classical writers into Italian.

The next step was to compose original productions in the Italian language, and it must be owned that good comedies of this period are even rarer than tragedies— perhaps because the dignity of the subject and the importance of tragic action served in some measure as a cloak for the many defects of their composition. But with comedy, where the personages often belong to plebeian or private life, and where the action is more familiar and domestic, a grace and vivacity of style and a happy ingenuity of plot are required to prevent the drama either from degenerating into what is insufferably dull and strained, or else from falling into the opposite defects of coarseness and vulgarity. Lest the words or jokes should fall flat, the actors would try to secure, by low and impudent buffoonery, the approbation which the composition itself could not command, until, when we take into consideration the unrestrained licence of the age, we can imagine to what depths comedy had to descend to obtain applause of this nature.

But the blame does not belong to the actors alone. The writers, servile in their imitation of their Greek models, carefully copied their defects in this respect also.

> " Des succès fortunés du spectacle tragique,
> Dans Athènes naquit la comédie antique.
> Là, le Grec, né moqueur, par mille jeux plaisants,
> Distilla le vénin de ses traits médisants.
> Aux accès insolents d'une bouffonne joie,
> La sagesse, l'esprit, l'honneur furent en proie."
> BOILEAU, *L'Art Poétique.*"

To judge from the best critics of Italian literature, it would seem that these lines might well be applied to the Italian comedians of this century.

It would be a fruitless task to inquire into the numerous indifferent productions of the various Siennese academies—*Dei Rozzi, Degli Intronati, Degli Insensati*— who made it their especial business to promote this kind

L 2

of comedy. These institutions were under the particular patronage of Leo X., who, with a delight in this species of representation scarcely becoming his position, summoned them year by year to Rome to perform the comedies composed by their various members.

It is probable that Leo X. had early acquired this taste from his tutor, Bernardo Dovizi da Bibbiena (born 1470, died 1520),[9] the writer of the first Italian prose comedy, "La Calandria." In the prologue Bibbiena defends himself for having written in prose instead of verse, declaring that the freedom of prose better befits the ease of everyday life than the restraint of rhyme. Also, this comedy "being intended for general representation to the world at large, the author does not write in Latin, but in the natural language which GOD has given us and which is therefore not less worthy of esteem than Latin, Greek, or Hebrew; nor is our language inferior to any of these if we polish it and bestow upon it the same care which the Greeks bestowed upon theirs." Bibbiena was the friend of Ariosto, Sadoleto, and Bembo, the patron of Raphael, to whom his niece would have been married if the world had not been deprived of this unrivalled painter while yet in the flower of his youth. The "Calandria" was represented for the first time before Henry II. of France and Catherine de' Medici on the day of their solemn ingress into Lyons, in the year 1548.

It is to be noted that the comedies of this century were generally reserved for the festive occasions connected with the births or marriages of the princes and princesses of the various Italian States, where they were represented with every kind of magnificent display.

We read of Alphonso I., Duke of Ferrara, causing a theatre to be erected after a design of Ariosto for the purpose of representing the comedies which were the minor productions of that great genius. It is a question whether Ariosto's comedy of "La Cassaria" did not precede "La Calandria"—at all events they were nearly contemporaneous. Ariosto may in truth be looked upon as the real father of Italian comedy, for, with his powerful

* His portrait by Raphael is No. 158 in the Pitti Gallery at Florence.

intellect and all the bold confidence of genius, he struck out a new path for the comedy of Italy, while her tragedy was still labouring on in the old track. If he did avail himself of the classic models, he made their ideas his own, and then expressed them with native vigour and freedom, using them with the same power, says an old writer on the Teatro Antico, as Terence when he latinized the plays of Menander. "La Cassaria" and "I Suppositi," two plays composed when he was quite young and written in prose, he afterwards remodelled and turned into verse so that they could not be recognized. "La Cassaria" was represented in 1517; "I Suppositi," in 1514; "Il Negromante," 1520; "La Lera," 1524; "La Scolastica" (finished by his brother Gabriel), 1528. But the discussion of their merits and defects would more properly belong to a paper which could treat of his great as well as his minor works.

The only other writer of comedy of this century who can dispute the palm with Ariosto, is his contemporary, the great historian and statesman, Niccolo Macchiavelli (born 1469, died 1527).[1] His comedies are considered by his countrymen of an importance scarcely inferior to his political and historical works, because they are written not so much with the object of diverting the mind of the reader, as with the intention of pointing still more forcibly the observations and reflections of his greater works upon the internal affairs of Florence. Macchiavelli did not intend by his comedies to ridicule the worthless or hypocritical characters of the world in general, but those which existed in Florence in his own time, with the practical purpose of working an improvement in the religion, and the public and private laws by which it was governed. Thus his original comedies, "La Mandragola" and "La Clizia"—which must not be confounded with his literal translations of Plautus and Terence—have not only a literary, but an historical value.

It was not to be supposed that this double claim upon our attention would escape the notice of the great historian and critic of our own time when, with his master hand,

---

[1] Ariosto was born 1474, died 1533.

he set himself to wipe away some of the black stains
which had so long clung to the character of Macchiavelli,
and to the policy which still bears his name. "'The
'Mandragola,'" says Lord Macaulay, "in particular is
superior to the best of Goldoni, and inferior only to the
best of Molière. It is the work of a man who, if he had
devoted himself to the drama, would probably have
attained the highest eminence, and produced a permanent
and salutary effect on the national taste. . . . By the
correct and vigorous delineation of human nature, it
produces interest without a pleasing or skilful plot, and
laughter without the least ambition of wit;" and speaking
of "La Clizia," he says: "Macchiavelli has executed his
task with judgment and taste. He has accommodated
the plot to a different state of society, and has very
dexterously connected it with the history of his own
times.²

We must refer our readers to one of the most brilliant
of Lord Macaulay's brilliant essays for a further analysis
of these two plays. Space will not admit of his criticisms being cited at full length in these pages, and we
could not attempt to render their meaning in words other
than his own.

The Italian theatre of this century is marked by a
third order of dramatic representation generally supposed
to be of native origin and peculiar to Italy.³

The *drammi pastorali* cannot be classed with tragedy,
nor yet with comedy, for successfully avoiding the defects
and errors to which either of these are respectively liable :
they preserve a distinct character of their own. Neither
the princely and heroic personages who pace the stage of
"gorgeous tragedy," nor yet the more humble individuals of private and domestic life, who jostle one
another through the merry scenes of comedy, are admitted within their pale. The time and place belong to

---

² "Critical and Historical Essays," vol. i. pp. 87–92. See also
Mr. Trevelyan's "Life of Lord Macaulay," vol. i. p. 136.
    ³ Tiraboschi declares that the only example of this kind of drama
among the ancient classics is the "Dafne" of a certain Sositeo,
whose origin, date, and country are alike unknown.—Tir. vii. p.
1305.

the imaginary blissful age of gold, and the *dramatis persona* are restricted to the shepherds, nymphs, and other simple characters of pastoral life of a refinement of taste and perception equally imaginary.

The first attempt at the representation of a fable of this kind was the "Cefalo" of Niccolo da Correggio, and passing by some other instances not of sufficient importance to be cited, we come to the Arcadian scene of "Il Sacrifizio" (1554), of Agostino Beccari—the "cori" of which were set to music by Alfonso della Viola—the "Aretusa" (1563) of Albertino Lollio, and the "Sfortunato" of Agostini Argenti (1567). These were all destined to be thrown into the shade by the beautiful "Aminta" of Tasso, to whose merits attention has already been drawn.[4] We only refer to it again that we may call attention to the contrast presented by its unaffected simplicity, purity of style, and natural grace when compared with the artificial character of its pertinacious competitor the "Pastor Fido" of Guarini.

Battista Guarini (born 1537, died 1612), in more than one point the rival of Tasso, has, however, shown no lack of generosity towards him. Compassionating deeply the grievous misfortunes of his fellow-poet, he had himself corrected many of the grave errors which, owing to the author's unhappy imprisonment, had crept into the stolen editions of the "Gerusalemme Liberata," with as much care as if the immortal poem had been his own work. Guarini knew that it was not in his power to rival Tasso on such ground as this, but with the "Aminta" he thought he might successfully compete. He therefore laboured assiduously on his "Pastor Fido," polishing and repolishing the dialogues of his characters, transporting into their pastoral abodes the manners and customs of the Ducal Palace where he lived, making the shepherds borrow the thoughts and language of statesmen, and endowing the nymphs with a series of stilted phrases sufficient to furnish a whole school of rhetoric, till, with the exception of their names and their garments of skins, nothing rural remained to declare their pastoral origin.

---

4 See page 74.

From the very first scene Guarini's imitation of Tasso, and his determination to place himself in opposition to him, becomes apparent. Where Tasso's heroine (Sylvia) rejects the counsel of her adviser, Guarini places his hero (Sylvio) in an exactly similar position. Tasso had disguised his own actual condition under the character of "Tirsi," to expose his treatment at the Court of Ferrara. Guarini, choosing the name of "Carino," avails himself of the same means to compass the same end ("Pastor Fido" act. v. sc. 1; "Aminta," act i. sc. 2). Finally Guarini places himself in decided and direct opposition to Tasso in the famous chorus from "Aminta," "O bella età dell' oro" (act i. sc. 10; compare "Pastor Fido," act iv. sc. 9), in which he imitates exactly the number of strophes, the metre, and the rhyme of his great rival.

The "Aminta" does not pretend to be anything more than a *pastorale*, and the unity, simplicity, and decision of purpose suggested by the title are maintained throughout the piece. The "Pastor Fido," on the other hand, by the very complexity of the title of *tragicommedia pastorale*, presents to our minds all the incoherent, detached, and heterogeneous elements of which it is composed, and which cannot be brought into unison by the mere surface varnish of a polished style. The happy grace and natural ease of the "Aminta" are ill exchanged for the fantastic idealism, strained metaphors, and forced sentiment of the "Pastor Fido." But after pointing out so many defects in the construction of the latter, it is only fair to call attention to the poetical execution, which is remarkable for harmony of verse, variety of metre, and skilful use of the blank verse in which Guarini excelled. Above all we must notice the famous and beautiful speech of Mirtillo (act iii. sc. 1), beginning—

"O Primavera gioventu dell' anno!"

which, had its author written nothing else, would in itself have served to immortalize his name.

As may easily be imagined, a crowd of imitators followed in the wake of Tasso and Guarini, but few, if any, of their compositions have survived, and their names are only to be found by referring to histories of literature.

We must now pass on to the *drammi musicali*—or, as we should call it, the melodrama—an invention as peculiar to Italy as the *pastorali* we have just mentioned. The writer is aware that these *drammi musicali* would find a more fitting place in an essay on music. But, leaving the consideration of their musical character in other and abler hands, these papers will only treat of their connection with the drama. The union of poetry and music, dating from time immemorial, and reviving in Italy with the troubadours and minstrels of the Middle Ages, had step by step become more intimately connected, the improvement in the one keeping pace with the advance of the other. We read in the "Divina Commedia" of Dante's Canzone, "Love that discourses in my thoughts" (Purg. ii. 107, 108), being sung by Casella. We next hear of Petrarch's "Trionfi" being adapted for the musical festivities of the Carnascialeschi; then we have the *cori* of the tragedies and the *intermezzi* of the comedies, while the *madrigali* of the *pastorali* of Tasso and Guarini prove by their delicate harmony how eminently the Italian language, now brought to its perfection, would accord with song.

Here was the adaptation of music to poetry.

But as the science and theory of music became more understood, its immense and wonderful capacities developed themselves till it ceased to be the subservient art, and the poetry was composed with an especial regard to the musical rendering of the drama. Florence, ever first among the Italian States for brilliancy of invention, gave birth to the society which was to unite in happy concord the two sister arts of poetry and music.

Under the auspices of two Florentine nobles, distinguished alike in birth, literature, and musical science, Giovanni Bardi (Conte di Vernio) and Vincenzo Galilei, father of Galileo—no less of a musician than his son, and scarcely inferior to him as a mathematician—Jacopo Peri, and Girolamo Mei, famous musical theorists, this combination was carried far on its road to perfection. The Grand Dukes of Tuscany, ever liberal in their patronage of the arts, lent every encouragement to a society whose united efforts were eminently calculated to

promote the splendour of the entertainments with which
they were wont to celebrate their marriage feasts.[5]

The Conte di Vernio, poet as well as musician, prepared more than one musical drama for occasions of
similar festivity. The strict character of these *drammi
musicali* consisted, it would seem, in *intermezzi*, or
musical interludes, introduced into the comedy chosen
for representation. The *intermezzi* had no connection
with the comedy, although with some ingenuity they
were made to represent in themselves a separate and
continuous story, which was carried on at the end of each
act of the drama. Thus, if the subjects, like those chosen
by the Conte di Vernio, were selected from mythology,
they were made to hang together, and to follow each
other in proper historical order.

Such was the nature of the first *drammi musicali*, but
a great step was yet to be made before they fulfilled the
idea which the name of musical drama or opera would
now suggest to our minds.

Hitherto the music employed for the *intermezzi* appears
to have been of the nature of part-songs, introduced
abruptly one after the other, with nothing to carry on the
idea of harmony, or lead from one passage to another;
the music entirely ceasing, and then beginning again in
the same style. But continuous scenes carried on between
several characters in a musical language capable of attaining to the rapidity of dialogue and the force and
vigour of declamation, without ceasing to be music, and
whole compositions entirely planned on this scheme, this
had not yet been attained to, nor indeed was it to be
reached for many years. Songs there were, and a certain
knowledge of harmony and of the theory of music, but
the "recitative" was the final discovery of that age of
great discovery, the sixteenth century.

Unhappily for himself, the Conte di Vernio, who had
done so much toward promoting the *drammi musicali*,
being summoned from Florence to Rome to attend on
Pope Clement VIII., was unable to witness their
wonderful progress. His musical, dramatic, and literary

⁵ See Sir Robert Phillimore's translation of Lessing's "Laocoon,"
Preface, pp. 44, 45.

society transferred itself to the house of Jacopo Corsi, his worthy successor in Florence, under whose roof the first "opera," "Dafne," was produced, in 1594. Ottavio Rinuccini, the young poet of the day, wrote the *libretto* with such an especial care and choice of words, both with regard to poetry as well as music, that it is worth reading on its own account. Giulio Caccini, the inventor of the new musical language, to which Italian so eminently lent itself, supplied the "recitative," and Jacopo Peri composed the music.

The "Dafne" was immediately followed by another drama of the same nature, the "Euridice," with the more ambitious title of *tragedia per musica*, which was represented in the year 1600 at the feast given at Florence in honour of the marriage of Maria de' Medici with Henry IV. of France.

The novelty of the invention which excited the general wonder and curiosity of Florence, the fame of the literary and musical society which produced it, the occasion of the great festivity chosen for its representation, the exactitude of the execution by the best musicians and vocalists of the day; last, but not least, the poetical merit of the drama, which, up to the time of Metastasio, had no rival in grace of expression or musical harmony— it will easily be imagined how all these circumstances combined to render this dramatic spectacle one of the most striking that Italy had yet witnessed.

It is a fact worthy of notice that, just as the "Orfeo" of Poliziano had given the first impetus to the drama at the close of the fifteenth century, so the same pathetic tale was chosen to illustrate the new dramatic discovery of the year 1600.

Thus ended the remarkable "Cinquecento." The fine arts by which it had been so conspicuously adorned— poetry, painting, and music—were all united in the melodrama, which, if by no means the most important, was certainly not the least remarkable specimen of the creative genius of the age.

But apart from a discovery whose individual merits and relative effect upon the drama deserve separate consideration, the Teatro Italiano Antico possessed tragedies

which, never deficient in power or pathos, often attained
to the sublime, comedies by whose sparkling wit the vices
and follies of the age were held up to unsparing ridicule,
and *pastorali*, whose brilliant imagery, delicacy of thought,
and grace of expression can never cease to please even
now, when the taste for that peculiar kind of drama has
died away.

PART III.

The Melodrama in Italy during the Seventeenth and Eighteenth Centuries—Apostolo Zeno—Metastasio.

A.D. 1600—1782.

> " Il faut aller à ce palais magique
> Où les beaux vers, la danse, la musique,
> L'art de tromper les yeux par les couleurs,
> L'art plus heureux de séduire les cœurs
> De cent plaisirs font un plaisir unique."

Tiraboschi, in the preface to his eighth volume, bids us
observe that whereas the literature of Italy during the
sixteenth century occupies three volumes of his history,
that of the succeeding age is easily comprised in one. Nor
does he attempt to disguise that whatever lustre this period
may derive from grave scientific discoveries, it is rightly
marked as an age of decadence in literature.

This remark seems particularly applicable to the drama
of Italy, which, during this century, can stand no comparison with that of France, then carried to the zenith of
its fame by Corneille, Racine, and Molière. Still, while
we admit this, it must be remembered that in the preceding age Italian tragedy and comedy had both attained
to a certain degree of merit before such compositions were
even known by name in France.

Although the general style of the Italian Dramatic
School of the seventeenth century is much to be deplored,
Tiraboschi considers that there are some few exceptions to
the rule which are worthy of passing notice. Several
tragedies published by the Bolognese Melchiore Zoppio
(died 1634), who was the founder of the Accademia de'

Gelati in Bologna :—the "Tomiri" of Angelo Ingegneri, though it has more claim to our sympathy as the composition of the friend who preserved Tasso's works from destruction than on account of its own individual merit ; the sacred Rappresentazione of "Adamo" by Andreini,[6] which is supposed to have suggested some of the most sublime ideas of "Paradise Lost"—the envy of Satan on beholding man's happiness in Paradise (book v.), the battle of the angels against Lucifer (vi.), the council of demons (ib.): all these are to be found in the "Adamo," whence it would seem that Milton has taken the gold, leaving behind the dross which disfigures the Italian tragedy. Two other rather obscure and unknown Italian Rappresentazioni, "La Scena tragica d' Adamo e d' Eva," by Troilo Benacense, and the "Angeleida" of Erasmo di Valvasore, are said to have also furnished Milton with some of those descriptive figures so unrivalled in their richness, which adorn the "Paradise Lost."[7] The Italian critics bestow some approbation on the "Tancredi" of Rodolfo Campeggi (published 1614), and the "Solimano" of Prospero Bonarelli, a member of the Accademia degli Umoristi, which, like the more ancient Siennese institutions, was originally founded for the purpose of promoting the comic drama. Some fifty sacred and profane dramas by the Sicilian Ortensio Scamacca (died 1648) came next in order, while Sarpi's rival historian of the Council of Trent, the Cardinal Pallavicino, found relaxation from his graver labours in writing a tragedy called "Ermengildo." The list shall be completed by four tragedies, the works of Cardinal Giovanni Delfino—of which the first, "La Cleopatra," was considered worthy of a place in the "Teatro Italiano"—and by the "Aristodemo" of Carlo de' Dottori, represented in Paris, 1657, by a celebrated actor, "Pietro Cotta, detto Clelio," with the intention of restoring the Italian tragedy to the high position which it had once occupied. But it was a vain effort, and still less can be said for the comedies of this century, which had degenerated into the lowest kind of

[6] Giovanbattista Andreini, born 1578, published his "Adamo" at Milan, 1613, and dedicated it to Maria de' Medici.
[7] See Walker's "Hist. Memoir of Italian Tragedy," pp. 160—175.

buffoonery, without any attempt at unity of plot or delineation of character, and were universally bad, with the exception of "La Tancia" and "La Fiera," two comedies by Michelangelo Buonarotti, a great-nephew of the famous sculptor.

As to the *pastorali*, "La Filla di Sciro," by Guidobaldo della Rovere, is considered the only specimen of the seventeenth century which can bear any comparison with the "Aminta" and the "Pastor Fido," those great original models of this order of drama. Although if one of these, the "Pastor Fido," is open to censure on the score of its occasionally artificial and affected style, the "Filla di Sciro" has copied this defect to an excess in accordance with the prevailing bad taste of the seventeenth century.

The deterioration of the drama during this period must in a great measure be ascribed to the predominant popularity of the melodrama, which had the effect of almost excluding for the time every other kind of dramatic representation from the stage. But this unbounded popularity, far from promoting the advance and improvement of the new discovery, was so highly prejudicial to it as almost to cause its total and immediate destruction.

The melodrama very early lost the charm with which it had been invested by the graceful poetry of Rinuccini and the careful musical compositions of Caccini, Peri, and Mei. In the hands even of their immediate successors, these intellectual enjoyments were exchanged for the mere wonder excited by startling scenical decorations, assisted by an almost stupendous apparatus of machinery.

If the authors who immediately succeeded Rinuccini had been content to follow in his steps, and like him had carefully weighed how far the effect of the melodrama upon the imagination might safely be assisted by this kind of scenic effect, they would have placed some check on their inventive faculties, and would thus have established a new kind of drama, pleasing to the fancy, without being at variance either with sound judgment or common sense.

But as it was, everything was sacrificed to the wonderful *mise-en-scène*.

The subjects were chosen for representation merely with

this object in view. On this account they were chiefly
taken from two sources—the mythology of the ancients
and the romantic and legendary lore of the Middle Ages.
In this last especially an inexhaustible store of scenery was
to be found suggested by the enchanted palaces and forests,
the tournaments, feats of arms, and manifold adventures
of the knight-errant ; while, of *dramatis personæ*, there
was an equal abundance in the magicians, giants, and
dwarfs, fair maidens, and gallant knights and squires ever
ready to succour "Beauty brought to unworthy wretched-
ness through Envy's snares or Fortune's freaks unkind."
It was an easy step to transport into the drama

> " Le donne, i cavalieri, l' armi, gli amori,
>   La cortesie, l' audaci imprese,"

permanently engrafted into the literature of Italy by the
immortal poems of Ariosto and Tasso, and there to invest
them with all the pomp of splendid decoration and scenery
which naturally appertains to them. The music which
had now become inseparably connected with the poetry of
these dramatic representations, combined to enhance the
effect. But at first it was difficult to make the combination of the two arts assume either a natural or plausible
appearance before the unaccustomed eyes of the audience.
Therefore the authors in choosing their arguments,
either from the realms of fancy or mythology, purposely
sought to place as wide a difference as possible between
the spectators and the circumstances of the action of their
drama, so that the improbability of the musical dialogue
might not so conspicuously challenge the attention. Thus
if it was contrary to nature that the heroes and heroines
should sing their parts instead of speaking them, they
transformed their men and women into gods and goddesses;
if the earth was an unlikely place for such conversations
in music, they laid their scenes in the Elysium or Hades
of mythology. Abandoning as hopeless the chance of
awakening the interest of their audience by depicting
character and passion, they sought only to gratify their
eyes and ears, and despairing of satisfying their reason,
appealed instead to their imagination.
But if the advance of poetry and music was thus

thwarted and hindered by the imperative necessity of producing a drama which must depend for its success on the magnificence of its scenic effects, painting and architecture were in the highest request. The art of perspective, so indispensable to create the space and distance necessary to keep up the illusion of the scenery, was carefully cultivated in the various schools of painting in Italy, while architecture had ample space for its development in theatres worthy of Ancient Rome. To cite only two examples : The theatre at Piazzola, a small town ten miles from Padua, erected by Marco Contarini, was particularly famous for its capacious stage. In 1680 and 1681 there were representations which brought upon the scene triumphal cars, drawn by magnificent horses, 100 Amazons, and 100 Moors, hunts and tournaments, and every gorgeous spectacle of the kind. The theatre of Parma, built by the Duke Ranuccio Farnese, is perhaps the most conspicuous example of all. It was designed in the year 1618-19 by Giambattista Aleotti from an ancient model, and not only the general plan, but all the details were carefully fashioned from the classical accounts of the Greek and Roman theatres. It was afterwards enlarged by Bentivoglio, till in the year 1690, on the occasion of the festivities given for the marriage of Odoardo Farnese, it was calculated to contain 14,000 spectators. To this day, it is said, may be seen the syphons and conduits by means of which water, sufficient to float barks of a considerable size, was turned on the scene. On another occasion horses were made to perform military evolutions in such numbers that they appeared to represent a real army. Notwithstanding its vast size the acoustics of this vast building are said to have been so perfectly managed that the ordinary tones of conversation could be heard as distinctly at the opposite end of the theatre as if shouted at the top of the voice.

Venice was especially distinguished among the cities of Italy by the magnificence of her musical and dramatic feasts, which prevailed during the carnival, and attracted crowds of strangers to the city. One of these, " La Divisione del Mondo," represented, 1675, by Giulio Cesare Corradi in the theatre of S. Salvadore, is a striking example of this kind of drama. Another, the "Pastore d' Anfiso," displayed the Palace of the Sun, built in perfect architectural proportions, of crystals of dazzling brilliancy. A third, "Il Dario," by Francesco Beverini, portrayed various striking scenes in the life of the Eastern monarch, his camp with elephants carrying towers filled with armed soldiers, the palace and terrace at Babylon, the pavilion of the king, the mausoleum of Ninus, and numerous cavalry and infantry drawn up in battle array. The "Glorie di Firenze" and the splendours of "Il Cielo di Cristallo" smiled on the nuptials of the Grand Duke of Tuscany, while the royal palace at Turin was turned into a theatre to represent with due effect the various scenes of the double drama of "Il Vascello della Felicità e l'Arianna."

It was indeed no wonder that an invention which combined the arts of poetry, music, painting, and architecture should have had such universal success and should have spread with marvellous rapidity over all the countries of Europe. France, Spain, England, Germany, and Russia lost no time in making this new and wonderful discovery their own.

But this paper can only afford to sketch, and that very slightly, its rise and progress in Italy.

The "melodrama," even in the debased form which it assumed during this century, was not only pleasing to the Italians on account of its novelty and varied charms, but also because it filled the total dramatic void of this period. The "Teatro Antico" had entirely decayed, and the theatre which then existed had, as we have seen, nothing to offer, either in tragedy or comedy, worthy of representation. It was, therefore, only natural that they should turn to the "melodrama," which held out so tempting and pleasing a prospect.

In this way its very defects, the extravagant scenic decoration, and the elaborate machinery by which it was oppressed and stifled during the seventeenth century, came to be considered as merits. The plot and style of the drama ceased to be of any importance, and the poets and musicians only vied with one another as to which could produce the greatest number of wonderful spectacles in one piece upon the stage.

M

But it was not in the nature of the divine arts of poetry and music to remain for any length of time in this slavish subserviency. Their triumph became directly manifest when the true poet and musician with heaven-born gifts arose to assert their claims, and the mere accessories of the melodrama assumed their right pro-portions, and fell back into their proper place. No sooner did Apostolo Zeno appear than the taste for extravagant scenery began to give place to a desire for a higher order of dramatic composition. He was the first to replace the drama on its ancient footing of majestic decorum, to be quickly followed by Metastasio, whose melodious poetry was seconded by such sweet harmony as the great masters of the Neapolitan school of music knew best how to produce. But we must not omit to give a few moments' consideration to the poet who first prepared the way for this the climax of perfection in the melodrama.

Apostolo Zeno was born in Venice in 1669. His father, Pietro Zeno, was a doctor of medicine; his mother, Catarina, belonged to the family of the Sevasti. His graver studies in history and various abstruse sciences—the fruit of which appears in his " Giornale de' Letterati," still highly thought of in Italy—did not inter-fere with his attaining his greatest celebrity in that reform of the melodrama, already alluded to, which was so urgently needed. The graceful poetry of his lyric compositions recommended him to the notice of the Emperor Charles VI., who summoned him to Germany, intending to make him poet laureate of the Imperial Court. Charles VI. exercised an influence on the melo-drama at the period of its revival so special as to be worthy of attention. It will be noticed by those who read the works of Apostolo Zeno and Metastasio that, with very rare exceptions, they have always been careful to bring their dramas to a happy conclusion, and the reason of this is easily explained. Both poets were under the direct influence of the Emperor, and were well aware that their patron could not endure a tragical end to the melodrama. He wished it laid down as a rule that in this order of dramatic composition the last im-pression left upon the minds of the audience should

never be a melancholy one. The Imperial opinion became a law to the great masters of the reformed melodrama, and thus, in their hands, a guiding principle to
their successors. Apostolo Zeno during his residence at
the Imperial Court received constant marks of the
Emperor's favour, for when he declined to displace the
poet laureate of the day by accepting the honour which
had been offered to him, the Emperor made him his
historian. But notwithstanding these flattering distinctions, notwithstanding the deserved popularity of his
dramas, Il Zeno felt a longing which he could not restrain to end his days in his native country. He
obtained leave to return to Venice, there to enjoy the
full stipend of his office, under the sole obligation of
supplying the Imperial Court with a new drama every
year. He died in 1750 at Venice. We must pass over
his more profound labours, his various biographies, his
indefatigable efforts to improve the Italian language, his
careful researches among old manuscripts, to speak of
his dramas, with which this paper is especially concerned.
In all these compositions, and they were sufficiently
numerous to fill ten volumes, Apostolo Zeno was particularly careful in the choice of his "arguments." Thoroughly acquainted with historical lore, whenever its
pages offered striking examples either of patriotic zeal,
desire for glory, generosity of soul, fortitude in adversity,
faithful friendship or tender compassion, he made use of
them as fitting subjects for the drama in place of the
extravagant nonsense which had been generally chosen
for representation during the preceding century. His
style is considered correct and sustained, his imagination
fertile, his plots carefully developed. Sacred subjects
were treated by him with a care and reverence hitherto
unknown, for even in the spiritual oratorios first introduced by San Filippo Neri, at Rome, although the music
was the work of the great masters, the poetry was considered of little or no consequence, and intrusted to
indifferent writers. Apostolo Zeno bent all his powers
to the task of investing the sacred dramas, so far as it
was possible, with all the solemnity and dignity which
their subjects would inspire. " Il Giuseppe," " Il Sisara,"

"Il Danielo," "L' Ezechia," "Davide," contain some remarkably fine passages, and the paraphrase of the first chapter of Isaiah [8] in the " Profezie d' Isaia " is very striking :—

> " Cieli, udite, udite o genti :
> Iddio parla. Attenti, attenti—
> Ho nudriti ed ho esaltati
> Figli iniqui, e figli ingrati.

> " Il giumento e il bue comprese,
> Nel presepio il suo gran Dio.
> Nol conobbe e non l' intese
> Israello, il popol mio," &c.

Still it must be owned that Apostolo Zeno is more to be praised for the laborious industry with which he raised the melodrama out of the deplorable state into which it had fallen than for any very remarkable genius. Critics have found considerable fault with his dramas for the length of the scenes, the unnecessary multiplication of incidents, often sufficient to furnish two or three tragedies, the dryness and stiffness of his characters, and an occasional harshness of versification in passages intended for recitative. Perhaps, however, these defects did not seem so conspicuous till Metastasio appeared to complete with his unmistakable genius the reform which Zeno had begun, and to carry the melodrama to a perfection which it has since been impossible to surpass.

Pietro Trapassi—called Metastasio—was born in Rome, January 28th, 1698. His parents, of humble origin and scanty means, stinted themselves in every way to provide for his instruction in the first rudiments of education. From his earliest years he was accustomed to recite scraps of Italian poetry. It is said that, when one day declaiming a favourite piece, he was accidentally overheard by Vittorio Gravina, one of the tragedians who had endeavoured, though without success, to raise the tone of the drama of the seventeenth century. Gravina knew how to appreciate in others the talents in which he was himself deficient. He undertook to educate the young Trapassi, and, having obtained the parents'

---

[8] " Hear, O heavens, and give ear, O earth, for the Lord hath spoken," &c.

leave, finally adopted him as his son. He changed his name from "Trapassi" to "Metastasio," a Greek word which, being equivalent to "trapassamento"—i.e. a transition from one state to another—was probably selected partly as a play upon the old name of his *protégé*, and partly with reference to his change of circumstances. The patron had no occasion to repent of his benevolence. His adopted child, with every external advantage of looks and manner, a countenance beaming with intelligence, a sweet and melodious voice, was a general favourite, and his extraordinary gifts soon made him famous in Rome. Gravina was careful to cultivate the early promise of his talents by an excellent classical education ; he encouraged him to employ them in original compositions, and the tragedy of "Giustino" (the only tragedy ever written by Metastasio) was composed at the age of fourteen, in compliance with his patron's request[9] The plot was taken from Trissino's "Italia Liberata," and the young author is scarcely to be blamed if he fell into the errors of languor and heaviness which had marred the original poem. Still the "Giustino" contains sufficient merit to make it an astonishing production for so young a writer, and to excite regret that he should never, in his more mature years, have attempted another tragedy. Metastasio, in common with the great classical poets of Italy, was destined for the law, and pursued with diligence the dry and difficult study of jurisprudence. But in 1718 the death of his patron left him at liberty to follow his own inclinations, which speedily diverged into those more pleasant paths of learning, the ancient classics and those of his own country. Among the latter Torquato Tasso was ever his favourite. Gravina filled up the measure of his benevolence by making his adopted son heir to all his worldly possessions, so that Metastasio was no longer in need of a profession to earn his livelihood. Among his numerous writings a touching tribute of gratitude to his patron is to be found in the poem, "La Strada della

---

[9] Metastasio protested against the publication of this tragedy with his other works, as quite unworthy to see the light. "Opera," vol. x. p. 3. Paris edition of 1782.

Gloria," [1] written immediately after the death of Gravina, in which Gravina (whom he apostrophizes with the fondest affection) appears to him in a dream, and bids him follow without ceasing the path of fame. The genius of Metastasio taught him that his special gifts would find their best scope in the improvement of the melodrama. This, once again brought within the rules observed by Rinuccini in his "Dafne," and enhanced by music like that which was composed for it by Peri, Caccini, and Mei, appeared to Metastasio to offer a wide field for his exertions, and a prospect of new and glorious laurels. But his scheme met with a sudden check. Unaccustomed to wealth, and consequently believing that his inheritance could have no limit, he, in a short time, squandered so much of his fortune that he found himself once more compelled, by absolute necessity, to return to the study of the law, which he had abandoned with such delight. Leaving Rome and the false friends who had led him into his extravagant way of life, he repaired for this purpose to Naples, at that time famous for its school of jurisprudence. There were, however, other schools at Naples more congenial to Metastasio's taste. Three out of the four famous musical Conservatorios [2] were still in existence, and among the pupils at that time were Gaetano, Jomelli, Caldara, Predieri, and Vinci, who would one day set his dramas to music.

Naples was in a state of festive gaiety to celebrate the birth of a daughter to the Emperor Charles VI., and Metastasio was selected as the poet to compose the drama which was to be represented in honour of the occasion. It was in vain that he refused, and at last, on the condition of his secret being strictly kept from his master of jurisprudence, he wrote "Gli Orti Esperidi," his first melodrama. The universal applause excited by this drama made it impossible to keep the author's name a

---

[1] Vol. iii. p. 475.
"Del buon Maestro il venerato aspetto,
Riconosco la guancia scolorita,
Del lungo studio," &c., &c.
[2] 1. Conservatorio dei Poveri di Gesù Cristo. 2. Conservatorio di San Onofrio. 3. Conservatorio di Santa Maria di Loreto. 4. Conservatorio della Pietà dei Turchini.

secret; more especially as the famous *cantatrice*, Maria Bulgarini, called "La Romanina," who had acted the part of Venus, declared she would leave no stone unturned till she had discovered the name of the poet who had won her such a shower of laurels. When at last her efforts were crowned with success, she used all her arts to persuade him to dedicate himself exclusively to the composition of the melodrama, for which he appeared to have so remarkable a talent. Metastasio could not withstand her urgent entreaties; he finally abandoned the law, and gave himself once more heart and soul to an occupation for which he was in every way so eminently fitted. La Bulgarini insisted upon receiving him into her own family during the interval which must elapse before he could earn a sufficient livelihood by his new profession, and showered benefits upon him. At her house he learned from the great Porpora some of the science of music, and thus stimulated and encouraged, he wrote "La Didone Abbandonata," in which La Bulgarini again performed the heroine's part, and drew tears from the eyes of the audience. It was afterwards represented in Russia before the Empress Catharine II., being set to music on that occasion by Galuppi of Venice. The Empress, at the conclusion of the piece, sent the great composer a present of a casket of rubies with a message to the effect that the unfortunate Dido, at the point of death, had left them as a legacy to him. La Bulgarini next transferred herself and family, always accompanied by her *protégé*, to Venice, and thence to Rome, where Metastasio's next composition, "Catone in Utica," was represented. This drama was an exception to the now accepted law that the melodrama should end happily, and was censured on that account. Shortly after its representation a squib appeared inviting "La Compagnia della Morte" to give the corpse of Cato, now lying dead in the theatre, "a decent burial." Metastasio, nothing daunted, produced for the carnival of 1729 "L' Ezio" and "La Semiramide," in the following year, "L' Alessandro nelle Indie," and "L' Artaserse," which have all been set to music,[3] some by good, some by indif-

[3] Forty different compositions of "Artaserse," and thirty-six of "Alessandro," are quoted in Clement's "Dictionnaire Lyrique."

ferent masters. Later in life he improved these dramas, which, when they first appeared, had some of the defects of his early marner, a too artificial style, an intricacy of plot, and an occasional weakness of dialogue. By this time his fame was widely spread, and Apostolo Zeno, on taking leave of the Emperor, begged to propose as his successor the "best dramatic poet of Italy," the author of "Didone" and "Artaserse." Metastasio was, in consequence, invited to the Imperial Court (1729) to fill the proud position of "Poeta Cesareo," with the offer of an annual salary of three thousand florins.

His first composition at Vienna was the oratorio of "S. Elena al Calvario," a sacred drama on "The Invention of the Cross,"[4] set to music by Caldara, and represented in the Imperial Chapel during the Holy Week 1731. In this, as in all of his sacred dramas, there are many beautiful passages.[5] Those taken from the Old Testament are "Giuseppe riconosciuto,"[6] "L' Isaaco,"[7] "La Morte d' Abele, Gioas,"[8] in which he is said to have borrowed some ideas from Racine's "Athalie." That from the New Testament, for the "Santissimo Natale," recalls some of the varied and beautiful ideas of Milton's "Ode on the Nativity." In that same year he composed "L' Olim-piade" and "Il Demofoonte," two of his masterpieces, written in the best period of his second manner, showing more precision and simplicity in the dialogue, a greater sobriety of narration, and a combination of vigour and delicacy in the ariette. In 1734 Metastasio was engaged upon another sacred drama, "La Betulia Liberata," treating of Judith and Holofernes, when intelligence reached him of the death of his friend and patroness, La Bulgarini, also that she had left him all her worldly possessions. But Metastasio at once renounced this second inheritance in favour of the husband of the famous cantatrice. He was deeply affected by the death of one who had been so

---

[4] Observed in our Calendar, September 14.
[5] "Giuseppe riconosciuto," Metastasio, "Opere," vol. iii. pp. 33, 54, 61. "Morte d' Abele," ibid. 78, 82, 101.
[6] Set to music by Predieri, represented 1740.
[7] Set to music by Porsili, represented 1733.
[8] Set to music by Reutter, represented 1735.

real a benefactress, to whom, in fact, he owed his present fame, and "La Betulia Liberata" bears the stamp of the sorrow which her loss occasioned in him. It contains arguments worthy of a theologian as to the belief in the true God, winding up with the conclusive reply to the idolater's disbelieving questions,—

> "Se Dio veder tu vuoi
> Guardalo in ogni oggetto,
> Cercalo nel tuo petto,
> Lo troverai con te.

> "E, se dov' ei dimora
> Non intendesti ancora,
> Confondimi, se puoi,
> Dimmi dov' Ei non è." [9]

He borrows all the ornaments of Eastern imagery to enrich his dialogue, while the beauty of the inspired words, "Sing unto the Lord, for He hath triumphed gloriously," are recalled to our minds by the chorus—

> "Lodi al gran Dio, che oppresse
> Gli empj nemici suo.
> Che combattè per noi
> Che trionfa così."

"La Clemenza di Tito" (set to music by Caldara) was another production of this year, which Voltaire esteemed so highly as to declare that it rivalled the most sublime passages of Corneille and the most finished touches of Racine. Many others followed in quick succession, among others "Le Cinesi," his single comic opera.

In 1736, on the occasion of the marriage of Maria Theresa with Francis, Duke of Lorraine, he wrote one of his cleverest and most amusing dramas, "L' Achille in Sciro," in which, by representing the hero as torn in pieces by the passion of love contending with the desire for military glory, he seized the opportunity of paying the bridegroom a graceful compliment. It was not thrown away upon Francis, who in return offered to make the

---

[9] "La Betulia Liberata," parte seconda, p. 545. The writer has refrained from translating Metastasio's *ariette*, partly because they would lose so much of their grace and delicacy in the process, partly because they are so simple in their beauty that any one can understand them.

poet count, baron, privy-councillor, anything, in short, he
liked. But Metastasio refused all honours, and continued
steadily at work upon his dramas, which had now obtained
a European fame. The death of Charles VI., the Seven
Years' War which ensued, public calamities, and private
infirmities arrested his labours for a time, but resuming
them in 1749, he finished his "Attilio Regolo," and sent
it to Hasse to be set to music. It was his favourite production, and he used to declare that if he could only have
saved one out of all his dramas, he would have chosen the
"Attilio." To the general reader it does not offer so much
attraction as many others. After this his poetical genius
did not reach any loftier summit of perfection. He sustained his second manner through the "Re Pastore," the
"Trionfo di Clelio," the "Nittetti," "Romolo," "L' Ate-
naide," and "L' Egeria," composed for the coronation of
the Emperor Joseph, in which Maria Theresa said she
recognized the undiminished vigour of his great genius.[1]
But in his declining years he had a third manner inferior
to the second, of which "La Festa Teatrale" and "Il
Ruggiero" are the most favourable specimens. Two odes,
one of sympathy with the Empress on the loss of her
husband, the other in praise of her villa at Schönbrunn,
procured him two notes of graceful compliment from
Maria Theresa;[2] nor must we pass over the slight thread
which connects him with the youngest Archduchess of
Austria, afterwards the beautiful Dauphine, and finally
the noble and hapless Queen of France. The undying
sympathy which her fate must ever excite bids us pause
with affectionate interest over the well-known couplet
with which Metastasio ushered her birth into the world,[3]
and the graceful "Complimenti," as they were called,
which he wrote for her to repeat when only five years, to
celebrate her parents' respective birthdays, in the year

---

[1] Vol. vi., "Opere di Metastasio," p. 260.
[2] Ibid., p. 263.
[3] Vol. xi. p. 273.   To the Empress Maria Theresa :—
       "Io perdei: l' augusta Figlia
       A pagar mi ha condannato
       Ma s' è ver che a Voi somiglia,
       Tutto il mondo ha guadagnato."

1760. They were set to music by Hasse, and arranged by Metastasio as a miniature drama, to be performed by the two sisters, Maria Carolina, afterwards Queen of Naples, and Marie Antoinette. The heavier of the two parts seems to have fallen on Maria Carolina, then eight years old, who tries to prepare her sister for the august ceremony, to which the youngest archduchess replies—

> " Prepararmi e perchè ?
> *Arciduchessa I.*   Che dirai ?
> *Arciduchessa II.*   Io gli dirò che l' amo,
>   Ch' essergli cara io bramo,
>   Che m' ami io gli dirò,
>   Ch' altro nel cor non ho."[4]

In the beautiful edition of Metastasio, published at Paris in 1780, and dedicated to Queen Marie Antoinette, a few graceful stanzas by Giuseppe Pezzana recall to her memory how in her childhood Metastasio used to teach her his *soave note*, and beg her to smile upon this new edition of his works from that lofty throne which she now adorns with every grace and virtue.

After the death of Maria Theresa, the Emperor Joseph continued to extend the same favours to Metastasio which he had enjoyed during the two preceding reigns, but his long and distinguished life was fast drawing to a close, and on the 12th of April, 1782, he died at Vienna, in the eighty-fourth year of his age.

Metastasio is considered by the greatest of his native critics to have surpassed all the other dramatic poets of Italy in the delicacy with which he painted the passions, and the refinement with which he has expressed the affections of his *dramatis personæ*. There is no depth of the soul which his eloquence does not reach, no secret feeling which does not respond to his touch, and on this account he was prized by all readers, of all ages, and all conditions of life. This tender feeling may be said to be the leading feature of all his poetical works ; but although his lyrics[5] would alone have won for him distinguished laurels, his fame really rests upon his dramas, which of

[4] Vol. xi. p. 256.
[5] See especially his Ode to the Spring. " Gia riede Primavera," " Opere," vol. ii. p. 525.

their special kind are models of excellence. The plot of each drama naturally and simply unfolds itself—a verse, a word even, often suffices to make it clear. From the very beginning he is careful to inform the audience what it is needful for them to know, explaining the past and present, and preparing the way for the future with an ease and a dexterity quite unrivalled by any other dramatic poet. The opening scenes of the "Temistocle" and the "Artaserse" are worth referring to as specimens of this peculiar merit. The dialogue is smooth and rapid, avoiding equally the long narratives of the tragedians of the sixteenth century, and the ambitious ornaments of the modern French school, and bringing that vivacity of action on the scene which is the very life of dramatic representation. The plots are so carefully worked out that even those melodramas which were prepared with an especial view to musical rendering can be given, equally well and with the same effect, when merely recited. He has left his own opinion on record as to the secondary place which music should occupy in the melodrama. "When music," he says, "aspires to hold a position of equal importance with poetry in the drama it ruins the drama as well as itself. It would be as great an absurdity to suppose that the dress of the person is of as much consequence as the individual himself. My dramas are proved, throughout Italy, by daily experience, to be more sure of a good reception when recited by actors than when musically rendered." [6] In this same letter he refers to the amount of music employed in the old Greek tragedies, a subject upon which he enlarges at full length in his careful extract from the "Poetics" of Aristotle. This extract, or rather analysis, was made in the first instance for his own instruction to guide him in the composition of his dramas, according to those strict rules of art which he was always careful to maintain. It was afterwards printed at the request of his friends. The operas which are best known to have been also declaimed are the "Didone," the "Clemenza di Tito," "Siroe," "Catone in Utica," "Demofoonte," and "Alessandro

---

[6] "Lettere sopra la Musica," vol. ix. p. 365.

nelle Indie." Goldoni, in his youth, was asked, when at Feltri, to choose a drama for representation, and he selected the "Didone" and the "Siroe," which were represented, but *senza musica misi soltanto le arie in recitativo.*[7] On these occasions the final choruses were omitted, but the airs were retained as connecting links of the dialogue. Indeed the Italian language, whose very prose is poetry, and whose poetry is music, almost naturally falls into recitative, and the ease with which Metastasio's compositions adapt themselves either to the opera or the drama would seem to prove this point. Again, the constant transposition of the parts of speech gives the Italian language an immense advantage, when employed either in oratory, poetry, or music, because the arrangement of the words is not governed by the natural order of the ideas, but according as the rounding of the period best pleases the ear. Take, for example, the opening lines of the "Orlando Furioso," already once cited in this paper, "Le donne, i cavalieri," &c. Every one perceives how the harmony of the verse is perfected by placing the words "io canto" at the end. Place them at the beginning, in their natural grammatical position, and who would recognize the pen of the immortal Ariosto? Of course this, like every other rhetorical art, is liable to be abused, as in truth it was by the "Cinquecentisti," the "Speronis," "Dolces," and "Casas" of the sixteenth century. But Metastasio knew well how to avail himself of this inversion peculiar to the Italian language without carrying it to excess. He knew also how to make full use of the other great facilities for poetry in which it was naturally prolific, the imitative character of its phrases, the richness and variety of its terminations, the flexibility afforded by the augmentatives and diminutives, and profiting by each and all of these advantages, he wove them into a style so clear and sparkling, into verses so flowing and melodious, that without the effort of learning them they remain indelibly impressed on the mind. Not only did Metastasio overcome the difficulty of expressing with freedom and vigour

7 " Mem. del Sig. Goldoni," t. i. p. 98.

in poetry those shades of affection and desire which it
would have been no easy task to clothe in the ordinary
language of prose, but he also contended successfully
with the difficulty especially connected with his order of
poetry, namely, that of adapting it to the music on which
the success of the melodrama must in a great measure
depend. Every sort of arbitrary rule interfered to
hamper his genius—the supposed necessity of limiting
each drama to a certain number of verses, of making each
scene end with an air; the prohibition that one air should
follow another on the lips of the same personage, the
restriction of the *recitative*, within brief limits broken by
the alternate speeches of each person as he appears on the
scene, and many other artificial and irksome laws, which,
however unnecessary they may appear, had to be carefully considered and adhered to by the then writers of
the musical drama. These were some of the difficulties
with which he battled. and over which he won so complete a triumph, that Italy is not only indebted to him
for his compositions as a poet, but also for the high
summit of musical perfection attained by the melodrama
during this century.

The famous composers of the age were no doubt to
a great extent inspired by Metastasio's genius. They
caught, as it were, the rays of his brilliant poetical fancy,
in order to reflect them and repeat them in their own
divine art; and no one ever succeeded better than
Metastasio in making the Italian language lend itself to
the requirements of music. Discarding all words which
were unsuitable for song, either from their length or from
the harshness of their sound, he chose only those which
by their sweetness, or by the position of their accent, as
ardì, piegò, sarà, were peculiarly adapted for musical
rendering. He divides the verses to shorten the periods
and render the pause more agreeable; he makes a discreet
use of the rhyme, so as to please the ear, without becoming monotonous. Then, seconded by music, he has
the art of making his verses exactly accord with the
affections he wishes to describe. - If he would paint the
enervating influence of the tender passion, each line seems
to shadow forth the fulness of a feeling which can scarcely

find utterance in speech;[8] the full, quick throb of courage, and his words succeed each other with bounding rapidity;[9] the delighted measure of hope; the low, sullen sounds of despair; the loud clash of anger; the dread blast of revenge; the soul-subduing voice of dejected pity; the veering song of jealousy, which now courted love, now, raving, called on hate; or the mingled measure of pale melancholy, which stole

> "O'er some haunted stream with fond delay
> Round a holy calm diffusing,
> Love of peace and lonely musing
> In hollow murmurs died away."[1]

Thoroughly understanding the character of the opera, Metastasio knew how to make it combine the claims of lyrical and dramatic poetry. It is to be noticed how carefully he reserves his figures and metaphors for his narrative and descriptive scenes, never employing them when he wishes to make the affections speak. How rarely he introduces his comparisons into the *recitative*, leaving them for the *ariette* when the music requires imagery and warmth. We will select only one, and that the most perfect specimen, of the countless examples of lyric beauty which his dramas afford.

> "L' onda dal mar divisa
> Bagna la valle, il monte
> Va Passagiera
> In Fiume,
> Va Prigionera
> In Fonte.
> Mormora sempre, e geme
> Finchè non torna al mar,
> Al Mar dov' ella nacque,
> Dove acquistò gli umori,
> Dove dai lunghi errori
> Spera di riposar."[2]

We have seen how perfect was the harmony established by Metastasio between music and poetry, but he did not rest satisfied until he had made the sister art of painting also contribute her services to perfect his work. The

---

[8] "Zenobia," act ii. sc. 5.
[9] "Olimpiade," act iii. sc. 4.
[1] Collins's "Ode to the Passions."
[2] "Artaserse," act iii. sc. 1.

dexterity shown by him in managing this interesting portion of the melodrama is worthy of attention. His careful choice of the circumstances of his scenery, the masterly manner with which he varies the local situations, the study of contrast in those scenes which appeal more to the eye than to the ear, the intimate knowledge of the geographical position, manners, customs, dress of the different nations—everything, in short, which may lawfully enhance the effect of his *mise-en-scène*, every sort of ingenious contrivance, every kind of pleasing picture may be found in the scenical directions for his dramas.

These were some of the striking features of the great reform worked by Metastasio in the taste of Italy, but the high religious and moral tone of his works exercised a still more beneficial, as well as a more lasting, influence over his country. Never, surely, was the truth conveyed to men's minds in more *molli versi* than by him. Never was virtue depicted in more amiable or more glowing colours than in those characters which he places before us for our imitation.

Apart from his manifold charms, this alone would suffice to maintain him his place in the opinion of worthy minds, more especially as the effect is spontaneous, and not forced, as it is in some of the French dramatists. It seems to be the self-evident conclusion of each dramatic work ; as, for instance, in the "Ezio," where the whole moral of the play naturally sums itself up in the concluding lines :—

> "Della vita nel dubbio cammino,
>   Si smarrisce l'umano pensier,
> L' innocenza è quell' astro divino,
>   Che rischiara fra l' ombre il sentier."

Then, if we consider his power in representing the affections, no one has depicted them with more grace and delicacy, so that Metastasio has ever been the favourite author whose works all alike may read and enjoy. No one knew so well how to appeal to the heart ; no one could better invest his characters with the motives which would naturally guide them. His touches are always those of a great master—clear, distinct, tender, and sublime.

Perhaps this extreme facility may have occasionally led

him into a snare. He has been reproached with introducing too great a number of romantic episodes into one
piece. Not content with one primary plot or passion, on
which the whole drama turns, he gives each of the subordinate characters—as, for example, in the "Semiramide"
—its separate romance ; so that in these secondary positions it becomes hackneyed, frivolous, and insipid. The
passion of Timante for Dircea ("Demofoonte") is real,
pathetic, tender to the last degree ; so is the primary
romance in the "Zenobia" and the "Temistocle ;" but
when all the subordinate characters play the same part,
the force of the predominant interest of the play is
weakened.

This is the principal cause of the want of power in
Metastasio's characters—a want which is sometimes made
more apparent by the smooth, gliding verses and the trip-
ping *ariette* in which the courtly poet makes his Roman
and Carthaginian heroes. to say nothing of the one-eyed
monster, Polypheme, pay their addresses to their respective
ladies.

To the same cause may be attributed an occasional
superfluity of scenes, merely inserted for the sake of
giving fresh scope for his favourite passion, and which,
far from advancing the general action of the drama, only
retard it, break the unity, and divert the threads which
were converging towards the central point of interest.
These slight defects might be illustrated by passages from
the dramas, but the space has been already occupied with
the more pleasing task of pointing out beauties which are
quite inimitable, and before which these trifling flaws fade
into insignificance.

His justly-earned fame won him not only the unanimous
applause of his own country, but also that of most of the
crowned heads of Europe, who invited him to their courts,
and vied with one another how best to do him honour ;
but he remained faithful to the German sovereigns who
had first befriended him, and who had bestowed upon
him the proud title of "Poetà Cesareo," which he enjoyed
for so many years. Pure and loyal in the midst of the
temptations of a courtier's life, free from the ambition and
envy which sometimes mar the character of great literary

N

men, modest when applauded to the skies, he preserved that gentleness and simplicity of character which, often transpiring in his verses, imparts to them so much of their charm. He proved the truth of his own maxim—

> " Un alma grande
> È teatro a sè stessa. Ella in segreto
> S' approva, e si condanna,
> E placida, e sicura
> Del volgo spettator l' aura non cura."
>
> *Artaserse*, act ii. sc. 2.

PART IV.

TRAGEDY AND COMEDY DURING THE SEVENTEENTH AND EIGHTEENTH CENTURIES; SCIPIONE MAFFEI AND ALFIERI.

A.D. 1600—1800.

> " The verse adorn again,
> Fierce War and faithful Love,
> And Truth severe by Fairy Fiction drest.
> In buskined measures move
> Pale Grief, and pleasing Pain,
> With Horror, tyrant of the throbbing breast."
>
> GRAY, *The Bard.*

THE consideration of the melodrama, in the attractive form presented to us by Metastasio, has caused us to pass by, for the time, those dramatists who laboured during the seventeenth century to restore the legitimate drama to the position whence it had been driven by its more fascinating sister. Martelli, Scipione Maffei, and Conti form the connecting links between the *Teatro Italiana* and the great dramatic poets of the eighteenth century. Upon them, as forerunners of Alfieri, Monti, and Goldoni, devolved the arduous task of reasserting the claims of tragedy and comedy on the public attention. It was no easy matter to contend with the prevailing preference for the musical dramas ; a preference so marked that the great public theatres—the "Aliberti" of Rome,

the "San Petronio" of Bologna, the "San Carlo" of
Naples, and the "Fenice" of Venice—were appropriated
to their sole use. The actors were in the pay and formed
part of the establishment of the respective Courts, while
the ordinary tragedies and comedies were excluded from
the royal stages, and driven back on the minor theatres of
the cities. They were performed by strolling players, who
wandered from city to city, turning everything into the
lowest farce as the surest method of gaining the popular applause, on which their very existence depended.
Ignorant and ill educated, these actors of Bolognese, Lombard, or Genoese origin spoke a garbled mixture of
dialects, and had no notion of pronouncing the pure
Tuscan of "Il bel paese là dove il Sì suona." Nor could
any grace or dignity of gesture be expected from players
of this class, to make up for the defects of their pro-
nunciation. Such was the state of the Italian drama
at the end of the seventeenth and at the beginning of the
eighteenth century. The merit of having raised it from
so ignominious a position belongs chiefly to the "Accademia degli Arcadi," founded at Rome by Vincenzo
Leonio (1690), and one of the most famous of these
literary institutions which flourished all over Italy during
this century. The beneficial influence exercised by the
"Arcadi" over literature in general was especially centred
in the reform of the drama; and, under the shadow of
this great literary society, the dramatic writers once more
ventured upon the abandoned field of tragedy. Pier
Jacopo Martelli (b. 1665, d. 1727), a member of this
Accademia, is the first to claim our notice. Fired by
emulation of the French stage, he thought by taking the
great writers who had formed it for an exact model,
he could produce dramas equal to theirs in his own
language. He did not even confine his imitation to the
general method of developing the plot, but carried it
so far into detail as to copy faithfully the metre they
employed, with its rhymes in stiff couplets—a kind of
verse hitherto unknown to the Italian stage, and ever
afterwards called from him "Martelliani." One example
will serve to show how ill the long Alexandrine metre
agrees with the spirit of the Italian language :—

" Signor vedi a' tuoi piedi, il tuo fedel Rustano,
 Che t' annuncia vicino, l' arrivo del Sultano."

Even as a novelty this metre had little charm for the
Italians, and very soon they discovered how wearisome
was the " monotonia della cesura e la rima troppo fre-
quente, e sempre accoppiata." Martelli himself, when he
perceived their unpopularity, observed that—" With a
pair of scissors the mistake could be remedied ; for, by
dividing the verses exactly in the middle, they could
be reduced to the short metre employed by the old
tragedians, pre-eminently by Speroni in his ' Canace.' " [3]
Martelli's Theatre was published at Rome in 1715. Its
merits were recognized by no less a critic than Goldoni,
who observes " that Martelli might have endowed his
country with a *teatro completo* had he not had the folly
to introduce a new kind of versification into Italy." [4]
Nevertheless, fifty years afterwards, Goldoni employed
the same metre in his play of " Molière," for the singular
reason that in a drama of which Molière was the hero it
was fitting to imitate the metre so often employed by the
French dramatists.

The compositions of Martelli embrace every kind of
drama ; and it is to be regretted that, after all his efforts
to improve the Italian stage, and the sterling merit of
many of his tragedies, he should have so far stooped to
the depraved taste of the age as to write a farce called
" Lo Sternuto d' Ercole," to be played with wooden
figures ! Goldoni describes how, in his youth, he himself
represented this comedy with a puppet-show which had
been given to him for his amusement. The plot is
simple. Hercules is represented as travelling through
the country of the Pigmies. The little people, terrified
at the aspect of what appeared to them a moving mountain with arms and legs, hide themselves in the clefts of
the rocks, till, perceiving the giant asleep on the plain,
they emerge from their hiding-place, and, armed with
pigmy weapons, march in myriads over the body of their
sleeping enemy. He awakes with a sneeze, which, like

---

[3] Maffei, "Storia della Lett. Ital.," vol. ii. p. 622.
[4] " Memorie del Sig. Goldoni," p. 68.

that of Gulliver, terrifies and disperses the invading army.
" Ecco," says Goldoni, " la commedia finita e scommette-
rei che nessun altro fuori di me s' immaginò di eseguire
la *Bambucciata* del Signor Martelli."[5] Gian Vincenzo
Gravina, already alluded to in the preceding paper as
the patron of Metastasio, immediately followed Martelli,
and laboured conscientiously at the task of restoring the
fallen drama. But in this respect his rules were of more
use than his actual compositions; for, by adhering to a
stiff imitation of the classical models, he fell into the same
error which had marred the works of so many of his
fellow-dramatists.

A decided success was, however, destined to attend the
next dramatic production of Italy, the " Merope " of
Scipione Maffei, which marks a distinct epoch in the reform of her tragedy. Verona, the birthplace of Scipione
Maffei (b. 1675, d. 1755), has good reason to be proud
of her distinguished son, more especially when he devoted so large a portion of his labours and talents to the
honour of his native city. It does not come within the
scope of this paper to treat of Maffei's " Verona Illustrata,"
with its exhaustive account of her celebrated Roman remains, and of her history from the time of Charlemagne ;
nor yet of his other great archæological and literary works,
save where they touch upon the drama. In his treatise
on the " Teatri Antichi e Moderni," Maffei defended the
existence and use of theatres with successful eloquence
against the indignant attack of a Dominican padre,
Concina, who looked upon them as the primary cause of
the vicious social condition of Italy. Maffei's triumph
was sealed when the Pope (Benedict XIV.) addressed
him a formal epistle expressing entire approval of Maffei's
defence, and his opinion that, in such hands, the drama
might be made to fulfil a useful and edifying purpose.
Maffei laments in his treatise over the " Pasticci drama-
tici," as he called them, of the day, which, he said, " do
not deserve the name of either tragedy or comedy, and.
worse than that, they propagate vice by the bad examples
they represent." He first compiled his " Teatro Italiano,"

. [5] "Memorie del Sig. Goldoni," p. 68.

consisting of the best dramas of the sixteenth century, and some of them he caused to be represented on the stage. But they only served to convince him of the inferiority of the Italian drama as compared with that of other European nations, and, in the determination to wipe away this reproach from his country, he composed his "Merope." Although not free from defects, this tragedy, for the beauty and force of the argument, the happy development of the plot, and the careful, sustained style. became universally popular; and a decided change for the better in the dramatic taste of Italy may be fairly said to date from its first representation at Venice in 1713. It was repeated forty times in one carnival, and has since passed through sixty editions. Nor was its fame confined to Italy, for it spread all over Europe, and was translated into many languages. The greatest tribute paid to Maffei was the adaptation of "Merope" to the French stage by Voltaire. Persuaded, however, that in its native simplicity it would not have the same charm for a Parisian as for an Italian audience, Voltaire composed a "Mérope" of his own, rearranging the scenes, and adding a few incidents to increase the interest. Then, preserving all the grand passages, which he rendered in his own language, while he pared away what was harsh or abrupt, he produced one of the most striking tragedies that have ever been represented on the stage. In the letter prefixed to the first edition of his "Mérope," Voltaire acknowledges his debt to Maffei:—"Si la 'Mérope' française a eu le même succès que la "Mérope" italienne, c'est à vous, monsieur, que je le dois; c'est à cette simplicité dont j'ai toujours été idolâtre, qui dans votre ouvrage m'a servi de modèle. Si j'ai marché dans une route différente, vous m'y avez toujours servi de guide."[6] But this handsome recognition is marred by subsequent conduct more in keeping with the spiteful wit of Voltaire, when, under the feigned name of De la Lindelle, he addressed a letter to himself, in which he reviles the Italian "Merope," and takes occasion to point out all its vulnerable points. Goldsmith pronounces

---

[6] "L' Italia Letteraria Artistica," p. 207.

Maffei's " Merope " to be "the most finished tragedy in the world,"[7] and " supposes that the author learned from the ' Samson ' of Milton, and the ' Athalie ' of Racine, to construct a tragedy without a love intrigue." It is a strong proof of the power of Maffei's mind that, without such an episode, he should have succeeded in winning the public favour at a period when a romance of some kind was considered indispensable to any drama. Maffei wrote his " Merope " with the intention of proving that, it was possible to excite the sympathy and sustain the interest of the audience by a plot depending entirely on the strong affection existing between mother and son, when brought out and placed in a vivid light by situations of extreme peril. Some of the scenes show great power and force of contrast. Yet it must be owned that there is something revolting in the fury of a queen who wishes to kill the murderer of her son with her own hands—something to excite horror rather than sympathy, and not to be excused even by the force of the situation, when the supposed murderer proves to be her son himself, whom she is about to destroy. Voltaire contrives to soften the impression conveyed by the queen's violence in this scene, till it merely appears undignified ; but with Maffei her conduct appears in all its rude barbarity. Eager in the pursuit of learning, and anxious to compare the litera- ture of other nations with his own, Scipione Maffei travelled all over Europe. Frederick Prince of Wales welcomed him to England with marked courtesy, and in return he dedicated to the Prince the first book of his translation of the " Iliad " into Italian. He visited Pope at his villa on the Thames, and found him engaged in the study of " Merope." The University of Oxford conferred a degree on the illustrious Italian, with an elaborate public oration in his praise, from which, however, says a satirical biographer, " he could not have derived much gratification, as, owing to the barbarous English method of pronouncing Latin, he did not understand a word they said."[8] He died at Verona in 1775, in the

7 Goldsmith, " Present State of Polite Literature," p. 48.
8 " L' Italia Letteraria Artistica," p. 208.

eightieth year of his age. His "Merope" raised the whole tone of the Italian stage, and the tragedians who succeeded him set it steadily before them as a standard of excellence. But they were not equally successful in gaining the popular applause; and the only tragedies which in any way rivalled that of Maffei were those of " Giulio Cesare " and " Giunio Bruto," by Conti. Antonio Conti, a Venetian nobleman (b. 1677, d. 1748), was a contemporary of Maffei ; but it was only in the decline of life that he turned his mind to the drama ; and so it came to pass that his " Giulio Cesare " was not represented till 1743, whereas " Merope " had appeared in 1713. The former of these two tragedies was highly popular when first performed at Venice, and the critics praise the simple grandeur of his characters by contrast with the affectation which clings to the modern dramatists in their treatment of classical subjects. " The true Roman speaks with natural nobility of character, beautiful because it is unconscious ; but in our modern tragedies the heroes are great and noble with so vast an effort that they collapse, and become mean and little in the attempt, displaying their foreign origin when they most wish to appear as Romans. The great merit of Conti consists in a wise adherence to those details of the manners and customs of the time which stamp the character of the piece, and in which the French dramatists are often very deficient." [9] A few tragedians, whose names are not of sufficient importance to find a place in this paper, stimulated by the examples of Maffei and Conti, continued to cultivate the tragic muse with praiseworthy zeal worthy of better success.

Translations of French and English plays were also written in great numbers at this time. Among others, the " Mahomet " and " Sémiramide " of Voltaire were rendered into Italian by Cesarotti. But such foreign aid could not impart sufficient life to sustain the tottering native drama. On the contrary it only served to confirm the prevailing opinion, that although here and there an occasional good tragedy might give promise of better things, Italy would never possess a permanent tragic theatre ; that tragedy

---

[9] Maffei, vol. ii. p. 624.

was not in accordance with the genius and character of her language. This despairing verdict was destined to be immediately called in question, and afterwards com pletely overthrown by the genius of Alfieri. " Why," he asks, with all the passionate eagerness of his character, " must our divine language, so bold and vigorous in the mouth of Dante, become languid and effeminate on the tragic stage; why should Cesarotti, whose poem of "Ossian ' is full of life and fire, become at once tame and insipid in his tragedies of " Semiramide" and " Mahomet " ? Of one thing I am sure, that, wherever the fault lies, it is not in our beautiful, flexible, ever-varying Italian speech." He proved the truth of his own words ; for, after the publication of his tragedies this reproach could never again be cast upon the dramatic literature of Italy. His immediate predecessors had laboured vainly in the same cause, copying, now the classic and now the French stage, but to no purpose. He bent his genius to the task, and it was done. Despising the mere surface work of imitating the foreign drama, he began by making himself thoroughly acquainted with his own language in its finest models, and then moulded it with masterly vigour to serve the great end he proposed to himself. But this result was only accomplished by years of labour. His early educa-tion was little calculated to develop his talents. He was born at Asti, January 17, 1749, of noble parents ; and it was the opinion of those days that for that class of life the smallest amount of education would suffice—that " ad un signore non era necessario di diventare un dottore." Eight years of " ineducation," as he himself terms it, had their fruit in a wild ungoverned youth ; but with this period of his life we have no concern. It occupies three epochs of his autobiography, and the fourth, which em-braces thirty years of manhood and middle life, gives a faithful account of the studies of his maturer years and of their fruit in his works. The representation of "Cleopatra," his earliest tragedy, performed in Turin in 1775, brought out forcibly its many defects, and made manifest to Alfieri the necessity of retracing his steps in those paths of learning from which in youth and indolence he had turned aside. " The thick veil," he says, " which had hitherto so effectually blinded me fell from my eyes, and I made a solemn vow to spare myself neither pains nor trouble, until, like a true son of Italy, I had mastered my own language." Beginning literally with the grammar, he proceeded steadily, verse by verse, through the Italian classics. Dante was too difficult at the outset, and was laid aside for Tasso ; Ariosto succeeded ; then Dante without the help of commentaries, followed by Petrarch, diligently noting the fine passages of each, and never pausing in his work ; so that in a year he had an accurate knowledge of these, the four great poets of Italy. And for sixteen years they continued to be his daily study. To his mind they contained all the elements of poetry, with the exception of the actual mechanism of blank verse, which, he observes, " can be easily extracted from the combination of the four, when taken together and manipulated with a little art." [1] Later in life he found another model for blank verse in the " Ossian " of Cesarotti, which had a great attraction for him. His friends, who watched his labours with interest, next recommended a study of the best prose writers ; and finally, still in the pursuit of his language in its purest form, he betook himself to Tuscany to accustom himself " a parlare, udire, pensare, e sognare in Toscano, e non altrimenti mai più." Like all true Italian scholars, he could not away with the French Italian, which in his time, as now, prevailed in Italy ; and which has such a mischievous effect upon the language, weakening its fine nervous idioms, and spoiling all its originality. Against these " gallicisme " Alfieri waged a ceaseless warfare, more especially because, owing to his Piedmontese birth and education, they were a special stumbling-block in his own path. The first use he made of the knowledge of his own language was to re-write the two tragedies of " Filippo " and " Polinice," which in his youth he had written in French. " Filippo " is now considered one of his best tragedies, and the dialogue between the King of Spain and his minister (act ii. sc. 5), a masterpiece of vigour and brevity, rivals Corneille's famous challenge

---

[1] Alfieri, " Opere," vol. ii. p. 109.

scene in the "Cid." The hateful character of Philip II. is portrayed with a powerful hand. To the study of his own literature succeeded that of the ancient classics; and the result of this was the tragedy of "Antigone." "Antigone" offers another striking instance of conciseness (act iv. sc. 1). The second scene of the second act is one of great power, and is famous for the one sentence: "Il reo d' un delitto é chi 'l pensa." Still keeping on classical ground, he wrote "Agamennone," and pursued the narrative in the tragedy of "Oreste." Aware that the subject had already been treated by Voltaire, he endeavoured to borrow the French tragedy from a friend, who refused to lend it, advising him to write his own play first, on the ground that, in that way his "Oreste," whether better or worse than the French one, would be at all events his own. "I took this excellent advice," says Alfieri, "and it ever afterwards became a rule with me, if I wrote on a subject already treated by modern writers, never to read their tragedies till I had composed my own. Thus I preserved an originality which none can dispute." However, every rule requires an exception to prove it, and, in the case of "Merope," Alfieri had read Maffei's tragedy on the same subject before composing his own. And his wonder that such a tragedy should have obtained so great a reputation induced him to see whether he could not do more justice to the subject. Like Maffei, he dedicated his tragedy to his mother in token of filial affection; and by a few masterly strokes he adds vigour to a subject which seemed to have reached its culminating point of interest in the hands of former tragedians. "Sofonisba" and "La Rosamunda, the earliest tragedies of the *Teatro Antico*, were again invested by him with their "sceptred pall." He relates with much candour how, on reading his first "Sofonisba" to a friend, it was such an evident failure that he threw it into the fire. He afterwards re-wrote it, though never to his entire satisfaction. "La Congiura dei Pazzi" was next suggested to him as a subject for a tragedy, by his friend Il Gori. Alfieri read the account of this conspiracy for the first time in Macchiavelli's History, and was so enraptured with the vigorous style of the narrative as to lay aside his dramatic works for the time, and to write a treatise on " La Tirannide," which he published in later years. Although his more mature judgment taught him to look upon the subject of his work in a modified light, and to wish that his wild invectives against princes and potentates had been strengthened by reasonable arguments, he would not allow himself to temper with "il gelo degli anni" the passionate cry for liberty which breathes in this ardent work of his youth. No one desired more earnestly than he did the freedom of his country, no one was more intolerant of the yoke of oppression under which Italy had groaned so long. Of the sincerity of these convictions he gave a remarkable proof. There was a law at that time in Piedmont that subjects of Alfieri's position and station in life might not leave the kingdom without permission of the Government. This was sufficiently galling to a man of Alfieri's restless, independent spirit; but another law, which prohibited, under penalty of a heavy fine, the publication of any books out of the kingdom unless revised by the State, touched him still more nearly. " In these circumstances," says Alfieri, "it was evident that I could not be both an author and a subject of his Piedmontese Majesty. Of the two I chose to be an author." He was also aware that the principles of liberty which he insisted upon so earnestly in his writings—in the " Tirannide," for example, and in his tragedy of " Virginia," one of his most powerful compositions—were not calculated to win the approbation of the Piedmontese Government. His proud, independent genius could brook no restraint of this nature, and he resolved to shake off the galling chains at whatever cost; to bid adieu to his country; in short, to make use of the word which he coined for the occasion—" di spiemontezzarmi." This self-banishment involved the renunciation of his inheritance and all other worldly possessions ; but the greatness of the sacrifice did not stagger his purpose. He deliberately made over to his sister Giulia (wife of the Conte di Cumiana) the whole of his property, on condition of her allowing him an annual pension of 14,000 lire. At one time it seemed doubtful if the Government would allow him to draw this pension, and

the chapter which he devotes to this extraordinary incident,[2] relates in an amusing manner the various economies
he strove to practise, and his calculations as to what profession would best secure him a livelihood. His passion
for horses—second only to his love of literature—and his
great gift for managing them, led him seriously to consider whether the trade of a horse-breaker would not suit
him. It was, he considered, one of the least servile of
occupations, and most easily combined with that of a
poet, "since a tragedy may be as well written in a stable
as in a court."[3] But at length his affairs were arranged,
and his sister, deeply lamenting the step he had taken,
was allowed by the Government to pay him the annual
pension he had asked for. Alfieri was now free. His
movements were no longer restrained by arbitrary rule.
His writings might express his bold uncompromising
sentiments without fear of restraint. The completion of
the "Congiura dei Pazzi," hitherto only planned, was the
first fruit of this liberty, written, as he himself expresses
it, with "febbre frenetica di libertà." But this cannot
excuse the false colours in which, to serve the cause of
freedom, Alfieri represents an action acknowledged by all
historians to have been the most dastardly of crimes. To
borrow the words of Roscoe—for none more forcible
could be found—" What shall we think of a dramatic
performance in which the 'Pazzi' are the champions of
liberty ? in which superstition is called in to the aid of
truth, and Sixtus consecrates the holy weapons devoted
to the slaughter of the two brothers ? in which the relations of all parties are confounded, and a tragic effect is
attempted to be produced by a total dereliction of historical veracity, an assumption of falsehood for truth, of vice
for virtue ?"[4] Still, while lamenting the general principles it inculcates, we must not be deterred from pointing
out the beauty of some of the individual parts. The scene
between the two Medici brothers, Lorenzo and Giuliano,[5]
which contains a tribute to the founder of their family,

[2] Vol. ii. pp. 58—71.
[3] Ibid. p. 68.
[4] Roscoe's " Life of Lorenzo de' Medici," note to p. 212.
[5] "Cong. dei Pazzi," act ii. sc. 1.

the great Cosimo, and a masterly description of a tyrant's method of crushing his people into submission—displays his gift of eloquence in a striking manner. "Don Garzia" followed the "Congiura," and is again made the engine for an attack upon the Medici. His next tragedy, "Maria Stuarda," he wrote for the singular reason that he did not like the subject; but with that indomitable will, so characteristic of him, he determined to see if he could not do justice to it, in spite of his disinclination. The experiment failed as a whole, although the principal characters, Queen Mary, Darnley, and Bothwell, are well drawn. The subordinate parts of Ormond and Lamorre are creations of his fancy, for it is in vain to seek them in history. He continued his work with astonishing rapidity; in ten months (1782) he wrote seven tragedies, arranged the plan of two new ones, and revised and corrected the fourteen which he had composed altogether. From time to time he judged of their effect by reading them aloud in a mixed society, inviting the criticisms of the learned, profiting even by the "yawns, coughs, and restlessness" of the rougher or more ignorant elements of his audience, to note for alteration such passages as were dull and heavy, and could not command general interest. But hitherto, with the sole unfortunate example of "Cleopatra," none of his tragedies had been put upon the stage. At last he was stimulated to make the attempt by the representation of a version of Thomas Corneille's "Comte d'Essex," by a company of dilettanti in the private theatre of the Duca Grimaldi, at Rome. Poor in the original, the play appeared even worse in a translation; and Alfieri longed to substitute one of his own, written with native fire, in his own beloved Italian language. He offered his "Antigone" to the amateur *corps drama-tique*. It was readily accepted, and the company not being sufficiently strong for all the parts, that of Creonte, usurper of the throne of Thebes, fell upon himself. The success of the piece· surpassed his expectations, and induced him to venture on what he terms the *terribile prova* of printing and publishing his works. The first edition consisted of one volume, containing his first four tragedies, published at Rome in 1783, and followed immediately by six more tragedies published in two volumes at Sienna. He was immediately assailed by the fire which he had expected of literary criticism, correspondence, and newspaper comments. The *pedanti Fiorentini*, as he calls them, gave him to understand that, if his manuscript had been corrected by their Academy, it would have had a better chance of success. An exception must be made in favour of Il Calzabigi's just and enlightened criticisms, which, far from angering the author, were of great service to him in his subsequent compositions. To this critic Alfieri wrote a reply, and the correspondence serves as an admirable preface to the first volume.[6] After the publication of these tragedies, Alfieri paused in his labours, and set out on extensive travels to France and England, not, as he tells us, from any curiosity or wish to see either of those countries, but partly from sheer restlessness, and partly for the purpose of buying English horses. This passion, already alluded to, was sufficiently strong to supersede for a period of eight months at a time the books and poetry which were at other times of such absorbing interest. During his sojourn of four months in London (1784) he bought fourteen horses (as many horses as he had written tragedies), which, with infinite labour, he transported to Sienna. He feelingly describes all the miseries the poor animals suffered in the transit, and his careful passage of Mont Cenis, which offered no small difficulties and danger to the high-bred English horses, "vivaci e briosi oltre modo."[7] On his way through Piedmont, the reigning King of Sardinia, Vittorio Amadeo II., sought in vain to lure the voluntary exile back to his native country. Liberty of thought and liberty of action were more than ever prized by Alfieri after his sojourn in England, and the royal courtesies were in vain, although later, in 1796, when the king was hard pressed by the French arms, Alfieri would have been glad had it been possible to render him any service. Breathing more freely when he had left Piedmont behind him, Alfieri began anew his rambles

[6] Alfieri, "Tragedie," vol. i. pp. 19—2.
[7] Alfieri, "Vita," vol. ii. p. 123.

over Italy and Europe. The fame of Voltaire's tragedy of "Brutus" stirred up a spirit of rivalry in the Italian tragedian. "Voltaire write on Brutus!" he exclaims; "I will have a Brutus of my own; nay, I will have two; and we will see if I cannot outdo this Frenchman of plebeian origin." And so "Bruto Primo" appeared, dedicated to Washington, followed by "Bruto Secondo," dedicated to "Il libero Popolo Italiano." They are noisy and tumultuous tragedies, where the stage is perpetually crowded with Roman citizens clamouring for freedom; and although they contain some fine declamations in favour of liberty, they are the least happy of Alfieri's works. His tragedies were now nineteen in number, and Alfieri, who had originally intended to limit their number to twelve, resolved to abstain from writing any more, and to publish them all in a new and complete edition. He was in Paris at the time of this resolution (1787), so he entrusted the publication of the new edition to Didot, a Frenchman of whose taste and talents the fastidious author had a high opinion. It was three years in preparation, owing to the care and pains which were lavished upon it, and it was still in type when Didot's press suddenly stopped for want of hands. The workmen, plunged deep in the politics of that exciting time, spent "whole days," says the indignant author, "in reading the newspapers and expressing their ideas as to the government of the kingdom, instead of attending to their business of setting up the types." But these were only the first signs of the awful storm of the Revolution from which Alfieri on his return to Paris, in 1792, narrowly escaped with his life. His "Memoirs" describe the well-known events of the 10th of August, the massacre of the Swiss Guard, the pitiless treatment of the Royal Family; his own flight, accomplished five days afterwards with the utmost difficulty.[8] The atrocities he had himself witnessed, supplemented each day by some new tale of horror as it reached Italy, filled to overflowing the measure of Alfieri's hatred of and contempt for the French. It was not till he had relieved his mind by an

---

[8] Vol. ii. pp. 188, 207.

apology for the unhappy Louis XVI., then a prisoner, and a furious invective against the whole nation, entitled " Il Misogallo," that Alfieri could again turn his attention to Italian literature. Still it was his unhappy fate twice before he died to see the objects of his especial hatred enter Florence—once in 1799, and again in 1804, when he peremptorily refused the French general's request to make his acquaintance. In the spring of 1793 we find him aiding personally in the recital of his tragedies by a society of dilettanti in Florence. He made great progress in the art of declamation, giving the light and shade, inflection of voice, and variety of action necessary to make the characters he personated stand out distinctly and vividly before his audience. " Saul " was his favourite tragedy. After reciting it several times, he was prevailed upon to play the part of the Hebrew king, in a private theatre at Pisa, and there he tells us "rimasi quanto al teatro, morto da Rè." Authors do not always give the preference to their best works. but the Italian critics confirm Alfieri in his predilection for " Saul," esteeming it the best and most powerful of his tragedies. Alfieri made a previous study of the character of Saul in Holy Writ, and the inspired language seems to have been present to his mind throughout the composition of the piece. We recognize it in the beautiful song of David, which stills for a while the king's madness, of which we can only give a faint idea in translation :—

"O Thou who in eternal power dost reign
O'er all created things dread Lord Divine,
Thou, at whose word I was from nothing ta'en,
How dare I lift my trembling eyes to Thine !
Thou, from whose gaze the depths of earth contain
No secret paths, and night as day doth shine:
Speak but Thy Word, and worlds in chaos close,
Stretch forth Thine arm, and scatter'd flee Thy foes.
Borne earthwards on the rushing fiery wings
Of myriad cherubims Thy chariot stayed,
And with Thy Word, which mightiest power brings,
Didst Israel's leader once vouchsafe to aid;
Wisdom and speech didst give from living springs,
And Thou Thyself his sword and buckler made.
Let but one ray of Thine effulgent light
Pierce through the clouds and strike our dazzled sight."
                                          Saul, Act iii. Sc. 4.
                                          O

Again, we frequently find it in the expression of the deep religious feeling which is the mainspring of each and all of the characters. "Miseri noi! che siam, se Iddio ci lascia," David exclaims, in his pity for Saul (sc. 1). "Col Rè sia pace" is Jonathan's salutation to his father. "E sia col Padre Iddio," adds Michal. "Meco è sempre il Dolore," replies the unhappy king. The dream of Saul, the departure of David on the eve of the battle, are worth referring to, as they abound in the rich metaphors which give such an Eastern colouring to the drama.

An interval of ten years elapsed between the nineteen tragedies which were published by Didot and the two last compositions, the "Alceste Prima" and "Seconda." These were the results of his Greek studies late in life, and Alfieri was not a little vain of having learnt Greek at the age of forty-six. "Better late than never," he observes in the chapter devoted to the account of this new accomplishment ; and in his mature years he read for the first time, in the original, the story of Alcestis " brought from the grave." It took such a hold of his imagination, that he breaks the vow which he had solemnly made never to write another tragedy, and gives us a finished composition remarkable for a soft delicacy foreign to his other works. The return of Alcestis to life in the concluding scene is beautifully told, recalling by its tender feeling the last scene of the " Winter's Tale." When, like Hermione, Alcestis

> " Bequeaths to death her numbness,
> For from him dear life redeems her,"

and is reunited to her husband, for whose sake she had laid down her life, while her children cling round her in rapt and wondering delight, the pathos of the scene is unrivalled. " Eccola ; mira ; Alceste viva è questa ! " and Alfieri puts the finishing touch when he makes the sight draw tears from Hercules, the mighty hero, who had snatched her from the very grasp of death.

> " It was the crowning grace of that great heart
> To keep back joy ; procrastinate the truth,
> Until the wife, who had made proof and found
> The husband wanting, might essay once more,

Hear, see, and feel him renovated now,
Able to do, know, all herself had done,
Risen to the height of her: so hand in hand
The two might go together, live and die." [9]

Thus once again embarked in literary labours, Alfieri,
at the close of his career, wrote six comedies, and was
engaged in revising them when the illness overtook him
of which he died at Florence, October 4th, 1804. But
these comedies did not add to his reputation, nor did the
rather "puerile vanity," as he terms it, which prompted
him to celebrate his lately acquired Greek scholarship by
the invention and self-investment of an Homeric Order of
Merit. This consisted of a chain, or, collar, from which
hung a cameo representing Homer, and bearing on the
reverse a Greek distich, invented by Alfieri, and translated
also by him into Italian rhyme :—

"Forse inventava Alfieri un ordin vero,
Nel farsi ei stesso Cavalier d'Omero."

But as the most eminent tragic writer of Italy he is
worthy of the highest honour. Full of vigour and power,
he breathes new life into the languid scenes of Italian
tragedy. He will have no imitation of French gallantry,
no Spanish rhodomontades. Italy must have a theatre of
her own, speaking her pure idiom, and representing her
own ideas on either classical or modern subjects. With
one sweep he clears the stage of all confidants and
secondary personages ; so that, if you run your eye down
the list of characters, you see that they rarely exceed six
or seven, and are generally limited to four. "In my
tragedies," he says, " you will find no convenient eaves-
dropper ready to hear and reveal the secret on which the
whole plot depends, no mysterious characters (with the
one exception of Egisto, in ' Merope') unknown either to
themselves or to others. I have not availed myself of
either supernatural or physical aid ; no flitting ghosts
haunt my scenes ; no thunder and lightning enhance my
catastrophes. I have abstained from unnecessary murders
and massacres. In short, I have rigidly denied myself
the usual licence permitted to dramatic writers." But

[9] " Balaustion's Adventure." Robert Browning, p. 147. See also
Mrs. Heman's Translation of the Alcestis, p. 124.

the very simplicity of his tragedies laid him open to
attack on account of their uniformity of method ; and the
author does not deny that he pursues the same system
with each and all alike, trusting to the variety of subject
and character to obviate this monotony. His own opinion
of his works, as deliberately expressed as if he was discussing those of another author, was constantly corrected
by contemporary criticism. He recognized the justice of
the enlightened comments of Il Calzabigi and of Cesarotti,
whose blank verse had served him for a model ; but to
the captious fault-finding of the Florentine Academy he
was perfectly indifferent.

> " Uom se' tu grande o vile ?
> Morì e il saprai,"

are the concluding words of the sonnet in which he describes for posterity the strange mixture of good and evil
in his character. And if the critics busied themselves with
his works during his lifetime, they dissected them after his
death in the most unsparing manner. The French revenge
themselves with bitter invective for the abuse Alfieri had
heaped upon their nation. Schlegel is scant of his praises,
and only selects the " Saul ". as worthy of favourable
comment ; but the opinion of his own nation, as summed
up in the discourse of Pietro del Rio, is of more consequence. " You must not look," he says, " for dazzling
variety of metaphor, nor yet for persuasive forms of
speech ; but you will always find a magnificent power in
the style, life and vigour in the action of the drama, force
in the dialogue, vivacity and truth in the characters, and
occasional passages of astounding eloquence."

PART V.

TRAGEDY AND COMEDY DURING THE SEVENTEENTH AND
EIGHTEENTH CENTURIES ; MONTI, GOLDONI, ETC.

A.D. 1600—1800.

VICENZO MONTI followed close upon the footsteps of
Alfieri in the *terribil via* struck out by that Michael

Angelo of the Italian drama. The "Aristodemo," Monti's best tragedy, was inspired by the recital of Alfieri's "Virginia" in Rome (1782). Deeply impressed with the beauty and vigour of that play, Monti, immediately on his return home, sketched out the plot of "Aristodemo," King of Messenia, which appeared to him an equally fine subject for a tragedy. The discussion among the *litterati* of the day as to the merits and defects of Alfieri's style stimulated Monti to improve upon the rugged asperities and strained inversions which occasionally mar the grand passages of his fellow-tragedian. And his success was signal; for Signorelli, an eminent critic, remarks that when Alfieri's noble conceptions are illustrated by Monti's polished style, Italian tragedy at last attains to the summit of perfection. "Aristodemo" carried away the gold medal offered by the Duke of Parma for the best drama, a distinction which, owing to the general inferiority of tragical composition, had not been claimed for two years. The style is noble and sustained, the versification fluent, the dialogue easy and polished, the plot clearly and rapidly unfolds itself; but, above all, the passions are delineated with the hand of a master. The anguish of Aristodemo, soothed by the tender compassion of Cesira, to whom, while still unaware that she is his daughter, he feels drawn with the strong chain of parental affection ; the attachment shown by the faithful servant Gonippo—all these, in the hands of an author who writes as if entranced with his subject, make a series of beautiful and pathetic pictures ; so that the interest is wrought up to the highest pitch by those alternations of terror and compassion which are the great elements of a well-sustained tragedy. It is an awful drama ; and if the mere perusal of it is sufficient to stir the strongest emotions, the effect when represented on the stage can easily be imagined. In the third Act (scene 7) there is a remarkable discourse upon suicide between Gonippo and Aristodemo, and the same scene contains the description of the apparition of the spectre to the unhappy king, one of the most powerful passages in the drama. The accessories of spectres and tombs have since been objected to as a kind of tragic terror too hackneyed for use ; and the entrance of Cesira into the

tomb has been censured as an unnatural act of courage on
her part ; but Monti urges in her defence that the desire
to save her father is sufficient to outweigh all the ordinary
fears such an action would inspire ; and we must here
observe that, like " Merope," the whole interest of
" Aristodemo " centres in filial affection. " Aristodemo " is
looked upon as undoubtedly the best of Monti's three
dramas, although the other two—" Caio Gracco " and
" Galeotto Manfredi "—have also obtained distinguished
laurels. ' The " Gracco " owed its reputation in some
measure to its patriotic sentiment, which was in accordance with the spirit of the age.   It has besides great
intrinsic merit, showing a vigour and power in depicting
the Roman character which can only have been derived
from deep study of the classics.   It would seem as if the
ardent spirits of this century in Italy looked back fondly
to the past, as though to learn from their Roman ancestors
how to gain that liberty for which they sighed in vain.
But Monti is careful to draw the distinction between the
true liberty established on the basis of truth and justice,
and the lawless licence at that time so vividly portrayed
in France, founded on crime, and only maintained by the
daily perpetration of new atrocities.   This " libertà di
ladroni e d' assassini " is sternly condemned by the Mother
of the Gracchi.   " 'They have," she says, " their country's
name for ever on their lips, and never in their hearts "
(act i. scene 3).   In his description of the assassinated
Consul (act iv. scene 6), Monti has literally borrowed the
well-known forcible language in which Shakespeare paints
the murdered corpse of Gloucester.

" But see, his face is black, and full of blood."

"Ma qui, il vedete ! tutto quanto il viso
    Dell' infelice n' è ricolmo e nero."

" His eyeballs farther out than when he lived,
    Staring full ghastly like a strangled man."

" Mirate le pupille
    Travolte, obolique, e per lo sforzo quasi
    Fuor dell' orbita lor."

" His hair upreared, his nostrils stretched with struggling."

" Notate il varco
    Delle narici dilatato, indizio di compresso respiro."

" His hands abroad displayed, as one that grasped
And tugged for life, and was by strength subdued."

" e queste braccia
Stese quanto son lunghe, e queste dita
Pur tutte aperte, come d' uom che sente
Afferrarsi alla gola, e si dibatte
Finchè forza il soggioga." [1]

The Italian tragedian does not attempt to render the

" Well-proportioned beard made rough and rugged,
Like to the summer's corn by tempest lodged ;"

but he concludes his description with a beautiful contrast
which diverts the thoughts from the preceding horrors.
An English translation can scarcely convey the soft and
peaceful picture presented by the Italian :—

" Not thus, not thus, my friends, a just man's soul
Parts from its earthly home. It flees not thence,
Like some invading foe whose iron tread
Leaves ruthless footmarks in the trampled soil,
But gently lays its mortal burden down,
With lingering looks of love. So have I seen
One who has travelled o'er some distant way,
Reaching the goal at last, take tender leave
Of the beloved companion of his toils,
Bidding him fond farewell."

The imitation of Shakespeare again appears in "Galeotto
Manfredi, Principe di Faënza," Monti's third and last
tragedy, the character of Zambrino, the wicked courtier,
resembling closely the Iago of " Othello." But he is also
painted from the life as a portrait of the author's personal
enemy. By the character of Ubaldo, the contrast to
Zambrino, Monti intended to represent himself ; and it is
said that on one occasion when the tragedy was being
played the allusion struck the spectators so forcibly that
they insisted upon the repetition of the whole scene
between the faithful and false courtiers.[2] The argument
of the tragedy, the author tells us, is taken from Ten-
ducci's " Storia di Faënza." [3] It had a great attraction

[1] " King Henry VI.," Part II. act iii. sc. 2; " Caio Gracco,"
att. iv. sc. 6.
[2] " Galeotto Manfredi," act iv. sc. 6.
[3] Also to be found in Roscoe's " Life of Lorenzo de' Medici," vol. ii.
pp. 168—172.

for Monti, who had spent much of his time in that brilliant and cultivated city, and had seen with his own eyes the chamber where Manfredi was murdered. Monti was born in Alfonsina, near Ravenna, in 1754 ; he was educated at Faënza. His talents early procured him the notice of the papal legate at Ferrara, Cardinal Borghese, under whose protection he went to Rome. There he resided some years, and became secretary to the Duca di Nemi, nephew to Pius VI. He obtained a high reputation as a poet some time previous to the appearance of those tragedies already mentioned ; but the limits of our subject will not admit of the mention, except by name, of his famous poem, "La Bassvigliana," written in the "terza rima" of Dante, and of the same visionary character as the "Divina Commedia." The subject was the death of the French envoy at Rome, Ugo de Bassville. It was published in 1793, the year of the murder of Louis XVI., and contains a striking description of the death of that unhappy monarch.[4] Monti witnessed the rise and fall of Napoleon, some of whose victories he celebrated in his poetry. In the zenith of his fame he recognized and acknowledged the bright star of the rising genius of Manzoni, and Manzoni, making allusion to the classical subjects of Monti's poetry, takes leave of the last tragedian of the eighteenth century in the graceful couplet—

> " Salve, O divino, a cui largì natura,
> Il cor di Dante, e del suo Duca il canto,
> Questo fia il grido dell' età ventura
> Ma l' età che fu tua tel dice in pianto."[5]

We have seen how great an effort was required to restore Italian tragedy, but it was a yet more difficult task to give stability to her comedy. The great writers of the fourteenth and fifteenth centuries, Bibbiena, Ariosto, and Macchiavelli, had once given it the shape and form of dramatic composition ; but their improvements were confined to their own comedies, and, with very rare

---

[4] Very forcibly translated by Mrs. Hemans. Poems, p. 121.
[5] " Hail, Bard divine ! at once to thee were given
   The heart of Dante and his leader's theme ;
   Meet salutation for the age to come,
   Thine own, o'er glories past, must weep and dream."

exceptions, no writers worthy of note continued the task which these had begun. Thus in the seventeenth century we find the comic drama of Italy chiefly depending for its reputation upon the old *commedie dell' arte*, which still maintained the position they had acquired by their classical origin. Goldoni conceived the ingenious idea of enlisting harlequin and his troop in the service of the true drama, availing himself of the licence they enjoyed, and the immunities they claimed from long prescriptive right. This was a work of time, and required all the skill and ingenuity of the greatest of Italian comedians before he could substitute the dialogues and plots of his own invention for the extempore jests and grotesque wit of the personages of the old Italian "Mascherata." We find the account in Memoirs which rival those of Alfieri in candour, and make so lively and sparkling a narrative, that Gibbon pronounces them " to be a great deal more comic than the comedies themselves." Carlo Goldoni was born in Venice in 1707, and from his childhood gave unmistakable signs of his passion for the drama. We have already seen how he employed the puppet-show which had been given to him for a toy, and at the age of eight he wrote his first comedy—so good that his father would not believe it was his unassisted work. At thirteen he composed a prologue to the comedy " La Sorellina di Don Pilone," by Gigli, in which he acted the part of the prima donna. It was represented at the Jesuit College at Perugia, the scene of his early education. He pursued his studies at Rimini, under the tutelage of the Dominican fathers, and there he fell in with a troop of comedians, with whom he rapidly made friends. Every night he attended their performances, and was in such despair when their engagement at Rimini came to a close that he accepted their invitation to accompany them to Chiozza, under pretext of seeing his mother, who had taken up her abode there. His voyage of three days in the *Barca dei Comici* seems to have influenced the whole of his after life. At college he spent the time he ought to have devoted to his studies in reading all the plays he could lay hands upon, in every language ; and perceiving the inferiority of the Italian drama to that of other nations, he determined that it should be the work of his life to place it on an equal footing with theirs. When dismissed in disgrace from college for a satirical dramatic composition, called " L' Atellana," in imitation of the old Roman farces, he nearly fled to Gravina at Rome, in the hope that he would take him, as a second Metastasio, under his protection ; but not having sufficient funds for the journey, he was obliged to return to his parents at Chiozza. What were they to do with him ? From his father's profession he had already turned with loathing ; he thought in a moment of despair of entering a monastery, but as quickly abandoned the idea. There seemed some chance of success for him in the legal profession, when, after passing his examination at Padua, he became enrolled in the corps of advocates at Venice. But his career as a lawyer came to an abrupt end, and although it was afterwards resumed with some distinction, it has been entirely eclipsed by his fame as the greatest writer of Italian comedy. He began, however, by writing an opera. " The authors of comedy," he tells us, " were ill-paid, while the Opera offered a prospect of an immediate fortune." [6] And so he wrote his " Amalassunta." He read it aloud to the director of the opera, who pronounced it to be a complete failure as an opera. " You have written it," he said, " on the true principles of tragedy, but you did not know that in the composition of an opera you must be guided by rules, which, however destitute of common sense they may appear, are none the less essential to the construction of a musical drama." And then he proceeded to enumerate all the arbitrary arrangements and restrictions as to the number of ariette, and their distribution among the actors and actresses, which Metastasio had managed to observe without marring the poetical effect of his drama. Made wiser by experience, Goldoni consulted a musical composer before he wrote his second opera. This he called " Il Gondolier Veneto," and it appeared as an intermezzo to an opera called " Belisario," shining all the more by contrast with this indifferent composition. Goldoni offered to re-write " Belisario ; " his offer was accepted with joy by the troop of comedians,

[6] " Mem. del Sig. Goldoni," p. 103.

and when the "Belisario" was represented at Venice
(1714), the effect it produced surpassed their highest
expectations. "Questa, questa," was the unanimous
choice of the audience, when, according to the custom,
the stage-manager appeared before the curtain to an-
nounce the performance for the ensuing night. The
"Belisario" had been supplemented by two "opere
buffe," also by Goldoni, a kind of dramatic composition
which, although well known in Naples and Rome, had
not yet made its way into Northern Italy. This novelty
added to the popularity of the performance, and the
comedians discovered that Goldoni was henceforth indispensable to their dramatic arrangements. He lived
with them on the most friendly terms, writing parts to
suit this person and that, gratifying the whims and
fancies of the prima donnas, and turning their very
jealousies and quarrels to account; thus feeling his way
by degrees to the reform which he had long meditated.
The first step consisted in composing what he called a
commedia di carattere, to be performed without masks,
by contrast with the *commedia a soggetto*, the name given
to plays with skeleton plots filled in at the pleasure of
the actors, just as charades are now performed in private
theatricals. The Italian comedians were very tenacious
of this privilege. They considered it an insult to their
talents to be given a written part to perform, and much
disliked the trouble of learning it. They struggled with
pertinacity for their rights in this respect, and Goldoni
never obtained a complete victory over them, although
he fought hard for it all his life. In his first *commedia*
of the reformed kind he entrusted the principal parts
to two actors, late additions to their company, of whose
talents he had a high opinion, and it had an eminent
success. After this attempt Goldoni tried another opera,
"Gustavo Vasa," about which he consulted the great
Apostolo Zeno, then in his old age, and living in retirement at Venice. The tacit discouragement of so excellent
a judge, and the lukewarm reception of "Gustavo Vasa"
by the people, proved to Goldoni that comedy was the
best field for his genius, for in it he could command
the success which did not always attend his other

dramatic compositions. "Il Prodigo" was another *commedia di carattere* of the same kind as his first experiment; but the comedians again complained that this cla-s of drama took the bread out of their mouths, and gave them nothing to do. To pacify them, he wrote "Le Trentadue Disgrazie di Arlecchino," to be played by their best actor, Sacchi. It was very well received, and the comedians were for the time satisfied. It was followed by another of the same kind. But in the succeeding one, "Il Fallimento," intended to expose the swindling speculations at that time prevalent in Venice, a much larger proportion of the drama was written than in either of the preceding *commedie di carattere*. Thus little by little, now yielding, and now taking advantage of his concession, Goldoni advanced steadily on his way to the reform he contemplated. He devotes a chapter of his Memoirs to the account of the origin of what he calls the "four masks of Italy," deriving his information from a manuscript containing a hundred and twenty *commedie d' arte*. Four personages were indispensable to the plot of each of these comedies — Pantaleone, a Venetian merchant; Il Dottore, a jurist, or Doctor of Law of Bologna; Brighella and Arlecchino, Bergamese servants, one a knave and the other a fool. Il Pantaleone and Il Dottore represent the parts of the old men, or fathers in the comedy; the other two are subordinate. Pantaleone, the merchant, has always worn the Venetian costume, Venice being the most ancient mercantile city of Italy. Il Dottore, the lawyer, from the famous University of Bologna, is meant to draw the contrast between the man of learning and the man of commerce. He was always disfigured by a most hideous mask. The servants are Bergamese, because in Bergamo the two extremes of knavery and stupidity are most conspicuous. Brighella wears a kind of livery, and a brown mask, as a caricature of the sunburnt skin of the inhabitants of those high mountains. Arlecchino, as has been already said, wears a coat of many pieces, to represent a beggar who patches his torn coat with rags and tatters of all colours and kinds. Goldoni then laments over the necessity of the masks, as concealing all the play of feature and change of countenance, which often convey better than words the desired impression to the audience. For this reason Goldoni determined sooner or later to extirpate the masks from Italian comedy. Meanwhile he continued indefatigable in providing for the public amusement, and in return he was a general favourite. His popularity stood him in good stead when, on his appointment to the consulship of Genoa, he left Venice (1741) to take possession of his new office. Italy was involved in the war of the succession of Austria, and the country was full of hostile troops. Goldoni and his wife fell a prey to the rapacity of the Austrian soldiers, and were robbed of all their goods; but they obtained immediate redress when the Commander-in-Chief discovered that he was the author of the comedies at that time so universally popular, and moreover presented him to Lobkowitz, the Commander-in-Chief of the Imperial Army, who placed in his hands the direction of the theatrical entertainments provided for the troops. At Pisa the comedians asked his leave to perform the "Trentadue Disgrazie d' Arlecchino," but this being a comedy *a soggetto*, and depending in great measure upon the talent of Sacchi, who had played harlequin before, now fell completely flat. Goldoni, in a moment of disgust, resolved to abandon as a hopeless task the reform of the *comici*, who would always insist upon representing *commedie a soggetto*, regardless whether their actors were good or bad. There was at that time a branch of the Accademia degli Arcadi resident at Pisa; the Arcadians received Goldoni with open arms, and invited him to join their society, assuring him that his talents might be far more worthily employed than in writing comedies. By their advice, he resumed the forsaken practice of the law; his clients steadily increased, he was making himself a name as an advocate, when, fortunately for the Italian drama, his scheme of life was again changed by tidings from Sacchi that he had returned to Venice. This letter from his favourite actor had the effect of a trumpet upon a war-horse. Sacchi begged Goldoni to write a comedy for him to act; moreover, he proposed the subject, "Il Servitore di Due Padroni," but Goldoni should treat it exactly as he pleased, even to the writing of the whole play, so as to leave nothing to be marred by the comedians. The temptation was not to be resisted. For a little while Goldoni still clung to the law, pleading by day and writing by night; but the arrival of a fresh troop of comedians at Leghorn settled the question for ever in favour of comedy. If Goldoni would only write for them, Médébac, their director, would engage the theatre of San' Angelo at Venice purely for the representation of his plays. Thus the moment had at last arrived for the reform which Goldoni had long desired to effect. The theatre was opened in 1747, with three *commedie di caraltere*— "Tonin della Grazia," "L' Uomo Prudente," "I Due Gemelli Veneziani." The brilliant success of these three comedies aroused the jealousy of the other comedians in Venice, which vented itself in spiteful criticisms and parodies. Goldoni was equal to the occasion, and wrote a parody of their parody of "La Vedova Scaltra," and thus effectually silenced his enemies. But for a time their ill-natured criticisms had emptied the theatre of San' Angelo. Goldoni, to restore its popularity, bound himself by a promise to write sixteen new comedies for the year 1750, which promise he fulfilled. The first of these, "Il Teatro Comico," successfully exposed the defects of the *commedie dell' arte*, and the only one of all this number which met with a bad reception was "Il Giuocatore," because it reproved the gambling at that time common in Venice. Space will not admit of a review of each one separately, so we will content ourselves with saying that " Il Vero Amico " was esteemed by Goldoni as the best of the number. His unceasing labours brought on a severe illness, aggravated by the ingratitude of Médébac, who refused to allow him the copyright of his works. This piece of tyranny decided Goldini upon breaking with the manager as soon as his engagement expired. Among the last plays that he wrote for the Teatro San' Angelo we must notice " La Locandiera," one of his cleverest compositions. Médébac used every effort to retain Goldoni in the service of his theatre, but the author of " La Locandiera " was already employed by a Venetian nobleman to write for the theatre of San' Lucca, at that time in private hands. This was the period of Goldoni's greatest fame. Among many excellent comedies, we select as the best the inimitable " Smanie della Villegiatura," well known to all. It was invaluable at the time in exposing the extravagances of these *villegiatura*, which seem to have been carried to a height of folly scarcely credible. But with his increasing fame his enemies increased also. There were many who still upheld the old masks, and said that Goldoni had done his best to extinguish an entertainment which had been the boast of Italy from time immemorial. At Rome, where he was summoned to write for another private theatre, the masks still reigned supreme. Goldoni saw them in their glory during Carnival, and then had the mortification to witness the ruin of one of his best comedies, " La Vedova Scaltra," in their unpractised hands, His enemies attacked him also for his Venetian dialect. This he endeavoured to correct by a four years' residence in Florence, submitting the new edition of his works to the corrections of those most learned in the pure Tuscan dialect. He tried to console himself by comparing his fate with that of Tasso, whose works were so mercilessly analyzed by the Cruscan Academicians ; but we can hardly forgive him for making the misfortunes of that unhappy poet the subject of a comedy. The fame of his plays having reached Paris, he received an offer (1761) from the superintendent of the Royal Theatre of a two years' engagement, remunerated with a much larger salary than any which he had received in his own country. He could not afford to throw away so good a prospect, and in a short time his preparations were made for leaving Venice. The comedy which was acted the night before his departure was called " Una delle ultime sere del Carnevale," and had reference to the author's farewell to his country. Goldoni was moved to tears when the theatre rang with applause, mingled with shouts of " Buon viaggio : ricordatevi di ritornare, non mancate ! " But he never did return. At the close of his first engagement he received a royal pension, and for the remainder of his life—thirty years—he resided at Paris.

He saw the last days of the *ancien régime* in all its splendour under Louis XV., following the Court from palace to palace. Versailles, Fontainebleau, Compiègne, Marly, he visited in turn; the favourite for whom the rigid rules of etiquette were always relaxed, taking affectionate interest in the failing health of the Dauphin, father of Louis XVI.; deeply attached to Madame la Dauphine, who treated him with never-failing kindness; teaching Italian to the king's daughters, Madame Adelaide and Madame Sophia, who in return obtained for him from the Government an annual salary of four thousand francs. He refused the invitation of a London manager that he might not miss the marriage festivities of the Dauphin and Marie Antoinette, Archduchess of Austria. Like Burke, Goldoni saw the Dauphiness "just above the horizon," and unconsciously he employs nearly the same language to describe her—"decorating and cheering the elevated sphere she just began to move in,—glittering like the morning star, full of life and splendour and joy." But we must refrain from dwelling on his narrative of that interesting time, described with all the truth and liveliness of an eye-witness of the events he recounts. Goldoni continued to write comedies for the Italian theatre at Paris; but there, as in Italy, the comedians insisted upon *commedie a soggetto*, and Goldoni's old difficulties were renewed. He allowed them their way, but sadly avows that he never went to see their maimed representations of his comedies. He frequented instead the French theatre, where he beheld with a sigh the carefully-learnt parts and finished acting which did full justice to Molière's admirable plays. "One or two things," he exclaimed on leaving the theatre; "either my countrymen must imitate their method of representing comedy, or I will write plays in French for the French comedians to act." The continued obstinacy of the Italian comedians drove him to the latter course, and, in spite of his foreign origin, his recently-acquired French, the sharp contrast with Molière, in whose theatre his plays came to be represented, his "Bourru Bienfaisant" won for him a shower of applause and the high commendation of Jean-Jacques Rousseau and Vol-

taire. Goldoni calls it the lucky comedy which sealed
his reputation. It was his tribute to the wedding festivities already alluded to, and was represented in Paris,
November 4, 1771, and the following day at Fontainebleau,
where the royal approbation made itself manifest in a
present of one hundred and fifty louis-d'or. For the
first time Goldoni had the satisfaction of seeing full
justice done by the actors to his talents. He was called
before the curtain, and, in spite of the compliment, he
found it a painful and novel situation, for the custom was
not known in Italy. It was difficult to make the Parisian
world believe that the "Bourru Bienfaisant" was not
translated from the Italian, but written ; indeed, as the
author expresses it, "thought out" in French. Thus
encouraged, he wrote another French drama, "L'Avare
Fastueux," which, although well received, had not the
same brilliant success as the "Bourru Bienfaisant." He
also despatched from time to time comedies and operettas
to Italy. His dramatic labours were varied by his duties
at Court ; for the instructions in Italian which had once
been given to the king's aunts, were now renewed to his
sisters, Madame Clothilde, before she became Princess of
Piedmont, and Madame Elisabeth, whose docility seems
to have won Goldoni's heart. On his retiring from Court
in 1787 he received a renewal of the pension granted to
him by Louis XV., and with this year his Memoirs close.
It would seem as if his life of ceaseless activity had well
earned the peace and comparative affluence secured by the
royal bounty to his old age. But he had scarcely begun to
enjoy it when the Revolution broke out. It is needless to
say that his pension was rudely withdrawn from Goldoni
by the party which came into power, and in his extreme old
age he suffered severe privations. He died in his eighty-
third year, January 8, 1793, a fortnight previous to the
murder of his sovereign and benefactor. Too late—the
day of his death—the Convention Nationale restored the
pension which they had wrested from him ; but they
settled on his widow an annual stipend of 1200 francs.
Goldoni has enriched the dramatic literature of his
country with one hundred and fifty comedies in prose and
verse, all eminently true pictures of domestic life. Like

the good old fashioned novel, he is careful to make
unhappiness the inseparable companion of vice, and to
crown virtue, after the proper amount of vicissitude, with
its due reward. The rigid critics of his country pronounce
that, had Goldoni had knowledge equal to his great
natural gifts, had he written with more care, had his satire
been finer and more delicate, he might very well have stood
a comparison with Molière. As it is, only five or six of
his comedies, "Il Vero Amico," "Il Padre di Famiglia,"
"Pamela Maritata," "La Famiglia dell' Antiquario,"
"Le Smanie della Villegiatura," "La Locandiera," "Il
Bugiardo," are calculated to amuse a cultivated audience ;
the others are farces, more adapted for the entertainment
of the people.[7] If, on the one hand, this want of knowledge mars the effect of Goldoni's work, it proves, on the
other hand, how great must have been his natural gifts to
accomplish what he did in the reform of the drama !
These gifts are indisputable, and were never at fault. He
possessed the keen eye of a critic in discerning the social
defects which demanded reform, an inexhaustible genius
in finding varieties of character, a lively imagination to
paint them in the brightest colours, consummate ingenuity
in disentangling difficult situations, and, in addition to all
these, a keen sense of humour, manifesting itself in a
lively wit. which provokes the merriment of educated and
uneducated alike. A born comedian, his life was full of
comical adventures, or he made them appear so by his
whimsical manner of relating them. If any extraordinary
bit of good fortune fell to his lot, it was immediately
succeeded by some half-ludicrous, half-serious calamity.
He is made Consul of Genoa, to his immense satisfaction,
with all the emoluments of the office ; he sets off to take
possession of his consulship, and on reaching it after many
perils and disasters, discovers that these emoluments are
purely nominal. This he relates as an excellent jest. He
is cheated out of a large sum of money, and he writes a
play called " L' Impostore," which brings him in twice as
much as he had lost. One of his comedies is rudely
criticized ; in fourteen days he writes another, which

7 Maffei, " Storia della Lett. Ital.," pp. 649, 650.

turns these criticisms into a subject for a comedy. And so on through his life ; only his end, over which we would wish to draw a veil, was tragical, in keeping with the fearful times in which he died, but not in keeping with the forgiving spirit which never recorded an injury, or the gentle kindliness of disposition which in any other circumstances, at any other time, must have been a sure passport to a corresponding benevolence. As far as his own country is concerned, he filled up the one thing that was lacking to her dramatic literature. Metastasio had shown the grace and delicacy of the Italian language in melodrama. Alfieri and Monti had proved that the same language was capable of all the eloquence and power which are the elements of tragedy, and Goldoni has endowed it with some unrivalled specimens of the true wit and masterly delineations of character which are the life and soul of good comedy.

PART VI.

IL TEATRO ITALIANO CONTEMPORANEO.

" For ill can Poetry express
Full many a tone of thought sublime,
And Painting, mute and motionless,
Steals but a glance of time;
But, by the mighty actor brought,
Illusion's perfect triumphs come,
Verse ceases to be airy thought,
And sculpture to be dumb."
CAMPBELL, *Valedictory Stanzas to J. P. Kemble.*

IT is a self-evident fact that the drama, while it exercises an important influence over the national character, will take its colouring from the surrounding circumstances, either political or social ; and it is therefore only natural that the contrast between the " Teatro Italiano Contemporaneo " and the " Teatro Italiano Antico " should be as striking as that offered by the present political condition of Italy when we compare it with that of former times. The " Teatro Italiano Antico " originating in the Court,

P 2

remained exclusively in the hands of those princely patrons by whom it was fostered and encouraged. It was a brilliant spectacle reserved to inaugurate their solemn progresses or their royal alliances, to be represented either in their private palaces or in some gorgeous theatre erected according to royal command by Bramante or Palladio, and decorated by Vasari or Titian. In accordance with the same principle the dramatic literature was framed on the ancient classical models, so as to suit the fastidious taste of the highly-cultivated audience. But with an existence so highly artificial the drama could take no permanent root in Italy, and restricted within the narrow limits of a Court circle it could have no general influence upon the country. Thus when the " Teatro Antico " was supplanted by the melodrama on the princely stage and sought refuge among the people, it was long before they learned to appreciate the stately tragedies and finished comedies which sought to claim their attention instead of the ancient buffoonery of the masks hitherto, from time immemorial, their chief if not their sole diversion. In these adverse circumstances of the seventeenth century we have seen how struggling and uncertain was the existence of tragedy, while comedy there was none. Nor did it revive till Goldoni adopted the expedient, not always successful, of enlisting the sympathies of the people by incorporating their ancient entertainment into his dramas. Alfieri found it an easier task to invoke the spirit of liberty in tragedies of fierce patriotism, one of which he dedicates, in a prophetic spirit, to " Il Libero Popolo Italiano." Thus a new and vast field was opened for dramatic literature, and it became apparent that in powerful hands the thrilling scenes of tragedy might serve to stimulate the passions of the people and to encourage them in that great struggle in which the heart of the country was engaged. Ugo Foscolo (b. 1778, d. 1827) and Giambattista Niccolini succeeded Alfieri and Monti. The former echoed the cry of liberty with passionate enthusiasm, but his fame rests more securely on his lyric poetry, chiefly the well-known " Carmine de' Sepolcri," than on his dramas. The best of these, " Tieste," was represented in Venice January 4, 1797, the year before

" Il Leon Veneto fosse spento," one Italian biographer tells·
us. A contemporary review [8] records the rush of spectators of all kinds and classes to the theatre for ten
consecutive nights, more out of curiosity to see the work
of so young an author (he was only nineteen) than because
of its individual merits. But none can dispute the claim
of Niccolini to a high place among the tragedians of this
period. Born at Florence in 1809, he beheld all the con-
vulsions by which Europe was agitated during the next
quarter of a century, and the Italians consider that they
owe him a deep debt of gratitude for asserting the independence of their country in his beautiful classical dramas.
The countryman of Dante, he models his style upon ·that
of the father of the Italian language, and once again gives
utterance to the passionate desire of the great Ghibelline.
His drama " Giovanni da Procida," amplifies in forcible
and beautiful language the lament of Dante over the

> " Mala signoria che sempre accuora,
> Li popoli soggetti," [9]

which caused the desperate cry of " Mora, mora !" to arise
from Palermo the night of the Sicilian Vespers. Again we
recognize an imitation of the well-known " Era gia l' ora
che volge 'l disio " [1] in the pathetic lines—

> " . . . . . . It was the hour
> When the solemn chime brings fond remembrance
> Of the beloved dead at rest in peace,
> And straight there rises to the trembling lip
> The pious prayer of faith, the tender sigh
> Of love more strong than death " [2]

The scene is chiefly laid in the churchyard at Palermo,
and the account of Giovanni da Procida taking the sword
from his dead son's hand as he lies in his tomb is very
striking. The author's deep love for his country is repeatedly expressed,[3] and her well-known historical scenes
gain fresh life and colour when treated by his bold and
vigorous hand. The misfortunes of the unhappy Galeazzo
Sforza seem to have a new claim upon our sympathy

[8] " L' Anno Teatrale, 1797."
[9] Par. vii. 71.   [1] Purg. viii.
[2] "Giovanni da Procida," act. i. sc. 1.
[3] Ibid, act iii. sc. 2 ; act iii. sc. 2.

when his wife, who watches the ebbing away of his poisoned life, describes the sad presage which to her grief-stricken mind foretells his death:—

> " Vain is the feast of beauty nature spreads
> Before a captive's gaze, and dark the sun
> Seen through the mist of grief—Now from each plant
> The dry dead leaves fall scattered on the ground,
> Leaving the parent bough ; one sere and stray
> Lay at my feet, and to my heart it spake,
> Thus will thy suffering husband fade and die." [4]

In "Antonio Foscarini" those who are acquainted with the history of Venice, and have shuddered with horror over the dark mysterious tyranny of the "Consiglio dei Tre," will recognize the justice of the prophecy, the fulfil-ment of which Niccolini must himself have witnessed :—

> " Oh haughty city ! now in savage pride
> Erect thy lion stands. A day shall dawn
> When he shall crouch and fall, disarmed by years.
> No flash of wrath shall show his dying fire,
> No mighty roar proclaim a glorious end." [5]

And those who have once seen the marvellous city will recognize the place

> ' " Where sit in state the marble palaces
> Before the mirror of the clear lagoon
> Whose limpid depths give back each glorious pile." [6]

While they listen again to the ceaseless waves—

> " Rotte dal vento nell' Adriatico lido."

"Arnaldo da Brescia" unites in one dramatic action, and places upon the scene the fiercely-contending religious and political opinions of the age in which the martyr lived, for the purpose of forcibly illustrating the great struggle for liberty which was still at its height when this tragedy appeared (1843). Such were some of the best of Niccolini's tragedies ; but no one was better aware than their author of the great difficulties which beset the path of the tragedian during the early part of this century. The influence of foreign literature was gradually making itself felt in Italy, and the reaction from the violent hatred of the French schools, which Alfieri had so keenly

[4] Act i. sc. 2.   [5] Act v. sc. 4.   [6] Act ii. sc. 5.

felt and so vigorously expressed in his works, had already set in. "I know," says Niccolini, writing to a friend, "what a difficult task it is to write tragedies for Italy; if you depart from the conventional rules, the lovers of the classics at once open their fire of criticism; if you follow these rules, the romantic school attack you for a servile imitator of Alfieri. To my mind the age demands a class of tragedy which will combine the two; but who will be so fortunate as to find it, and to overcome the popular prejudice which will not believe in any but Alfieri's tragedies? As to the versification, I do not see why harmony should not go hand-in-hand with force and vigour, as we are taught by the immortal example of Dante." But although some of the passages already quoted may serve as illustrations of this successful combination, on other occasions, by his studious avoidance of the severity of Alfieri's style, he falls into the opposite extreme, employing a stately pomp of versification too monotonous to give sufficient play to the action and passion of the drama.

Another great name, that of Alessandro Manzoni (died May, 1872), which has more than one claim to honour in the roll of Italian literature, demands a place in this essay, as an eminent tragedian, the worthy successor of Alfieri, Monti, and Niccolini. His two beautiful tragedies, the "Adelchi," and the "Conte di Carmagnola," with their inimitable *Cori*, will be subsequently discussed in the short tribute to his memory, which occupies a few pages of this Collection of Essays. It would be trespassing on the indulgence of our readers to anticipate this, except to remark that these tragedies are living pictures of the times they represent in a style of unrivalled vigour and language of the richest metaphorical colouring. Besides these intrinsic merits, they were the means of a reform in dramatic literature, for which "Il Teatro Contemporaneo" owes Manzoni an everlasting debt of gratitude. In their composition he deliberately sets at defiance the hampering laws of time and place so pertinaciously insisted upon by the French dramatists:—

> "Qu'en *un lieu*, qu'en *un jour* un *seul fait* accompli
> Tienne jusqu'à la fin le Théâtre rempli." [7]

---

[7] Boileau, "Art Poétique."

When assailed by the criticisms of the indignant *savants*, he proves in an eloquent letter written in their own language, "qu'il n'existe, ni dans la nature de l'esprit humain, ni dans celle de art dramatique, de principe en vertu duquel on doive considérer l'unité de temps et de lieu comme une règle absolue et fondamentale de la tragédie."[8] Having disposed of "l'unité de temps et de lieu," he proceeds to call in question the third unity, "l'unité d'action," and to prove that it is not, as the French dramatists maintain, to be taken in its literal acceptation of a single action, but in its wider sense of a principal action resulting from the chain of events as they naturally unfold themselves in the drama. The reasoning of an "opuscule qui n'a pas seulement été composé en France . . . mais en quelque sorte pour les Français"[9] is so conclusive as to shake even the confidence of the French dramatists in their theory, while it emancipates, completely and for ever, the Italian drama from such tedious and useless formalities. Niccolini and Manzoni are the great masters of Italian tragedy during this century, and it is to be feared that the age will scarcely produce any works equal to theirs, even though their scholars and imitators have the double advantage of example as well as precept to guide them. The new era of dramatic literature had been inaugurated by Manzoni in the north of Italy, and the first tragic writer of any distinction who profited by his reform was the Piedmontese, Carlo Marenco. He tries to combine the vigour of Alfieri's style with the richness of Niccolini's versification, and the result is somewhat stilted and unnatural; but he renders his country service by placing upon the stage some of the most significant facts of her history, and succeeds in making them point a moral for the use of modern times. Some of his dramas are taken from the "Divina Commedia;" the hapless Ugolino, the murdered Buondelmonte, the tyrant Ezzelino, the turbulent Corso de' Donati, and the gentle Pia de' Tolomei are all brought upon the scene.

[8] Manzoni, "Opere," Lettre à M. Chauvet sur "L'Unité de Temps et de Lieu," p. 151.
[9] Ibid.

Many of the modern dramatists borrowed the subjects of their dramas from the same rich and inexhaustible mine. Leopoldo, son of Carlo Marenco, drew from thence "Piccarda dei Donati;"[1] Pietro Corelli, "Farinata degli Uberti;"[2] Luigi L'Indelli, "Pier delle Vigne," the Chancellor of Frederick II.,

> "Who held
> Both keys to Frederick's heart, and turned the wards,
> Opening and shutting with a skill so sweet,
> That besides me into his inmost heart
> Scarce any other could admittance find."[3]

But while rendering justice to many fine passages, it must be urged that none of these familiar and beautiful episodes, nor can any exception be made in favour of Silvio Pellico's "Francesca da Rimini," are adapted for dramatic representation. There are few, if any, of the great subjects of epic poetry which would not lose much of their distinctive character by being transported from thence into the drama, but in the particular instance of the "Divina Commedia," in which the characters as represented by Dante have remained for centuries the objects of universal admiration, such a transposition could not fail to have a most injurious effect. The great original conceptions of the poet's fancy stand out before our minds as he would wish us to imagine them, bearing the peculiar stamp of the genius which created them. Add one more touch, they lose their individuality, more especially when, as with Dante, their poetic grandeur does not lie in themselves, but in the manner in which he places them before us. His fine strokes of narrative and description cause the few verses to present us with a more complete picture than any the drama could offer us even when accompanied with all the accessories of scenic effect. Descending from the northern provinces of Italy we come to Rome, where the drama, until a very recent date, exposed to the strictest censorship, made little if any progress. The argument, the language, the allegorical meaning of the composition were narrowly scanned, lest any deduction should be drawn from them at variance with the policy of the Papal Government. Tragedy, in

[1] Purg. xxiv. 11.   [2] Inf. vi. 79.
[3] Inf. xiii. 55 et seq. Cary's Translation.

its conventional classical form, offered the most convenient disguise for political sentiments from such close and suspicious scrutiny. By his drama of " Caracalla," Gianbattista Marsuzi, following close upon the track of Alfieri, first instilled a hatred of tyranny into the Roman mind, and Giuseppe Cherchetelli endeavoured to teach the same lesson in several tragedies which are however more calculated to win him fame as a patriot than as a tragedian. The same remark is applicable to the few other writers who can scarcely be said to have flourished in this close and stifling atmosphere. It is a singular fact that in Rome, for eighteen centuries the centre of Christianity, the idea of religion is conspicuous by its absence from the scenes of her drama. The old pagan arguments are again and again produced upon the scene, and no spark of the Christian enthusiasm which inspired the pen of the noble-minded Manzoni, kindles into life the cold, dead scenes of Roman tragedy. Naples, in spite of the tyranny under which it groaned during the first half of this century, is far richer in dramatic genius. The " Medea," of Cesare della Valle, Duca di Ventigrano, is a tragedy almost worthy to be compared with those of Alfieri, upon whose style and plan it was carefully formed. Another classical subject, " Il Sophocle," was revived with success by Paolo Giacometti, and magnificently rendered by the famous Salvini, in the Teatro Niccolini, May 5, 1867. Those who have had the good fortune to see this wonderful actor, will not think the enthusiastic praise bestowed upon him by the writer of " Il Teatro Contemporaneo," overstrained. " Tommaso Salvini has surpassed himself in his conception of the character of Sophocles. Imagine that you see upon the scene some Grecian statue of one of her venerable sages endowed with life by a new Pygmalion, pacing the stage with majestic steps, declaiming the rounded periods of his splendid oration, and you will have some idea of the ' Sofocle Salviniano.' " [4] Passing by several other tragedies of no inconsiderable merit we must notice for especial approbation the " Girolamo Savonarola" of

---

[4] " Teatro Italiano Contemporaneo," p. 170. " Capuana."

Salvadore Mormone, which, like the tragedy of "Arnaldo da Brescia," powerfully illustrates the evils resulting from the temporal power. Mormone, however, approaches the subject with more calmness than Niccolini, and treats it with grave dignity, as if the author wished to convince the reason rather than appeal to the passions of his audience. Macchiavelli is among the *dramatis personæ.* and the scene between him and Savonarola is considered one of the best in the tragedy. This drama, entitled a tragedy, belongs more properly to that class of "Drammi Storici," which form so important a feature in the modern Italian drama, that they deserve a separate consideration. Framed on a slightly different plan from tragedy in the strictest acceptation of the word, they are not subject to the same stringent laws, and have therefore more scope to develop the political sentiments of the times. It seems probable that they will gradually take the place of tragedy in an age more easily impressed by the real examples of courageous virtue taken from history than by the ideal heroism of the ancient tragic stage, according to the philosopher's remark, that a good citizen may always serve and love his country, but he will not find it necessary to *save* her every day. "La Lega Lombarda," by Napoleone Giotti. one of . the best of the followers of Niccolini, is a striking example of this peculiar species of drama. The central figure of the drama, Federigo Barbarossa, with his indomitable will and giant strength, a very Cæsar in deed as well as name, forms a splendid type of a mediæval hero, while the triumph of the league is enhanced by their successful resistance to so formidable an enemy. The same subject is treated with less success by Giuseppe Ricciardi, who also wrote "Il Vespro," "La Cacciata degli Austriaci di Genova," and "Masaniello," whose character, notwithstanding the diligent efforts of the author, refuses to be endowed with any of the qualities indispensable to a hero, dramatic or otherwise. "Torquato Tasso," by Paolo Giacometti, finds a better position in this order of drama than in the comedy of Goldoni, more especially as the subject is treated with skill and care, showing a due appreciation of the character of the unfortunate poet. Music and painting are also placed upon the stage in the form of Michel Angelo and Gianbattista Pergolesi, by Domenico and Gennaro Bolognese; and approaching nearer to modern times we find "Silvio Pellico" and "Daniel Manin," resuscitated by the Bolognese Luigi Gualtieri. Before quitting the subject of the "Drammi Storici," we must not omit to notice the "Anna Maria Orsini" of Ludovico Muratori, not on account of any remarkable merit, but because it was written on purpose for the famous actress, Adelaide Ristori, to whose marvellous acting, like that of Salvini, the modern Italian drama owes so much of its fame.

The modern "Drammi per Musica," or as we should now call them, the operas, next claim our attention. In the last century we saw the melodrama at the height of its fame in the skilful hands of Metastasio. His operas formed on the principle which guided the first inventors of the art, fulfil as nearly as possible that ideal dramatic perfection which some philosophical writers have considered to lie beyond the reach of tragedy or comedy, and to be alone attainable by a judicious combination of music and poetry, with a due regard to the laws of dramatic art. Unhappily no one succeeded Metastasio of sufficient genius to maintain the melodrama in so eminent a position, and as the poets became more and more indifferent, the musical composers gained rapid ground, till the melodrama, wholly absorbed in music, lost its double character, and the *libretto*, in theory, the most arduous composition that can be imagined, became in practice the most trivial of all literary occupations. It is for other and more competent judges to decide whether music itself does not suffer in the end by this entire subservience of poetry in the loss of the beauty of poetical expression, especially in a language which offers, as we have already seen, such especial facilities for the combination of the two arts. Meanwhile it is impossible not to share the regrets with which the Italians view the diminished charms of their originally beautiful invention, as we trace the principal causes to which they attribute this unhappy result. They appear to be twofold. (1) The neglect of the careful study of the component parts of the opera in their due

relation to each other. (2) The nature of the audience.
Among the former, the disregard of the *recitative* or
declamation for which Italy was at one time so famous,
was the first indication of the decay of melodramatic poetry,
because in it the imitation, which is the end of dramatic
art, depends more upon the poetry than the music. In
order to give weight and effect to the language, the actor
should carefully observe all the rules prescribed by declamation as to noting the sense of the words, dwelling on
the poetical rhythm, giving all the inflections and changes
of voice which the music is only intended to sustain, that
the action may be in keeping with the rest of the drama.
Formerly, *recitative* was looked upon as the basis of
the opera, and it was the custom of many of the melodramatic writers, who succeeded Metastasio, to have their
operas declaimed before sending them to the musical
composer, that they might mark in the manuscript the
various impressions which the poetry was intended to
convey. Gluck,[5] who exercised for a short time an
important influence over the Italian opera, thought the
recitative so important that lest it should be marred
by a careless, hurried rendering, he would often sustain it
with a subdued violin accompaniment. But towards the
middle of the eighteenth century, the poets, neglecting
the *recitative*, turned their attention exclusively to the
lyrical strophes which were the motives for the airs in
their dramas. In this they were eagerly seconded by the
musical composers as likely to afford a wider scope for
the refinements of their art. Absorbed in these intricacies,
they soon lost sight of the necessity of making the music
express the meaning of the words.

"Parto," "Parto," repeats some beautiful voice over
and over again till nearly half an hour has elapsed, while
the sense of the dramatic action summons the actor
immediately elsewhere. Another performer will declare,
with interminable musical loquacity, while she runs up
and down the compass of her voice—

"Non ho più voce
Non so parlar."

---

[5] See "The Dictionary of Music and Musicians," p. 51.

This kind of solecism, far from being an unavoidable necessity, is entirely at variance with the original idea of the melodrama, which has been unjustly accused of inconsistencies and want of *vraisemblance*. These faults ought really to be ascribed to the incapacity of authors unable to surmount the difficulties of successfully combining the two arts.

Two schools of melodramatic writers succeeded Metastasio, those who were guided by the French taste in the melodrama, to which may be attributed much of its deterioration, and the followers, at a humble distance, of the "Poeta Cesareo." Among the last the most worthy of notice are Coltellini, Mattei, the celebrated Neapolitan musician, and Il Conte Gastone, who wrote a drama "Alessandro e Timoteo," a translation, or rather adaptation, of Dryden's "Ode to Music," with the view of proving—and a better illustration could scarcely be found —the increased grandeur of effect gained by the strict accordance of the poetry with the music. The best writers of the actual modern melodrama are Salvadore Camera and Felice Romani, some of whose couplets are considered by the Italians worthy of Metastasio. We select one from the well-known "Sonnambula" of Felice Romani, which will be remembered as specially graceful:—

> "Son geloso del zeffiro amante
> Che ti scherza col crine, col velo;
> Fin del Sole che ti mira dal cielo
> Fin del rivo che speechio ti fa."

> "Son, mio bene, del zeffiro amante
> Perchè ad esso il tuo nome confido
> Amo il Sole perchè teco il divido
> Amo il rio, perchè l' onda ti da."

But with these few exceptions, the *libretti* of the present time are scarcely subjects for literary criticism. Still less may be said in favour of the *opera buffe*, or comic operas. Those of Goldoni and Gigli and a few others are the best specimens of the fun and humour of a class of work which in less skilful hands must degenerate into buffoonery and bad taste.[6]

The comedies of the nineteenth century, and especially

[6] Goldoni, "Opere," vol. xii.

those which usher in its dawn, are more deserving of our attention than the melodrama in this debased form. There seemed at that time a fair promise that the school founded by Goldoni would not lack scholars of sufficient ability to carry on the reform which he had initiated. Among his immediate successors we may notice Alber-gatelli, Federici, Vêlli, Chiari, and Giraud, and a few other writers of more or less distinction. But the comic drama of Italy was still more permanently enriched by the contributions of Gherardo de Rossi and Alberto Nota. We select as the most favourable specimen of the dramas contained in De Rossi's four volumes, "Il Calzolaio Inglese" ("The English Shoemaker"). It is written in the purest Italian idiom, and the plot, intended to ridicule the follies committed by the rich English *parvenu* in Rome, is highly entertaining. Following the advice of a feigned antiquario, who is determined to cheat him out of his money, the Englishman is careful to admire always the most sombre-looking pictures, the statues most covered with dust, because that would be an infallible sign of age, and the buildings most in ruins, till one day the original fatal remark escapes him as to the Coliseum : " Quando quella fabrica sarà *terminata*, sarà un stupore. Turati quei buchi e imbiancata dev' essere un portento ! " [7]

Alberta Nota (born in Turin, 1775) manifested an early unmistakable taste for comedy in the constant recital of Goldoni's plays, but, unlike Goldoni, he did not suffer the comic drama to become his only profession in after life, al-though he found in it the best relaxation from the labours of the official appointments which he held under the Imperial Government at Turin in 1803, and at Vercilli in 1811. Thus in spite of the tragical events by which Europe was at that time agitated, his natural disposition to look always at the comical side of matters disposed him to dwell more upon the follies and absurdities than the crimes of the French Revolution, and to hold them up to ridicule in his clever and amusing comedies.

The best of these are contained in a volume of " Com-

---

[7] " It will be a wonderful building when it is finished, with the holes filled up, and whitewashed all over. " Il Calzolaio Inglese," act ii. sc. 4, vol. i. p. 192.

medie Scelte," in which the Parvenu, the Bibliomaniac, the Hypochondriac, the Coquette, are represented in their most ludicrous aspect.

The plot of each of these plays develops itself with a happy choice of circumstances, which succeed each other with natural ease, and lead up to the catastrophe without apparent effort, and unassisted by any *coup de théâtre.*

In the " Vedova in Solitudine " and " La Lusinghiera," there are scenes which exhibit a keen sense of humour, when he successfully ridicules the opposite schools of Pedantic Purist Italian and the slipshod affected Gallicisme of the other extreme.

His own style is extremely happy, careful without affectation ; he is considered equal to Goldoni in natural simplicity of expression, and superior in his choice of polished and correct idioms.

Nota was the last of Goldoni's immediate followers, who maintained the individual character of the Italian Drama. The French influence which during his life he had successfully combated, after his death made rapid progress, and ended by prevailing, greatly to the detriment of native originality. After the usual custom of imitators, the Italian dramatists copied the defects of the school they put before them for a model, and reproduced with exaggerated caricature on the Italian scene all the faults and follies of the French stage.

Paolo Giacometti, whose works as a tragedian we have already mentioned, found a new task for his flexible genius in the improvement of the degenerate condition of comedy. " Il Poeta e la Ballerina. Siamo tutti Fratelli," directed against the Socialists, " La Donna " and " La Donna in seconde Nozze," in which the simplicity of the Goldonian comedy is successfully reproduced, and adapted to the manners of the present day ; " Le Metamorfosi Politiche," intended to ridicule political *Trimmers*, would give the best idea of his success in this different line of dramatic writing. The author is guided in the choice of his subjects by a careful observance of the times, and no longer restricted by the characteristics of individual cities and provinces, his dramas are adapted for the profitable entertainment of the kingdom at large. The contem-

porary of Giacometti, and a still more popular comedian,
T. Gherardi della Testa, wrote many comedies in the pure
idiom of his native Tuscany, and like Giacometti, he took
Goldoni for his standard of excellence. True to nature,
and with the improvement of the social condition of his
country for his object, his dramas held up to playful
ridicule the follies of his time. A popular favourite ever
since the representation of "Le Scimmie," his first
comedy in 1844, his last, "Il vero Blasone," occupied the
stage for 200 successive nights.

Riccardo Castelvecchio, a dramatic writer of equal if
not superior merit, found it a more difficult task to win
the public favour, but several years of labour and patient
perseverance met at last with a reward in the reception
accorded to one of his best comedies, "La Cameriera
Astuta." We must close this first period of the modern
drama with the mention of three excellent comedies, by
V. Martini (commonly called "l'Anonimo Fiorentino"),
"La Donna di Quarant' Anni," "Il Cavaliere d' Indus-
tria," "Il Misantropo in Società." Born and brought up
in the midst of the cultivated society of Florence, the
"Anonimo Fiorentino" is able to give us such a perfect
picture in his dramas of its refinement of manners and
intellect, as to leave no cause for regret that he should
have restricted the range of his ideas within the circle of
a single city. His dramas illustrate the first period of
the "Teatro Italiano Contemporaneo" and represent the
Italy of the future, in that perfect aspect, political and
social, which was one day to satisfy the longing desires of
so many centuries. The dramatic writers of the second
period, while they still aim at the same end, the improvement of their country, endeavour to reach it by a slightly
different path. They substitute the real for the ideal, and
represent with a faithful hand, Italy as she is at the
present moment, now that no longer the scene of feverish
strife, she is able to enjoy her great position among European States in dignified repose.

Paolo Ferrari, Achille Torelli, Teobaldo Cicconi, Luigi
Gualtieri, Lodovico Muratori, and Giuseppi Costetti, are
the principal writers of this school, and many of their
dramas successfully prove that the best affections of which

Q

human nature is capable, and the most cherished interests of life when faithfully represented on the stage, can vindicate without the assistance of either discussion or argument, their unalterable claim to popular esteem,—a claim which has a double hold upon the sympathy of the audience, when the characters are taught by the genius of a Salvini or Ristori, to breathe, and live, and move. Nor must we allow the names of these unrivalled actors to overshadow those of Ernesto Rossi, Alamanni Morelli, and Luigi Bellotti-Bon, who re-endowed the stage with Goldoni's comedies, animating them with new life. Their author's signal triumph over a foreign language was revived after a lapse of nearly a hundred years by the French actor Sanson, in his excellent representation of "Le Bourru Bienfaisant" in the Teatro Niccolini.[a] It is, however, to be lamented that this happy alliance between the author and the actor should be the exception and not the rule, and that the same struggle which was productive of such vexation to Goldoni should still prevail in Italy. Till quite a recent date, the rights of the author over his own drama were supposed to be sufficiently acknowledged by a trifling honorarium, and the glory of seeing his composition represented on the stage. The " Comici," as in Goldoni's time, asserted that a further recognition of these rights would be the ruin of any theatre, and heartily coincided in the indignant exclamation of a favoured French actress of the seventeenth century, "Eh ! quoi, n'y aurait-il pas moyen de se passer de ces coquins d'auteurs !" · But Corneille, on the other hand, wrote to Voltaire, "Je suis saoul de gloire et affamé d'argent ;" and ever since Goldoni sold his comedies for thirty "zecchini" apiece, the Italian authors have echoed the same complaint. They protest that if an actor can make a livelihood out of the profits of his art, an author ought to have the same power, whereas in the present state of things any second-rate actor can easily earn a thousand francs in the course of the year, while no author can gain anything like those profits from a drama which must cost him on an average

---

[a] April, 1867, "Teatro Italiano Contemporaneo." It will be remembered that " Le Bourru Bienfaisant " was represented for the first time in Paris, November 4, 1771.

six months' labour. At last, however, this long-contested privilege was established by law,[9] and it remains to be seen whether under these favourable auspices a new dramatic era will dawn for Italy, whether some new Alfieri or Goldoni will arise to claim a national reward for their labours.[1]

Meanwhile, it has been the endeavour of the writer, in this slight sketch, the last of a series of papers on the Italian Drama, to render full justice to the merits of the "Teatro Italiano Contemporaneo." Although the modern theatre of Italy cannot claim the admiration excited by the more brilliant periods of her drama, it still deserves to be recognized as playing a prominent part in the political and social improvement of the country. The importance of such a theatre can hardly be too highly estimated, when we consider the extent of its influence over all classes of people. Many will learn from its speaking pictures salutary lessons, from which they would turn aside if presented to them in a less attractive form, and are thus insensibly led to appreciate those refined and better qualities of our nature which, by their ennobling influence may impart a sublime tone of thought and character even to the most trivial concerns of daily life. With such a task always in view, we can only hope that for many a succeeding age the Italian dramatists will still—

> " To sense and nature true,
> Delight the many, nor offend the few ;
> Through varying tastes *their* changeful drama claim,
> Still be its moral tendency the same :
> To win by precept, by example warn ;
> To brand the front of vice with pointed scorn,
> And Virtue's smiling brows with votive wreaths adorn."

---

[9] June, 1872.
[1] " The Italian Government has offered two prizes, one of 2000 and one of 1000 lire, for the best dramatic production of the year." —*Gazetta Uffiziale del Regno d' Italia*, January 20, 1876.

MANZONI.

A SKETCH.

" EI FÙ." Such are the opening words of that great effort of Manzoni's genius, the Ode on the Death of Napoleon, and they are now applicable to the poet himself. He *was*, he no longer *is*, the author of the greatest work of fiction in the Italian language, the poet whose best energies were employed in the praises of religion, the champion of truth and justice, the defender of the Christian faith against the attacks of infidelity; for on Thursday, May 22nd, 1873, at the great age of eighty-nine, Manzoni went to his rest.

" The city wears mourning" ("La città è in lutto"), was proclaimed in word and deed at Milan, and so it should be. Nevertheless the lamentations, which the loss of one at the same time so virtuous and so eminent would naturally occasion, are checked by the consideration that a life of singular honour and distinction, prolonged beyond the usual term of existence, with full possession of all the faculties, has been brought to a peaceful close at his native place, and surrounded, if ever man was, by all "that should accompany old age," "as honour, love, obedience, troops of friends."

The slight sketch which follows is intended to induce the general reader to pursue the study of Manzoni's life and character in his works, and, in however humble a degree, to contribute to their estimation.

Alessandro Manzoni was born at Milan in 1784. His father, whom he had the misfortune to lose in early youth, was Count Manzoni, his mother was the daughter of Beccaria, the author of a treatise on "Crimes and Punishments," once much, and deservedly esteemed. She inherited, and further transmitted to her son, a portion of the sound

wisdom and generous principles which animate that work.
It was not unbecoming the grandson of Beccaria to record,
as it will be seen he did later, his horror of torture, and to
expose the wickedness and uselessness of it as a judicial
mode of discovering the truth. Manzoni's ambition was
early fired by the example of the three great contemporaries who immediately preceded him in the difficult path
of letters—Vittorio Alfieri, Vincenzo Monti, and Ugo
Foscolo. He was barely twenty-one when, by an epistle
in blank verse, he proved himself worthy of being admitted
into that fellowship. In these verses he imagines that
he spirit of his friend appears to him after death, and, in
reply to the question as to whether he was not reluctant
to tear himself from this world, he puts into Imbonati's
mouth a fearless and spirited condemnation of those vices
which had already filled with disgust the youthful mind
of Manzoni. In them we see the first germ of those
feelings by which his life was influenced—the love of
truth and justice, and the abhorrence of oppression and
wrong—which appear in all his works, and which, first
professed at twenty-one, he maintained unchanged through
a life prolonged to its ninetieth year. These verses, while
by no means destitute of individual merit, are so remarkable on this account that a translation of some of them is
here given :—

> " Hadst thou my death
> Foreknown—for that foreknowledge and for thee
> Alone I should have wept—for otherwise,
> Why should I grieve ? Forsooth, for leaving
> This earth of ours, where goodness is a portent,
> And highest praise to have abstained from sin.
> This earth, where word and thought are ever
> At variance, where, aloud by every lip,
> Virtue is lauded and in heart contemned,
> Where shame is not. Where crafty usury
> Is made a merit, and gross luxury
> Worshipped—where he alone is impious
> Whose crime is unsuccessful—where the crime
> Loses all baseness in success : and where
> The sinner is exalted, and the good
> Depressed : and where the conflict is too hard
> Waged by the just and solitary man
> 'Gainst the confederate and corrupted many."

R. P.

In 1805 he accompanied his mother to Paris, where, by
his relationship to Beccaria, whose book had been commented on by Voltaire and Diderot, he attracted the
notice of Volney, Cabanis, De Tracy, and Fauriel. His
intercourse with these men, who represented the Atheist
school of thought of the eighteenth century, was attended
by an exactly opposite result to that which might have
been expected. It produced a strong reaction upon his
generous mind, and first incited him to become the champion of the truths which they attacked. It reflects no
small credit upon the natural rectitude of his principles
that he should have found safety in what might have
proved a dangerous snare. He met with an immediate
reward, for the light of the Christian faith, which he had
been able to descry amid the dark mists spread over it by
her enemies, dawned full upon his mind, revealing to him
the truth of those mysteries which the philosophers, in
their pride of intellect, could not discern, and enabled
him to utter them anew in hymns far superior in originality of thought and beauty of expression to any others
which had hitherto been written. The chief of these are
upon the vital truths of Christianity : The Nativity ("Il
Natale"), the Passion ("La Passione"), the Resurrection
("La Risurrezione") of our Lord, and the Descent of the
Holy Ghost ("La Pentecoste"), which last is considered
by his countrymen to surpass them all. More especially
the invocation of the Holy Spirit in the four concluding
stanzas, the Giver of that Peace "which no terrors can
disturb, no infidelity shake, which the world may deride
but can neither give nor take away,"[1] words almost of inspiration, which drew from Goethe the admission "that an
argument often repeated, and a language almost exhausted
by the use of many centuries, may regain their first youth
and freshness when a young and vigorous mind enters
upon the subject and adopts the worn-out language." In
1809 Manzoni published a poem entitled "Urania;" but
it was not till 1821 that he became a poet of European

[1]   "ai terrori immobile
E alle lusinghe infide,
Pace che il mondo irride
Ma che rapir non può."—*La Pentecoste.*

fame, when he wrote upon a subject of European interest
— the death of Napoleon Buonaparte. The opening words
of the "Cinque Maggio" have already been alluded to, in
which Manzoni announces to the world the death of this
extraordinary man ; and, after dwelling for an instant
upon the appalling effect which such an announcement
must produce, unrolls in the brief space of a few stanzas
the whole panorama of that marvellous life before our
eyes ; the passage of the Alps, the Pyramids of Egypt,
the plains of Madrid, the rushing Rhine, the snowy steppes
of Moscow, the Empire which stretched from the one to
the other sea ("dall uno all altro mar"); the alternations
of success and failure which attended his career, the glory
the greater because dearly bought, the laurel of the victor,
the flight of the vanquished, an Emperor's throne, or an
exile's banishment, twice at the summit of all human
greatness, twice levelled with the dust ("Due volte nella
polvere," "due volte sugli altar"). Nor are the feelings
of his own breast, as varied, as agitated as the actions of
his life, less eloquently described—the fluttering hopes
and fears which wait on a great enterprise ; the burnings
of his ambitious heart lest he should fail to grasp the prize
which it was madness to hope for ; the blank despair
when, in lonely exile, the whole flood of memory swept in
upon his soul. Once again he sees the breezy battlefield,
the fluttering canvas of the tents, the lightning-flash of
the infantry, the rapid rush of the cavalry, and above the
distant roar of the cannon the short stern word of command, obeyed as soon as heard. No wonder if the poet
should have thought the religious consolation which he
himself so dearly prized, the only balm for the bitter disappointment attendant on the train of such recollections
as these, and that he should conclude his ode with the
assertion that Napoleon's indomitable will bowed in
submission to the behests of that branch of the Catholic
Church to which nominally at least he belonged. Such
is the imperfect sketch of one of the finest pieces of
Italian lyric poetry, the greatest tribute which could be
paid to a great genius, while it invested him with a halo
of romance so brilliant as to dazzle the eye which would
search for his faults. The fame which this ode acquired

more than justified Manzoni's modest hope that "perhaps his lay would not die." It was translated into German by Goethe, and with care and spirit into English both by the late Lord Derby and Mr. Gladstone.

The fertility of Manzoni's genius was next displayed in two tragedies, "Il Conte di Carmagnola" (the story of the celebrated Venetian "condottiero" of the fourteenth century), and the "Adelchi," the subject being the expedition of Charlemagne against Adelchi, the last of the Longobardian Chiefs (772—774). These tragedies attracted great notice in the literary world. Both were carefully commented upon by Goethe,[2] and received from him the highest praise. The "Conte di Carmagnola" he makes the subject of a careful analysis, and in conclusion he compliments Manzoni upon having shaken off the old trammels and struck out for himself a new path in which he walks so securely as to make it safe for others to follow his footsteps. He praises him for his polished, careful details, the simplicity, the vigour, and the clearness of his style, and adds that, after a most careful examination, he could not wish a word altered. Nor was this all. Goethe wrote again upon the same subject to defend a young author, in whom he felt a deep interest, from the attacks of English critics in the *Quarterly Review*.[3] The "Carmagnola" was also commented on in the *Journal des Savants*, the *Revue Encyclopédique*, and the *Lycée Français*. Manzoni replied to his French critics in an elaborate letter on "l'Unité de Temps et de Lieu," written in French to Monsieur Chauvet, and pronounced by Fauriel himself to be "just, profound, and conclusive." The "Adelchi" shortly followed upon the "Conte di Carmagnola," and justified the expectations which had been raised by his first tragedy. Goethe, whose interest in Manzoni had been further stimulated by a personal acquaintance, and who also commented on the "Adelchi," now pronounced that "Manzoni has won for himself a most honourable

---

[2] Goethe's Werke, vol. xxxviii. pp. 252—305. "Neueste Italienische Literatur." These criticisms were first published in the "Kunst und Alterthum," an Art Journal, edited by Goethe from 1818 to 1828.

[3] No. xlvii., Dec. 1820. P. 86.

place among the modern poets; his beautiful and really
poetical talent is founded upon genuine human sympathy
and feeling."[4] Neither the "Adelchi" nor the "Carmagnola" is adapted for actual representation in the present
time, or in the present theatrical circumstances, but the
cori which they contain, and which, formed on the
model of the Greek tragedies, Manzoni first introduced
into the Italian, drama, are really noble specimens of
lyrical poetry. Speaking of the two in the "Adelchi,"
Goethe observes that they reveal to the mind in one
moment a chain of ideas, which stretches back into the
past, fills the present, and reaches forward into the future.
The first of these relates to the surprise of the Longobardian army by Charlemagne's troops, and concludes with
the author's condemnation of the theory that the deliverance of Italy from bondage would be secured by the intervention of a foreign power. The second, upon the death
of Ermengarda, the wife of Charlemagne, who, when
unjustly repudiated by her husband, took refuge in a
convent, is almost unrivalled in deep and tender pathos.
The following translation will perhaps suggest some of its
beauty to the reader, or at least induce him to consult the
original :—

> " Loose dishevelled tresses thrown
> Wildly o'er her panting breast,
> Drooping hands and marble brow,
> The dews of coming death confessed ;
> Rapt in holy thought, her eye ˙
> Sought, as she lay, with trembling glance, the sky.

> " The wailing ceased ; the solemn prayer
> Rises from the choral band,
> Upon the death-cold countenance
> Descends a gentle hand ;
> And o'er the azure eye-balls' light,
> Spreads the last veil of never-ending night.

> " Lady, from thy troubled mind,
> Chase each earth-born hope and joy ;
> Prayer, the broken-heart's oblation,
> Yield to GOD, and die !
> Far from realms of time and space,
> Is thy long suffering's resting-place.

---

[4] Goethe's Werke, vol. xxxviii. p. 296.

" Ah ! such thy unrelenting fate,
  Sad mourner here below,
Thy prayer for forgetfulness
  Ungranted still to know ;
At length affliction's sacrifice,
Unto the Lord of Saints, in sainted grief, to rise.

" When those sleepless shades among,
  That cloister's holy aisle,
Those altars ever worshipped
  By the virgin's holy toil ;
E'en there, amid the vesper strain,
Rushed on her thought the days that may not be again,

" While yet, beloved, and careless
  Of the morrow's treacherous chance,
In pleasure's maddening ecstasy,
  She breathed the gales of France ;
And mid the Salian daughters there,
Went forth the most admired, the fairest of the fair ;

" When, her bright hair decked with jewels,
  From some watch-tower's lofty place,
She beheld each object, instinct
  With the tumult of the chase ;
While, bending o'er his slackened rein,
The Monarch, with his flowing hair, came thundering o'er
  the plain.

" Behind him came the fury
  Of the fiery snorting steed,
The rapid flight, the quick return,
  Of hounds in breathless speed ;
And, from his penetrated lair,
The savage boar rushed forth, with fiercely bristling hair.

" Pierced by the Royal archer's shaft,
  His heart's-blood dyes the trampled plain ;
See, from the ghastly sight, she turns
  To her attendant maiden train ;
Her shrinking face, with sudden dread,
All lovely in its agony, with paleness overspread.

" Oh ! Aquisgrano's [5] tepid stream !
  Oh ! Mosa's wandering flood !
Where, the rough chase's tumult o'er,
  His mail unclasped, the warrior stood ;
Beneath whose ever-freshening wave,
His limbs, with noble toil-drops stained, the Monarch loved
  to lave.

---

[5] Aix-la-Chapelle.

" As the dew-drop softly falling
On the burnt and withered plain,
To the scorched and faded herbage,
Gives the vital juice again ;
Till in its former glory smile,
With renovated verdure, the once-parched and sickly soil :

" So o'er the harassed spirit,
Which an earthly love has broken,
Descends the gracious influence
Of a word, in kindness spoken ;
Until its gently healing art,
To another and a calmer love, diverts the aching heart :

" Alas ! but as the morrow's sun
Climbs the heaven's fiery way,
The still and heated atmosphere
Consuming with its ray :
Rewithering all around
The slender grass, just lifted from the freshly moistened
    ground.

" Thus, though lost in brief oblivion,
Will immortal love return,
And the spirit, unresisting,
With its wonted fervour burn ;
Recalling to their well-known grief,
The thoughts, that vainly wandering, sought a permanent
    relief.

" Lady, from thy troubled mind
Chase each earth-born hope and joy ;
Prayer, the broken-heart's oblation,
Yield to God and die ;
Die, and let the sacred earth
Thy tender reliques hide, the witness of their birth.

" Rest, Lady, rest ; in still repose
Grief's other victims lie ;
Wives, whom the sword left desolate,
Virgins betrothed in mockery,
Mothers (oh agony !) compelled to hear
The shrieks of dying sons yet writhing on the spear.

" Thee from Royal lineage sprung,
From th' oppressor's guilty race,
Who found in coward numbers strength,
In reason insult, and in right disgrace ;
In blood their privilege, their pride,
Remorseless to have lived, remorseless to have died :—

" Thee kind misfortune lower placed
Amid the suffering crowd ;
Have then thy rest – their pitying tears
Shall deck thy early shroud ;
No word of insult shall be said,
No act defile the ashes of the cold and blameless dead.

" Die, and to thy lifeless face
That peaceful calm restore,
Which, the future unpresaging,
Rapt in present bliss it wore ;
While with thyself alone,
Sweet converse held the happy thoughts beneath the virgin's
    zone.

" Thus, from the riven thunder-clouds
The setting sun unrolled,
And the shadowy mountains, mantled
In a flood of trembling gold,
Unto the pious swain betray
An omen, as he gazes, of the morrow's brighter day."

                                                    R. P.

There is only one chorus in the "Conte di Carmagnola,"
which describes in vigorous language the din and fray of
the battle, in the midst of which there is no confusion ;
and the poet contrives to carry his own conviction of the
wickedness of civil war home to the mind of the reader.
The rather obscure passages of history which serve as a
basis to each of these two tragedies are carefully illustrated
by the author in historical notes.

The work of Manzoni which is best known is probably
"I Promessi Sposi." It has been translated into all
European languages, and has been as popular—can more
be said ?—as an historical romance by Sir Walter Scott.
It was founded on the model which he furnished ; it had,
like his works of this kind, for its object to amuse, interest,
teach, and improve the reader, to make a particular
portion of history stand, as it were, alive before him.
History supplied certain facts and dates, imagination
peopled the place and the times with living persons
dressed in the manners and costumes of the epoch, whose
actions and fortunes were so interwoven with the true
facts of history as to make the reader interested in the
former necessarily acquainted with the latter. The object
of Sir Walter Scott and Manzoni did not end here, but

both strove to show that "Virtue alone is happiness below." Both refused to make vice attractive; both thought that to do so in the course of the romance, even though in the end it were punished, was high treason against morality and religion. Perhaps of Manzoni it may be more truly said than of any other successful writer of romance, that his work contained "no line which dying he could wish to blot." The scene of "I Promessi Sposi" is Milan and the neighbourhood of Como and the Italian lakes: the time is the early part of the seventeenth century. The love-story of simple good persons, Renzo and Lucia, affords the opportunity for exposing the vice and virtues, the customs and manners, lay and clerical, of the epoch, and of introducing an account of that most terrible of Divine chastisements recorded in history—the plague, which ravaged Milan and its "contorni" in 1630. To attempt to describe what Thucydides, Lucretius, Boccaccio, and Defoe had described was a bold undertaking, but it was successful, as any reader of the thirty-first chapter of the third volume may see, and mainly because Manzoni imbued his narrative with the spirit of contemporaneous and original memoirs which he carefully consulted. He speaks wisely, and with full experience of the living incommunicable "power" which such records possess.[6] The never-failing tendency of such a visitation to disclose the worst and the best features of corrupt humanity appears in these pages, as in the everlasting record of the plague at Athens. Among the many philosophical passages in this romance, the effect of famine upon the minds as well as the bodies of the sufferers, and the increase of its inherent evil by a legislation which vainly attempts to alter the laws of nature, are forcibly described. The romance would be well worth reading were it only for the study of the characters, which are in truth so well known that it is only necessary to touch slightly upon them. The author does not fall into the mistake of making either his hero or his heroine too perfect. Renzo, bold,

---

[6] "Forza viva, propria e per dir così incommunicabile vi sia nelle opere di quel genera comunque concepite e condotte."

enterprising, and impetuous, is weak-minded and easily
led into snares,—witness the scene in the "Osteria" at
Milan,—but misfortune tends to strengthen and develop
his character; and when at the last he shows himself
capable of a great and noble effort in the forgiveness of
his enemy, Don Rodrigo, the reader feels he has earned
the happiness in store for him. Lucia's character is
gentle and retiring, and her instincts, always good, are
strongly opposed to the kind of irregular marriage which
her mother compels her to attempt as a mode of extri-
cation from their difficulties. The account of the failure
of this attempt makes one of the most spirited chapters
in the book. This is the only instance of her principles
failing her. Afterwards they guide her straight through
the terrible dangers which beset her path, such as the
scene in the Innominato's castle, where by her firm faith
and simple eloquence she becomes the first instrument of
his conversion and change of life, while her gentle, loving
nature easily leads her to forgive those who had caused
her so much misery. The really fine characters which
claim, if it may be so said, the personal affection of the
reader, are Fra Cristoforo and Federigo Borromeo, Archbishop of Milan. The character of the first, to which the
clue is given in the history of his youth (chap. iv.), speaks
in his actions, the fruit of a life of self-denial and humi-
liation imposed in order to atone for the crime of his
youth committed in a moment of fierce passion. From
that time, from the moment of his asking forgiveness of
those whom he had wronged, and accepting the "bread
of pardon," a portion of which he preserves in his wallet
as a perpetual reminder of his fault, wherever there is a
good deed to be done we find him, comforting his poor
friends Renzo and Lucia in their hour of need, confronting
the villain in his castle, and for their sakes patiently
swallowing his insolent words, nursing for three months
the plague-stricken people in the Lazzaretto at Milan, and
dying from the exhaustion consequent upon these labours,
but not before he has forced Renzo to forgive his enemy,
and absolved Lucia from her rash vow. The character of
Federigo Borromeo claims at once admiration for the
holiness, harmony, and repose which are its chief features,

made more striking by contrast with the violent scene in the Innominato's castle, which immediately precedes the introduction of the Archbishop into the story. We feel, indeed, that "his life is like a stream of pure water issuing from the rock clear and limpid, pursuing its long course through various countries, without once stagnating or suffering its waters to be troubled, and throwing itself still pure and sparkling into the river. . . . He had the firm conviction that life is not intended to be a burden for many and a feast for only a few, but to all alike a serious business, for which each will have to give an account: and from his childhood he sought how he could best render his existence at once useful and holy" (chap. xxi.). And this beautiful description of his character forms a fit introduction for the affecting scene between the Archbishop and the Innominato. Don Abbondio, the weak priest, plays a middle part between the virtuous and the vicious in the story. Excluded from the first category by his selfishness and cowardice, his vices are not of a sufficiently positive nature to place him distinctly in the latter class. Still Manzoni is careful to point the moral, showing how great mischief may be caused by such mere negative qualities, as all the calamities in the story date from his refusal to perform his duties from motives of personal fear. The vicious characters are drawn with much vigour, and probably only too much truth. Two of the most remarkable passages in the work represent the agony of mind they undergo: Don Rodrigo when cut down by the plague in the midst of his career of crime (chap. xxxiii.); and the Innominato ("the Nameless One"), that other strange character, whose stony heart is melted by the prayers of Lucia, and who in the bitterness of his remorse is twice on the point of committing suicide, were it not for his half belief in "something after death" ("se c' è quest' altravita"). The changes which take place in his mind before he seeks the Archbishop are admirably portrayed. The minor characters—"Agnese," "Perpetua"—who often make the comic elements of the story, are so described as to give that light and shade which makes the particular charm of the work.

The " Colonna Infame " is an historical treatise, written
as a kind of supplement to the " Promessi Sposi,"[7] and
intended to illustrate that portion (chap. xxxi.) which describes the plague at Milan in 1630. In the panic caused
by the pestilence there grew up a strange popular belief
that the disease was purposely spread by persons who
were supposed to anoint (*ungere*) the walls of the streets
and houses of Milan with a fatal poison. Were it not
for the careful explanation contained in this chapter of
the " Promessi Sposi," it would be incredible that so pre-
posterous an accusation should have obtained any credit.
Manzoni traces it back to the very beginning of the plague,
which spread with such fearful rapidity because the
magistrates, who formed a Sanitary Commission, persisted
in denying the reality of the dreaded and horrible disease,
and refused to take the necessary precautions against it.
The belief that a class of persons existed capable of
deliberately spreading the infection by poison once established, the accusation was soon fastened upon some
unfortunate victims. Their innocence of a crime which
had never been committed, was of no avail in the eyes of
judges predetermined to find them guilty. After the
horrible custom of those times, they were put to the
torture and forced to denounce themselves. Nor did the
falsehood thus wrung from them avail them. They were
put to death with circumstances of horrible cruelty : the
house of Il Barbiere Mora, the supposed preparer of the
poison, was razed to the ground, and the " Colonna Infame " raised upon the site to record his infamy. Till the
year 1778, when it was pulled down, it might have been
said of this, as of our City Monument, that it,

> " Pointing at the skies,
> Like a tall bully, lifts the head and lies."

Manzoni proves in his treatise, where the contemporary
evidence of this disgraceful trial is carefully sifted, that
the Column of Infamy recorded the guilt of the judges
and not of their victims. Perhaps the preface to this
work is the most striking part of it. Pietro Verri, in his

---

[7] " I Promessi Sposi," chap. xxxii. vol. iii. p. 236. " Riserbando
però ad un altro scritto la narrazione di quelli (unzioni di Milano)."

" Observations upon Torture," which were suggested by
the same horrible occurrence just alluded to, draws an
inference as to the uselessness as well as the cruelty of
that method of procedure for the discovery of crime. But
Manzoni, Beccaria's grandson, goes deeper into the subject.
It is not so much the cruelty, though that fills him with
horror, as the flagrant injustice of the proceeding, which
is so revolting to his just mind : "The horrible victory
of falsehood over truth, of armed fury over defenceless
innocence." The labour which he has spent upon this
work will not, he adds, " be wasted if the indignation
and loathing which must result from the study of such
horrors are turned against those sinful and revengeful
passions, which cannot be discarded like false systems, or
laid aside like bad institutions, but which by the contemplation of the hateful end to which they lead, may on
other occasions be rendered less ungovernable in their
fury and less fatal in their results." [b] Manzoni's energies
were next employed in refuting an attack upon the
Catholic Faith contained in Sismondi's " Histoire des
Républiques Italiennes " (tome xvi. p 410). He entitled
the book " Osservazioni sulla Morale Cattolica," and it
refutes the position that attacks upon the dogma, rites,
and sacraments of the Church deserve to be called
Philosophy.

The life of Manzoni is best related in his works, for he
took no part in the political affairs of his country, and,
for the last forty years, has lived chiefly in retirement.
We only hear of his being made a Senator of the kingdom
of Italy in 1860 ; and in 1868, in spite of his advanced
age, he assisted in preparing a report on producing 1 nity
of speech throughout Italy, taking for a basis the Florentine language. There are but few details of his private
life either to be collected. He married, in 1807, Enrichetta Luigi Blondel, to whom he dedicated his tragedy
of the " Adelchi." She died in 1833, and he afterwards
married again. He appears to have left no son worthy of
the name, his son Pietro having pre-deceased him, to
whose children, Renzo, Vittoria, Giulia, and Alessandra,

[b] " Colonna Infame," Introduzione, p. 15.

R

he has bequeathed his manuscripts ("Autografi"). His will contained no disposition with regard to his funeral. It has been well said of Manzoni that he himself, like his hero of the "Cinque Maggio," took up his position between two ages ("s' assise tra due secoli"), and that the undying wreath which his genius prepared for the head of Napoleon really rests upon his own brow; certainly the events of the last few years have proved that his empire over the hearts and minds of his countrymen rests on a more solid foundation than that which was based upon the brilliant but ephemeral victories of Buonaparte. Manzoni questioned posterity as to the reality of Napoleon's glory—

> "Fu vera gloria ? . . . ai posteri
> L' ardua sentenza."

Posterity is answering, if it has not already answered, in the negative. Manzoni's laurels were never tarnished by envy, hatred, malice, uncharitableness, or wickedness. There is something inexpressively beautiful and elevating in his old age Retired from the tumult of the world, feeding himself on literature, cheered and animated by religion, modest in the extreme, receiving visits from every distinguished person who passed through Milan, accepting with courtesy, but without emotion, the homage of princes, with the one exception, it is said, of Victor Emmanuel, who had fulfilled the Poet's dream—the Unity of his much-loved Italy. He returned, and it is narrated as an exception, the visit of the King of Italy. For, says an eloquent writer, probably his friend Signor Bonghi, in the *Perseveranza* of the 29th of May, "He had two faiths —one in the truth of Catholicism, another in the future of Italy—and the one, whatever was said, whatever happened, never disturbed the other. In anxious moments, when the harmony between the two was least visible, he expected it the most, and never allowed his faith in the one or the other to be shaken. Rome he wished to be the abode of the King ; Rome he wished also to be the abode of the Pope. Obedient to the Divine authority of the Pontificate, no one passed a more correct judgment upon its civil character, or defended with more firmness, when speaking upon the subject, "the right of the State."

It is really not an exaggeration to say that Italy wept over his bier, while it has been calculated that a hundred thousand persons were actually present at his funeral. It is to be hoped that this intense appreciation of piety, patriotism, genius, and mental culture may supply a happy omen for the future of Italy, to use her lost poet's expression—

"Augurio di più sereno dì."

ADDENDUM.

An autograph letter by Manzoni hitherto unpublished has appeared in print since this Essay was written. It was edited by the Marchese Filippo Raffaelli, Bibliotecario della Communale di Fermo, and a translation of the letter is now appended to the foregoing sketch of the life of Manzoni, as a further illustration of the generosity of his disposition.

The circumstances which gave rise to the letter were as follows :—

A hostile criticism, entitled "Dubbi intorno gl' Inni Sacri di Alessandro Manzoni," by Giuseppe Salvagnoli Marchetti di Empoli, was printed at Macerata in 1829. Luigi Fratti di Reggio, a lawyer, undertook to defend Manzoni, but wrote to him previously on the subject, asking him to explain certain difficulties connected with the disputed points. To this Manzoni, after courteously thanking his would-be advocate, replied,—

" It has been my invariable custom to remain outside any disputes as to Italian literature, even when they professed to be merely amicable disputes, and not only to remain outside but to ignore them entirely when I found myself in any way the subject of them. Now your proposal is that not only should I embark in one of these disputes, but in one which entirely concerns my own humble efforts, and this adds a special repugnance to the dislike I feel to any dispute of the kind. You must therefore excuse me if I offer no explanation of the passages which appear to you difficult; indeed they are not worth the attention you propose to bestow on them, because words should speak for themselves in the first instance, and if they do not and require explanation, they are not worth it. Pray do not think I presume, either upon your good-will towards me, or on the privilege of my age and experience if I beg you to desist from an undertaking which is only prompted by too partial an opinion of my writings. The time and talents you propose to spend in this way could be far better otherwise employed. Just consider of what little importance is poetry in the world, and then the special insignificance of my share in it. What does it signify whether my verses are good or bad? Are they worth the dispute? Consider also that for the same reason such disputes become necessarily more complicated in a proportionate degree to their insignificance; the more heated the discussion they provoke, the more fruitless is the result. Such disputes arise from no other cause than from the necessary absence of that common general acceptance which appertains, as a general rule, to matters of greater importance, and which anticipates all dispute. From this alone may we expect a decision at once prompt, momentous, and lasting. Outside this category the points at issue may be manifold, variable, complicated, and their solution arbitrary, conflicting, and transitory, as must be of necessity the private opinions which they germinate; these form the elements of a decision only applicable to the disputed point and are no test for the future."

It is an accepted fact that Manzoni, as the founder of a new school, had both enthusiastic admirers and bitter detractors. There is not one of his works which has not been the subject of censure. But, as we see from the foregoing letter, the natural temperance and sweetness of his disposition forbade him either to enter the lists in his own defence, or to allow any one else to enter them for him.

Fratti unhappily was not dissuaded from his purpose. The defence of the Hymns was published anonymously, and was the cause of a fierce discussion upon their merits and demerits which was carried on in the newspapers and reviews.

But Manzoni adhered to his resolution of taking no

part in the discussion, and the only exception to his rule was made in favour of his " Morale Cattolica," which he justified from the accusations brought against it by Sismondi in his " Storia delle Republiche Italiane." Whoever reads the preface to this defence cannot fail to be struck by the delicacy of feeling, the modest wisdom, and the love of justice exhibited in the character of a man whose goodness of soul was only equalled by his natural genius and great store of acquired knowledge.

Frequently the target for criticism and attack, he never made any retaliation, but accepted all with Christian toleration, trusting to the intrinsic merit of his works for their ultimate triumph over unjust depreciation. Injuries and abuse he met with dignified silence, oblivion, and complete forgiveness. In this respect he has left an example which may well be imitated in the literary world.

ALEARDO ALEARDI.

" Pallida vita ! e tu saresti il grande
Avvenimento degli umani e il solo ?
Il Passato è una larva, a cui l' oblio
Va scancellando i languidi profili ;
Il Presente non altro è che il veloce
Avvenire che arriva."
(*Canti di Aleardo Aleardi.—*
" *Lettere a Maria,*" p. 155.)

ALEARDO ALEARDI has been described by a native critic,
like Napoleon in Manzoni's Ode, as alternately "nella
polvere" and "sugli altar." "Sugli altar," when his
poetry thrilled through Italian hearts, and nerved them
to the great struggle for the liberty of their country;
"nella polvere" when, that liberty being accomplished,
they could, from the safe shore of their assured freedom,
"turn to the perilous, wide waste, and stand and gaze."
But although the comparison may contain some elements
of truth, it would be an injustice to Italy to take it in its
literal sense.   Aleardi's countrymen would be the last to
strip the leaves from the poet's laurel, even though the
crown may have been hastily adjudged ; nor would they
be likely to scan with too cold a criticism the fervent
lines which emboldened them to break free from the
hateful foreign yoke.

Aleardo Aleardi was born at a period when that yoke
was most oppressive.   Venetian Lombardy had again
fallen into the hands of Austria ; and the faint hope
once cherished by the population as to the preservation of
those privileges which, as a Cisalpine Republic, they had
enjoyed under the Empire of the first Napoleon, was soon
dissipated.   Austria held them once more in her iron
grasp.   All trace of nationality, patriotism, or historical
tradition must be obliterated.   The Austrian flag waved

once again over the fair plains of Lombardy ; and under this banner the flower of her youth were compelled to fight in far-off countries whenever it was the good pleasure of a prince whose name was scarcely familiar to them, and for a nationality not their own.

Verona was chosen by the Austrian Empire for the headquarters of their administration, and here the surveillance was so strict that the press was subjected to severe censure, and all newspapers were forbidden except the *Gazetta di Milano*, the organ and instrument of the Government.

At this crisis, and in this the centre of the struggle between oppression and patriotism, Aleardo Aleardi was born. He was of noble birth, the last of his line, one of the oldest families in Verona, but his patrimony was small. His parents, Giorgio and Maria Canali, belonged to the class of small landowners which abound in Italy, and more especially in Lombardy, where the property is much subdivided.[1] The father, after having taken some slight part in the political strife to which his native country was a prey, saw the ancient Republic of Venice succumb before the French arms. He watched with anxiety the development of the new system of government introduced with such large promises of liberty by the invading foreigner, and, mistrusting their fulfilment, he withdrew from the field of politics to spend the remainder of his life in domestic retirement. He had two children only, one daughter, Beatrice, and one son, Aleardo Aleardi.

We pass briefly over Aleardi's childhood. It gave but little promise of the genius which was to show itself in after years. Removed from his home before he was ten years old, and placed in the College of Santa Anastasia, he pined for the love and tenderness of his mother, the delightful freedom of his country rambles, and drooped like a flower rudely transplanted from its native soil. He lost all the spring and joy of childhood, became taciturn and morose, was disheartened as to his studies, often in disgrace, the lowest in the school, nicknamed, by his schoolfellows, the " talpa " (mole), the more to signify

---

[1] " Epistolario di Aleardo Aleardi," pp. 101, 102.

his incapacity. For six years he was in this way the despair of his masters, the cause of the bitterest disappointment to his parents. The poetry of Virgil seems at last to have roused his dormant faculties. A new interest awakened in his mind, from which the clouds seemed suddenly dispelled; and his tutors, who had looked upon the slowness of his progress as a marvel, were now equally astonished by its rapidity.

The impetus so gained was sufficient to emancipate him from the trammels of the school which had been so irksome to him. He left Santa Anastasia, and pursued his studies at the most ancient and celebrated University of Italy. Padua, while under the wing of the Lion of S. Mark, had been the resort of the most learned profes· sors of Europe; but under the Austrian supervision it had lost much of its power and reputation, the Government being guided in their choice of the professors by political intrigue, paying little regard to their proficiency in science. Here, then, Aleardi continued his education, adding to the drier study of the law a careful training in the physical and natural sciences, the fruit of which often appears in his poetry. But while his mind became gradually enriched with different stores of learning, the idea of patriotism remained predominant. He read Dante, and then, casting a glance over his country, perceived how little the people, divided, oppressed, and enslaved, responded to those earnest appeals, which had struck a responsive chord. in his own heart; and the longing to inspire them with the same enthusiasm grew daily more strong within him. A few stray pieces of political po· try, while they revealed his patriotic aspirations, easily won for him the poet's laurel, and made him the central figure among his fellow-students. Even these trifling verses did not escape the vigilance of the Austrian police. Their suspicions, once awakened, fastened themselves upon the unhappy Aleardi, and from that moment he was closely watched.

His favourite walking-stick, in the top of which was inserted an ancient Italian *lira*, bearing a crown, and the inscription "Regno d' Italia," was looked upon with the deepest suspicion. One day it was missing; the next he was summoned before the police magistrate. "Did the walking-stick belong to him?" showing the luckless cane. "Why had it that emblem?" pointing to the *lira*. "Because it was the first money that ever came into my hand." replied Aleardi, undaunted. He was remanded, but from that day his name was recorded with a black mark in the Austrian books.

Aleardi, after this adventure, was more guarded in his conduct and kept a careful watch over the manuscript of the poetical composition in which he found a *sfogo* for his patriotic ideas. These were only circulated among his intimate friends, all more or less distinguished names in modern Italian literature, Prati, Gazzoletti, Fusinato, Somma, and Dell' Ongaro.

In the society of such kindred spirits, and in the midst of all the gay carelessness of University life, gifted with a boundless, restless imagination, he passed the years of his early manhood. But the closing years of his studies at Padua were darkened by a great sorrow, the death of his mother. Her loss was keenly felt by Aleardi. He sketches her portrait with reverent touches in some of his most pathetic lines : "Give me back," he cries, with passionate yearning, " the days of my youth—

"That I may see my Mother's tender gaze,
  Her full dark eye. Didst thou not seem to me
As some fair pilgrim passing through the earth,
Or as the sun's sweet ray immaculate
Upon a stagnant waste ; or like the petals
Of a fragrant rose, too swiftly scattered
O'er the stream of time, and borne away ?
Yet in the inner chamber of my heart
Thy perfume lingers yet. From thee first came
The fount of poetry which springs within,
And if perchance my Italy should shed
Some leaves from Fame's bright wreath upon my brow
The laurel crown shall wreathe thy sepulchre,
For it is thine." [2]

In a short time another domestic tie equally precious was severed. The husband only survived his wife two years, and Aleardi and his sister Beatrice were left orphans

[2] " Un' Ora della mia Giovinezza." p. 8.

in the world. Aleardi's early taste for poetry and his poetical gifts, instead of being a cause of pride, had always been a source of great uneasiness to his father. Twice over he warned his son most emphatically against putting himself "sulla via del poeta :"—

"It will lead you all astray, and your life will never cease to be restless and unhappy. Let poetry alone, and choose instead a more sober and a more certain companion for your life. Choose the law." [3]

Aleardi promised, though with great reluctance, to follow this advice, and, to please his father, on quitting the University of Padua, continued his studies in jurisprudence under the great jurist, Grassotti. For a little time he persevered, but Nature had made him a poet, or rather, as he says, with the modesty which characterized him, had planted in his soul a most irrepressible "passion for poetry, for it requires a good deal of courage to say that one is a poet," [4] and he was at last constrained to obey her dictates. But his poetry was to be no mere idle day-dream ; he meant to be a "poeta civile," his country's bard, destined, as he fondly hoped, in his youthful enthusiasm, to accomplish the deliverance of Italy.

With this mission clearly before him, he composed his first great poem ; but the moment was not yet ripe for an open display of his patriotic views : so he retraces his steps some 300 years, and borrows the robe of past history, with which to clothe them. The theme could not fail to be popular with Italians. It was the gallant defence of Cyprus by the Venetian Republic against the Turks, and particularly the siege of Nicosia.

Driven from pillar to post by the fierce attack of their enemies, the brave handful of Christians were gathered together in Nicosia, there to make one last stand against the Turks. This is the scene of Aleardi's poem entitled "Arnalda di Roca," from the heroine, a daughter of the house of Roca, one of the noblest of the Cypriote families. The Venetian historian Sagredi describes in a few quaint words the incidents which form the argument of the poem :—

---

[3] "Due Pagine Autobiografiche," p. xiii.   [4] Ibid. p. xiv.

"On July 25, 1570, the Turks besieged Nicosia. After fifteen vain assaults, at last, on September 9, they entered the city by the breaches. Fifteen thousand people were put to death, the rest sold for slavery. The ruin of the city had been foretold by a comet. One ship, amongst the other slave-laden ships, was freighted with a cargo of beautiful Cypriote women destined as a present for the Sultan. Among these Arnalda di Roca, worthy of a crown rather than of chains, free of soul, if fettered in body, seeing the fearful fate that was in store for her, set fire to the ammunition, and blew the ship into the air. 'Thus,' says the quaint historian, 'did she set on fire the funeral pile of her country, to be born again as a Phœnix to the glories of Heaven, and this was the last flame which celebrated the obsequies of what had once been the capital of a most flourishing kingdom.'"

This poem, "Arnalda di Roca," is supposed to have been written on the anniversary of the loss of Cyprus. On this day, and every other anniversary, which records either a past disaster, or a past triumph, in the history of the ancient Republic, the poet's fanciful conception describes the ghost of the old *Bucentaur* putting out to sea, carrying on board a goodly company of Doges and Venetian statesmen, who, rising from their long-forgotten tomb, set forth to revisit the scene of many a hard-fought battle both by sea and land.

> "This, then. is the day
> That Cyprus fell, and thus a priceless pearl
> Passed from the ducal diadem, to deck
> The jewel-hilted sword, the reeking blade
> Of yon Byzantine lord ! Lo ! yestere'en   5
> In the dead hour of midnight, solemn, still,
> While the forsaken gondolas lay chained
> To the deserted shore, nor sound nor tread
> Broke the deep silence of the quiet streets,
> The phantom semblance of the golden ship   10
> *Bucentaur* rose and glided by. Her sails
> Rent standards; and her oars, the rusting halberds
> Of a bygone age ; still from the high-curved prow
> The dying lion watched the fated course
> Whose broken wing flapped as an unfilled sail   15
> In that dead calm. The porticoes
> And stately steps, churches, and palaces,
> Seemed as if alive with shadowy forms

Rich in the garb of Doge or Senator;
Who ever, as the phantom ship drew nigh,   20
Went forth to meet it, o'er those dark, still depths
Passing with trackless feet. They reach the deck,
Weird welcome interchanged; the ship glides on.
But, as they pass the point where dash and foam
The breakers 'gainst the giant marble walls,[5]   25
A gale mysterious arose, and whence it came
None knew; which urg'd them swift as lightning's flash
Through the dark clouds of night. Like frighted steeds
The Istrian shores flee from their sight, and next
Pola's deserted amphitheatre,   30
Dalmatia's rock-bound coast: along the line
Point after point appears, recedes, is gone:
Only one fragrant breath Corcyra wafts
From valleys fair, and orange-laden groves.
Still must the ship drive onwards on her course,   35
And ever as she speeds past cape and gulf,
Scenes of Venetian combat oft renewed,
Rise as the witness of those sturdy fights
Torn planks, masts, oars, and figure-head,
Forth from their sandy grave, hid fathoms deep,   40
And follow, swimming, in the phantom's wake.
But as they reach Lepanto's well-known shore,
Behold Lepanto's towers; as if by touch
Of magic wand, that strong wind fell; the shades
In serried ranks drew to the vessel's side.   45
But vain the menace of the outstretched arm,
And vain the semblance of the glittering blade
Piercing the gloom; while through Morea's gulf,
Epirus' long shore, the mutt'ring sound
Of imprecation, fierce and deep outburst,   50
In agonized laments, which fill the air.
The breeze returning gathered up the sound
And bore it onwards. Onwards stood the ship
Devouring spaces in her headlong course;
Thy swelling hills, fair Cythera, they pass,   55
Where the soft murmur of the turtle dove
Wakes gentle echoes in thy myrtle groves,
And Crete, where still, unsepulchred,
Her hundred cities lie. The eyrie next
Of Christian eagle, Rhodes, whose battlements,   60
Once mightiest, now black and shattered stand,
And, if in midnight voyage some passing bark
Come 'neath that fort, haply her sails might catch
The dim, faint outline of the warrior souls
Keeping a ghostly watch; the crew, dismayed,   65

---

[5] These sea-walls, called *murazzi*, were built of solid marble in the
year 1776.

Seized with a mystic sense of loss and death,
Pause awe-struck, shiv'ring in the cold night breeze.
Cyprus at length stretched forth her rocky arms,
The ship ran in, her phantom voyage was o'er,
And the sad shades dispersed throughout the isle."[5]   70

Then follows the story. The scene is laid in Nicosia;
the time, September 9, 1576. It is night, and the city,
closely invested by the Ottoman armies, is wrapped in
the deepest obscurity. But there stands the palace of
the "Roca," one of the noblest of the Cypriote families.
Dark against the midnight sky, a single lamp burns in
one of the windows; it is flickering and paling before the
approaching dawn, which streaks with light the distant
Syrian sea. The beautiful Arnalda di Roca, the heroine
of the story, is seated at the balcony-window; the forgotten lute is by her side; the Bible, the "divin libro,
che primo

"Scritto dall' uom, fia letto ultimo in terra,"

is open at the account of Judith's return from the
Assyrian's tent. Arnalda gazes out upon the night, and
in her thoughts she envies the Jewish heroine, for she is
distracted by the prospect of the impending ruin of her
country, which she has long foreseen. From her childhood, the gay companions of her own age, fair Cypriote
damsels, like herself, have called her in sport a prophetess,
because she would predict coming events from long habits
of observation, and the careful study of the book of
nature, wherein she learned to love "Dio, la patria, i
parenti." All—her religion, her country, her father in
his old age, Nello (Sir di Saido), her betrothed knight—
are now threatened by the approaching catastrophe; and
if any thought of hope crosses her mind, it falls instantly dead, as the hapless bird which flies over the
Dead Sea. There are some moments, Aleardi says,
when the sorrows of life are so desperate that they appear
to lift one corner of the veil of futurity and to enable
you to see beyond it. Arnalda, overcome with the sad
thoughts suggested by her prophetic soul, tormented by
the hot vapours which rise from the scorching plain,

---

[5] "Canti di Aleardo Aleardi," pp. 448–450.

goes down into the garden, and there makes an agonized prayer for the safety of her country and those she loves. "Save, O Lord," she cries, "my father's hoary head, my Nello's gallant heart, and if one of our house must fall a martyr, let it be me alone." Absorbed in grief, she has not noticed the clash of arms, the soldier's quick step. Nello has heard the prayer of self-sacrifice, and stoops to comfort her. Hope will not die in his breast so long as there beats one loyal heart, or one lance remains to be broken. But Arnalda points to the vacant space on the top of the dome of the Santa Sofia of Cyprus, where the cross had been shattered by the enemy's cannon, too sure a presage of its future destiny in the infidel's hands. Then, in the full certainty that death is coming upon them, she relates to him an episode in her life, which she had hitherto concealed from him : how that, when on a pilgrimage with her father to the Holy Land, they had been overtaken by a sand-storm in the desert, and would have perished had it not been for a young Arab chief, then an exile in the desert, now the head of the Ottoman army. "He asked me," she adds, "for my love, but I had none to give him, only gratitude and pity. Oh, my Nello! I have one boon to ask of thee : in the fierce hour of battle do not aim thy blows at one who had compassion on my father as he lay fainting in the sultry desert!" The battle begins. Arnalda's father stands upon the ramparts of his castle with no thought but for his country and Arnalda. These two strong affections grapple to his soul as closely as the ivy which mantles round the ancient battlements on which he leans. But in vain the courageous defence of the handful of Christians against the hordes of Mussulman troops. "Oh!" exclaims the Italian patriot, with his heart full of his own country's wrongs, "is there a sadder sight upon this earth than when a hapless nation as one man marches with unflinching step into the very jaws of death, rather than become the slave of the conqueror?" The Conte dei Roca rallies his men for one last sally, is mortally wounded by an arrow sent from Assano's (the Arab chieftain's) bow, and is carried into a neighbouring church, and there stretched at the foot of one of the royal tombs, while the

setting sun streamed in purple rays through the painted
glass, the dying soldier opens his eyes to find his daughter
hanging over him. The dialogue between the father and
the daughter is very fine.[7] "Arnalda," he cries, "look
from the topmost window, what seest thou?" She,
struck to the heart with anguish, fearing to leave him,
yet anxious to obey his last commands, climbs with
tottering feet the stone steps in the belfry, gains the
highest window, whence she can see the whole of the city,
and the wide plain stretched out at its feet. The bat-
tering of the guns shakes the painted glass in the windows,
the vaults below give back the sound. There is a noise
of approaching steps. Arnalda descends in haste to
defend her dying father with her last strength. Nearer
and nearer comes the sound ; the gallop of a horse at
utmost speed.. It is here ; it is gone ; no, exactly in the
centre of the porch, it stays as of itself. For the first
time Arnalda turns pale. The dying Count recognizes the
well-known step. "Sir di Saïdo," he cries, "is, then, all
lost?" Their worst fears are confirmed. The father
confides his daughter to Nello's care, sees their hands
joined in betrothal, and expires. His eyes are scarcely
closed in death when the enemy bursts into the church.
Assano is at their head. "Sposa, siam perduti !" Nello
cries, as he springs to his feet to fight, sword in hand,
the last fight of despair. The crowd surrounded the two
combatants as at a tournament. The Lord of Saïdo gains
a vantage-ground on a piece of broken column, and fights
with desperate courage. The curved blue scimitar of the
Infidel is about to fall on his bare head, when the horse
of the assailant loses its footing on the smooth pavement,
and falls ; the hollow tomb beneath giving way beneath
his weight, horse and rider bite the dust. Nello's victory
is certain, when, from the farther end of the church, there
comes the hiss of a ball, and he falls to the ground. Then
all is over.

The third and last canto relates the fate of Arnalda.
When the fatal ball struck Nello she swooned ; and she
wakes from her trance to find herself in the power of the

[7] "Canti di Aleardo Aleardi," pp. 447, 448.

Mohammedan chief. In one instant the past flashed back, the future dawned, she felt at the point of death. "Ah! hapless Arnalda, dost thou not know that griefs, even the most awful, have *not* death at their call?" The Ottoman fleet returns to Constantinople; two ships, laden with prisoners, make their sad way over the sea. Among the Cypriote women the hapless freight of one bark is a poor lady, half-crazed with grief, to whom, disregarding her own depth of sorrow, Arnalda ministers. Because—

> " If e'er misfortune strike a noble heart,
> It straightway yields its purest treasure forth ;
> Treasures of love, unknown to happy days,
> Making it tender of another's woes.''

But if she is capable of the tenderest offices of pity, she is also equal to the most heroic deeds of valour. The vessel, continuing its voyage, passes the waters of Settaglia, calmed by the Sacred Relic, with which the Empress Helena assuaged their fury when returning with her inestimable prize from Golgotha. The imprisoned damsels are allowed to breathe the soft evening air on the deck ; and from a solitary height along the coast the bell rings the Ave Maria. They fall on their knees ; Arnalda recalls her mother's violated tomb, her father's unburied head, her Nello struck with mortal wound, and her lips move in prayer for the dying and dead. All the while the poor crazed soul measures the deck with her meaningless glance, accompanied with wild snatches of her native song. On a sudden, Arnalda is moved by an inspiration to attempt the deliverance of the unhappy captives. If she fails, the worst that can befall her is death. Her words, the prospect of liberty, have power to inspire the poor stricken does with the rage of the lioness; they incite the galley-slaves to revolt, among whom is Nello, not dead but wounded, with many of the warriors who had so lately fought for their country, who now, chained to the oar, are forced to conduct the vessel on her melancholy way.

Arnalda, with her own hands, sets Nello free. A desperate fight ensues. The Ottoman crew are overcome, and, for a brief period, the captive-laden ships are free. " Cipro vincemmo," the Lord of Saïdo once more utters his war-cry. " Fratelli, al remo !" In the delirium of joy, as he clasps the hand of his betrothed, the tears, which no misfortune could wring from him, spring to his eyes. Alas! how brief the joy. Another ship appears on the horizon. To arms! to arms! it is Hassan's ship; and silently, steadily, darkly, leaving a white track behind her, she comes on. , The fugitives crowd all sail in breathless agony and suspense, for there is no heart so brave which does not palpitate at the approach of death; and when the dissolution draws nigh, the soul flies upwards to meet "il Dio che s' avvicina." The chase is soon over; shot and shell fall like thunderbolts on the unhappy vessel; and in the brief succeeding pause the mountains give back the echo. Once again the enemy is on board, and the death-struggle begins. It is long and fierce; who does not know how desperately the free man will fight, whose arms still bear the livid impress of the captive's chain; and when the dawn arose it seemed as if only the hollow shell of the ship floated upon the waters.

Arnalda, where art thou? Art thou hidden? Assano seeks all over the wrecked ship for any trace of thee. Or has Death taken thee into his merciful arms? Silent, wounded, more deathly pale than the vestal tapers which burn before the altars, her only trust in God, the daughter of Roca yet lives, crouched in the corner of the vessel where a store of gunpowder remains unharmed, guarded to the last with jealous care. There in dead silence she waits for death. Alas! even this last asylum is no longer to be hers. The falcon has found the traces of the wounded dove, and swoops down. The Arab conqueror approaches with demoniac light in his eyes, followed by two Ethiopian slaves. One carries a bowl filled to the brim, and covered with cloth of gold. "I bring to my Houri the most precious gem the East can produce to lay at her feet." Then, with a demon's laugh, he threw back the cover, and displayed the bleeding head of her betrothed. Arnalda let no look betray the horror of her soul. She kneeled down; she raised her eyes to heaven, and made her prayer to the great God of her fathers. Then, with immovable calm, she took a pistol from her bosom, applied the short barrel to the gunpowder, and, with firm hand, drew the trigger. In an instant, living

s

and dead, the tyrant and the captive, tormentor and the victim, the swift ships, the scene of the late deadly strife, disappear amid a sheet of fire and clouds of smoke, like the " baseless fabric of a vision." The foamy waters part in circles to receive back in showers the fragments which tell the tale of that destruction. "Tutto passò." The calm which precedes the dawn smiles on the quiet waters ; the silence returns to the lately-troubled air ; the oranges and lavender upon the mountain-paths give forth their first fragrant morning perfume ; the lark rises singing to heaven's gate ; no trace of the late furious strife. misery, and bitter hatred remains but the faint cloud of smoke, which hovers over the water where the combat raged.

And now the phantom ship again puts forth to sea on her homeward voyage, and the stately shades troop back to their tombs to pillow their heads in dust ; the *Bucentaur* returns as she went forth, save that on her topmost yard she bears the relic of a martyr ; that martyr who, as a brilliant star, must ever shine in the firmament of the Cyprus skies. In these last lines Aleardi alludes to the still more famous siege of Famagosta, and the martyrdom of the hero Bragadino.

It was at one time his intention to have dealt with this subject in a dramatic poem. He worked at it when in villeggiatura with his sister Beatrice, to whom he was passionately attached ; but the manuscript was lost, and the poem never published.

His next poem, "Le Prime Storie," was dedicated to his father. It was written in 1845, though it did not see the light till 1857.

We have already alluded to the keen sympathy felt by Aleardi for the fate of Lord Byron. His romantic death in the cause of liberty, his enthusiastic poetry in praise of their country, were still fresh in the minds of the Italians, when Aleardi wrote one of his best poems, "Il Monte Circello," composed in imitation of "Childe Harold" It was originally written in four cantos, but only one of these, the last, was ever printed. Like "Childe Harold," Aleardi had wandered all over Italy, and knew every inch of her beloved soil. The scene of his poem opens with a description of the rock from which the poem takes its name, the ancient " Capo di Circe," at the western extremity of the Pontine Marshes. It was the gentle twilight hour, which seems like the kiss of peace to a fevered brow ; the evening vapours were rising from the steaming plain ; the golden cloud of insects—" nati al mattino e al vespero già vecchi "—had but just disappeared, when a vision passed before Aleardi's eyes. A phantom bard crowned with laurel stood upon that cloud-capped summit ; his long, hoary hair was confined by the Grecian band ; his garments were rude and old, and he seemed to feel his way like a blind man. When he struck the golden chords of his lyre, he turned his face to the sea. And then Aleardi recognized the blind bard, who, while the earth was yet in her infancy, was Emperor of Song, who told of the fierce wrath of Achilles, and Hector's cruel fate, the wanderings of Ulysses, his wisdom and his revenge. The vision disappears at the end of the song, and the sole vestige which remains of the mendicant bard whose tattered garment was worth the robes of a hundred emperors, is a branch of laurel.

Aleardi next descends into the famous Pontine Marshes, the grave of many a forgotten city. This description of the plain so fair and fruitful in appearance, but containing in every furrow the germs of death to the reapers who from generation to generation are sent down from the Abruzzi to gather in the harvest, is looked upon as a masterpiece by his native critics.

The Bay of Naples suggests the piteous fate of Conradine of Swabia, familiar to us in the " Purgatorio" (xx. 67-9), but whose portrait as painted by Aleardi awakens our sympathy anew :—

" The youth,
Pale, beautiful, his locks of curling gold,
His eyes the colour of the sapphire bay,
His open brow marked by misfortune's stamp.
    . . .   The Swabian star
Glittered in silver on his azure crest,
Still on his breast the Swabian eagle shone.

There on the scaffold pale and proud he stood,
And mid the surging crowd the gauntlet flung ;

Who took it up, none knew! but when the fated hour
Clashed from each steeple in Palermo's town,
That glove became a living hand, and tolled
The knell which summoned Anjou's hated race
Before the Throne of God." [8]

Terracina, Anzio, and the Appian Way, with its hundred
miles of monuments, temples, and tombs, bygone relics of
Roman splendour, are all treated in this, the one fragment
which remains to us of a much larger scheme. The poem
ends with an enthusiastic description of the dawn of
Creation and the origin of Italy. Some of the lines are
fine, but Aleardi was tempted by his love of physical
science to embark in an elaborate account of the geolo-
gical formation and development of his country, which
makes the conclusion complicated, and to the uninitiated
difficult to understand.

Aleardi's best composition was written in the following
year (1847): he called it "Lettere a Maria." It created
a great sensation in Italy at the time, and will probably
outlive his other works   It is divided into two parts,
" L' Invito," and " L'Immortalità dell' Anima." One of
Aleardi's biographers [9] tells us that originally there were
two more " Lettere a Maria," but that Aleardi in a fit of
passion, thinking they were not appreciated by the person
to whom he was reading them, threw them into the fire.
Their loss, says the biographer, is the more to be regretted
as the poet had often told him that they were the best
part of the work. We can judge what they must have
been by the two which remain, which contain some of his
most beautiful lines. Nor is this surprising, when we
learn that " Maria" was his " Laura," and that his attachment to her was as hopeless, as chivalrous, as romantic,
and as high-flown as that of Petrarch for Madame Laura
de Sade. Another biographer, writing in 1863, tells us
that the real Maria was at that time in existence, and that
after many years of harassing anxiety, and after having
advanced a long stage on the journey of life, she still
remembers with infinite delight her moment of triumph
when this poem first appeared, and made her the envy and

---

[8] "Canti di Aleardo Aleardi," p 78.
[9] " Prampolini," p. 7. See also " Epistolario," pp. 262, 263.

admiration of all her countrywomen. Who she was we are not able to say; that she no longer lives we gather from a later poem of Aleardi's.

Among many beautiful passages in the "Lettere a Maria" there is one which has a special interest for English readers, as it is evident from it that Aleardi must have been so impressed with Gray's "Elegy" as to reproduce some of the ideas either consciously or unconsciously in his own language.

The pathetic familiar features of the English churchyard, "the rugged elms," and the; "yew-tree's shade," have no place in the Italian imagination, but we find their counterpart in—

> "Quell' erboso ultimo lembo
> Chiuso da bianco muricciuolo dove
> Una selvetta pullula di croci;
> Quello è il nobile campo, ove anno i padri
> De la villa riposo."
>
> ("The rude forefathers of the hamlet sleep.")

We find the "blazing hearth" in the "Allegria del focolar loquace;" the "cool, sequestered vale of life" is rendered by the lines—

> "E alcun vi fu che ne la ingenua vita,
> Uniforme non seppe altro del mondo
> Chè quel campo, quel monte, e quella chiesa."

The "heart once pregnant with celestial fire" is suggested by—

> "Un Ildebrando, cui mancò la stola
> Venerabile e i tempi;"

and the parallel is very close between the "mute, inglorious Milton" and the "occulto Pindaro sanz' arpa," the "novo forse Napolëon, che non sortìa la spada," and—

> "Some Cromwell guiltless of his country's blood." [1]

During the years 1846-7, the date of the two poems we have just been considering, the Italians gave many a proof of their ever-increasing hatred of the Austrian rule. They longed for some one to give voice to their shuddering indignation, to protest against the cruelty of their oppressors. In Aleardi they found an apt representative of their aspirations, and thus he obtained the wish of his heart in becoming the bard of Italian liberty. When a new poem

---

[1] See "Lettere a Maria," p. 160. "Canti di Aleardo Aleardi."

by Aleardi was announced, a feeling of hope sprang up even in the most despairing hearts, and they blessed the young poet who was not afraid to plead, in eloquent and pathetic lines, the cause of his country. At the first outbreak in Venice, Aleardi was chosen by Manin to form part of the Provisional Government, and was afterwards despatched as ambassador on their behalf to Paris, to enlist the sympathies of France in the cause of Italy.

Louis-Philippe was still on the throne. Every courtesy was shown to the envoy, but Aleardi soon perceived that little else was to be hoped for from his cold, selfish policy; still less from the revolution of June that same year, when France was entirely engrossed with her own affairs. Yet indirectly the success of the French revolution of 1848 exercised a powerful influence upon the movement for Italian freedom. By this time Carlo Alberto had cast in his lot with Italy; he was at the head of affairs, and Aleardi applied to the new Government for his recall, as there was nothing to be gained by a longer sojourn in France.[2] He left Paris, bidding adieu to Béranger, Lamennais,[3] and Mickiewitz, with whom he formed an enduring friendship, and returned to Italy, pausing for some time in Florence, where a courteous reception from Giusti and Capponi consoled him for his disappointment in the failure of his embassy. Meanwhile the insurrection was spreading in Italy. Bologna had risen to arms, and Aleardi hastened to the scene of action, to render what assistance he could. But the unequal struggle was soon over, the city capitulated, and Aleardi returned to Florence, till the entry of the Austrian troops; thence to Genoa, where he would have been content to remain, had he not been summoned to Verona by the mortal illness of an old friend, who had been his tutor, and had stood almost in the place of a parent to him since his father's death. For his sake, Aleardi exposed himself to the fury of the Austrian Government against the revolutionist, and arrived in time to minister to his friend during his last moments.

Verona received Aleardi with open arms, as the patriot

[2] "Epistolario di Aleardo Aleardi," pp. 21—71.
[3] Ibid. p. 52.

who had done his utmost to ameliorate the condition of his
fellow-citizens. For some little time he remained undisturbed, till unhappily the Austrian Government recollected
that he had taken part in the too celebrated " Processi di
Mantua," and he was thrown into prison in October, 1852.
He was at first confined in the military prison of S.
Tommaso in Verona, from thence he was transferred to
Mantua. The treatment which Aleardi received at the
hands of the Austrians will be no surprise to those who
have read " Le Mie Prigioni," or Mr. Gladstone's eloquent
essays upon the sufferings of the Neapolitans.[4] Aleardi
was not chained to a fellow-sufferer, but in every other
point his condition seems to have been equally hard to
bear. The four prisons of Mantua being already choked
with victims of the Austrian tyranny, one cell only was
empty, so bad of its kind that it had hitherto been considered unfit for human occupation. Into this Aleardi
was now thrown. It was narrow, damp, and not only that,
but for eighteen hours of the day it was perfectly dark,
and during the remaining six a grey twilight was the
nearest approach to daylight. It contained literally no
furniture, save a mattress on the floor. His prison fare
consisted of two *pani* of black unleavened bread, which
were brought to him in the morning, and a plate of soup
later in the day. But neither solitude, nor obscurity, nor
the pangs of hunger, nor the restraint—to a person of his
disposition most cruel to bear—wrung from him a single
complaint. He bore all in patient silence, freely forgiving
in his heart those who were the cause of his sufferings.
These were not only physical but moral. For some time
he struggled against his anguish, and found some alleviation in composing poems, which he afterwards entitled
" Ore cattive." They occupy more than thirty pages of
his collection of poems,[5] but they are inferior to his other
works, and this is not surprising when we remember the
circumstances in which they were written. After more
than six weeks spent in this abominable cell, he was
allowed to leave it for a short time in order to see his sister

[4] Gladstone's " Gleanings," vol. iv. pp. 1—135.
[5] " Canti di Aleardo Aleardi," pp. 198—219.

in one of the guard-rooms in the presence of the soldiers. His eyes, accustomed to the darkness in which he had been confined, were so dazzled by the light of day, that at first he could discern nothing. But as soon as he saw his sister, he spoke to her with calm cheerfulness, and said he was in want of nothing, lest she should be miserable in thinking of his sufferings. On his return to his cell, however, when he was alone, he threw himself upon the ground, where he remained for some hours in an agony of grief and despair. After three months his prison was changed, and for the better. He was now removed to one of the highest stories, and here he had light and air, and could see the cornice of the Basilica of S. Andrea (the great work of Leon Battista Alberti), from whence the pigeons flew to and fro, suggesting thoughts of liberty to the unhappy captive.

He was still without books or means of writing, and had not been able to commit to paper the poems which he had composed. At last, as a great concession, he was given a German grammar and dictionary, to the study of which, glad of any occupation, he diligently applied himself. One night in December his sleep was interrupted by unaccustomed sounds, continued hammering, and marching to and fro; there appeared to be a general excitement. At last he became aware that these were preparations for the execution of some of the prisoners. A few days afterwards Aleardi and many others of the remaining prisoners were roused with the dawn, and conducted in prison-vans to the Castle, where they were drawn up in a row; the list of names was called over, and by the silence which followed upon the reading of some of the names, Aleardi discovered which of his fellow-sufferers had fallen victims to the Austrian bullets. They were then taken into a piazza, while the rain poured down in torrents, and their pardon was announced to them. Pardon!—for what? It will be remembered that from the moment Aleardi was thrown into prison till the moment of his freedom, there had been no question of examination or trial as to whether he was innocent or guilty.

The Mantuans who had crowded round the gates of the Castle, received the liberated prisoners with enthusiasm,

and offered them every kind of hospitality: Aleardi
declined, fearing to expose his host to the future suspicions of the Austrians, and the next day returned to
his native city. The hardships which he had suffered in
prison had by no means daunted his courage, or diverted
him from his self-chosen career.

"Le Città Italiane marinare e commercanti "[6] was his
next work. From the dissolution of the Roman Empire,
the time when Italy, as an Empire, was laid in the
coffin ("discesa imperatrice entro la bara "), he traces the
existence which rises new-created from her ashes, and
follows each Republic through its own gallant history.

First, the "queen with an unequalled dower," Venice,
whose future S. Mark sees in a prophetic vision as he
sails past the desolate lagune on his way to Aquileia.
Before his eyes the phantom of a Byzantine Church
hovers on the horizon of that labyrinth of sandy islands
and reedy shores. There will his bones one day find an
honoured resting-place beneath the golden cupolas, and
over the portico :—

> "Scintilleranno egregi e impazienti
> I destrier di Corinto."[7]

Or, in Byron's words, which might almost stand for a
translation,—

> "Before S. Mark shall glow his steeds of brass,
> Their gilded collars glittering in the sun."

And while rivals still slept, her galleys sped to bring the
gems from the "exhaustless East," and pour them in
sparkling showers into her lap. Ease and indolence
followed upon such stupendous wealth, and other cities
pressed forward to dispute with her the sovereignty of
the seas.

First of all, Amalfi, with her well-known *tavola
amalfitina* of Roman law, and her discovery of the
compass. Then Pisa :—

> "And from the Arno's shore fair Amazon,
> Pisa, all beauty, and all valour, came,

---

[6] "Canti di Aleardo Aleardi," pp. 173, 187.
[7] Ibid. p. 177.

> In the sea joust an eager combatant,
> Riding triumphant on her foam-dashed prows,
> As on the back of untamed battle-steed." [8]

Genova, *lionessa dell' onda*, the suzerain of Pera, and who, when the Old World did not yield sufficient wealth, unlocked the golden storehouse of the New Hemisphere, and cast its riches at the feet of Europe.

The Northern nations still lay wrapped in the slumber of the dark ages, restrained and repressed by feudal law, while the commonwealths of Italy were as hives of industry in the garden of the sunny South. Many a foreign palace glitters with Venetian crystals ; an empty heraldic decoration was the only repayment Florence ever received for the million of golden florins lent to the King of England in his need. Happy the warrior, of whatsoever nation he be, if in mortal fight his breast is covered with the corselet of Lombard steel. But now the crown of Venetian glory is cast down : the garlands of flowers which were showered upon her on the day of her annual marriage with the sea she scatters like a new Ophelia, one by one along her path. The tomb has closed over even this memory of her glorious past, and all that remains to her is " La speranza e Dio."

Early in the poem Aleardi alluded to the three successive stages of Italian life : first the Etruscan, next the Roman, and thirdly the Commercial and Maritime, when Italy was divided into many rival Republics. There was yet another existence in store for her, which he lived to see, when she became a nation's kingdom, in which the parts dissolved with the Roman Empire were again united, and the several communities, laying aside their rivalries and animosities, were combined in one whole ; so that at last the "gloria," which he prayed for in the concluding lines of the poems, did indeed dawn :—

> " Sui tre orizzonti della mia marina."

---

[8]   " Tremenda e bella
Tu pur scendevi alle marine giostre,
Balzando in cima alle spumanti prue
Come a selvaggi corridori in sella."

But in the year 1856, when the poem was first published, this conjuncture of all the States in one independent nation was characterized by contemporary writers as a " dream of enthusiasm and folly. Cavour was, however, laying the first stone in the building of the kingdom, by his protest against the Austrian system of repression and violent reaction, never relaxed since 1848-49, which he laid before the Congress of Paris. The Italians were momentarily calmed by the prospect of an amelioration of their fate, but the negative result of the Congress raised the revolutionary spirit afresh. Three years later, and the noble little Kingdom of Sardinia again risked her whole existence in the cause of her oppressed fellow-countrymen. This time France came to the rescue, and the era of Italian independence seemed about to dawn. Aleardi again held aloft the nation's banner, in spite of the perils with which he was surrounded, in his " Canti Patrii,[9] some of which, he says, in a letter to a friend, were written by twenty lines at a time with " i birri alla porta," and then concealed. Often the hiding-place was discovered, the papers destroyed, and the work had to be done over again. But as the destroyed papers were always replaced by Aleardi's fertile genius, it was not likely that he would be long left at liberty during this the crisis of Austrian rule of Lombardy. He was again arrested, his papers were searched, and he was first consigned to a prison in Verona, afterwards removed to Josephstadt, where he was again visited by his sister Beatrice. She was worthy to be called " Amore, Benedizione, Allegrezza serena della mia vita agitata." In these terms he dedicated to her one of his best compositions, " Accanto a Roma," which contains a magnificent tribute to Dante.[1] Another equally fine passage paints with living touches the portrait of the " divino infelice Tasso."[2] Two of his companions were already condemned to death, and the faithful sister was in an agony of anxiety. " But mind, Beatrice," said Aleardi to her one day when she was with him in his prison, " never entreat any one for my life.

[9] Pp. 259 –297.
[1] " Canti di Aleardo Aleardi," p. 106.   [2] Ibid. 113.

I would rather die a thousand times than owe my life to the favour of my country's enemy." [3]

The Peace of Villafranca, while it destroyed his hopes of the deliverance of his country, set him at liberty, together with all the other political prisoners at Joseph-stadt.

Aleardi repaired to Brescia, where he was the object of the warmest sympathy and many a patriotic demonstration. He was offered the chair of Italian Literature at the Instituto Filosofico, at Milan. This he did not accept, preferring the life of independence which he had from the beginning marked out for himself.

But the next year, from his place of retirement, Aleardi beheld the realization of his long-cherished hopes, beyond his utmost expectations. It was the year 1860; the whole interest of Europe fastened on Italy, when, says the "Annual Register," "we have to relate, not the obscure struggles of a faction, nor the abortive attempts of conspiracy, but the history of dynasties overthrown, of the union of the North with the South of Italy in one large kingdom, under the constitutional monarchy of the House of Savoy."

To Garibaldi, who alike single-hearted and single-handed, cut the cords by which Southern Italy was bound, and set her free for ever, Aleardi dedicated his poem, entitled "I sette Soldati." [4] The seven soldiers represent the seven nationalities oppressed by the House of Hapsburg—Hungarian, Pole, Bohemian, Croat, Austrian, Tyrolese, Italian—and in the morning after the battle Aleardi fancies himself walking over the battlefield, bending in turn over each of the dying heroes.

It is a long poem, and not equal to the occasion for which it was composed, though it contains many beautiful ideas, and some fine lines. Moreover, it was written in 1861, and Aleardi could not wholly rejoice in a freedom which was not shared by his own native province. A few years later, and Lombardy was also delivered from foreign rule. The day that (to quote the words of the late King)

[3] "Prampolini," pp. 4, 5. See also "Epistolario," p. 167.
[4] "Canti di Aleardo Aleardi," pp. 306—335. See also "Epistolario," p. 176.

"the Iron Crown was restored to Italy," and he rode triumphant into Verona, was celebrated by Aleardi in some of his best lines.[5]

The temporal power of the Papacy was the only stumbling-block which now remained in the way of the perfect unity of the Italian kingdom. This stumbling-block, in the true spirit of Dante, Aleardi set himself to remove ; but his efforts were no more successful than those of his great predecessor's, although six centuries of experience had served to prove the truth of the immortal lines :—

> " Come pesa il gran manto,
> A chi dal fango 'l guarda ;
> Che piuma sembran tutte l' altre some." [6]

But if the stern language of Dante fell upon unheeding ears, the imaginative metaphors of Aleardi were equally disregarded.

It was in vain that he employed by turns the language of persuasive entreaty and prophetic warning, first recalling to the recollection of Pius IX. the time when he was the desire of the people's hearts, when the people wept round the standard which he had blessed. Then his pastoral staff was worth all the sceptres of Europe, then . every Italian hearth was sanctified, all Italy joined in one hymn of thanksgiving.[7] But these high hopes were all shipwrecked on the rock of Gaëta, and for the time the Holy See lost its influence over Italian hearts and minds. And then Aleardi describes with a hardy metaphor the triple crown of terror, shame, and anathema, weighing heavily upon the head " d' un Vecchio infermo." The

[5] " Aleardo Aleardi," p. 393 ; " Epistolario," p. 239.
[6] " Purgatorio," xix. 104.
> " With what a weight that robe of sovereignty
> Upon his shoulder rests, who from the mud
> Would guard it, that each other fardel seems
> But feathers in the balance."
> (*Cary's Translation.*)

[7] " Canti di Aleardo Aleardi," pp. 402, 403 :—
> "Ogni privato ostello
> Diveniva una chiesa . . .
>   Italia,
> Era un inuo."

poem from which we have just cited was dedicated to the
"venturo Pontefice" (the future Pope); but long before
Leo XIII. succeeded to the Papal Chair the temporal
power had succumbed before the irresistible march of
events. Aleardi saw the last and noblest jewel restored
to the crown of Italy in her ancient capital, and the fulfilment of the prophecy which he had himself made to
the late King on one occasion when he was in his
presence.

"Voi potrete dire con sublime orgoglio, O Sire, a vostro
figlio : Umberto, ti io ho composto la più bella, la più
gentile corona d' Europa." He celebrated this last triumph
of Italian liberty in a poem called " L'Aurora Boreale del
25 Ottobre 1870."[8]   Moreover, he witnessed the recon-
ciliation of the Pope and the King before both passed,
within a few weeks of each other, from the world where
they had played such prominent parts, the succession of
the young Prince to the kingdom which his father had
made for him, and the election of another Pope to face
the still unsolved problem of his altered sovereignty.

Meanwhile Aleardi became a representative of the
"Italia Una," in whose cause he had spent his life. He
entered the Italian Parliament, held the chair of
Æsthetics in Florence, became member of the Upper
Council of Education, and was raised to the dignity of
Senator. But these new offices distracted him from his
art, for which indeed the prevailing motive had now
ceased to exist. He published very little. In the latest
edition of his works, printed at Florence in 1878, there
are only a few " Poesie Volanti " added to the collection
of poems published in 1867.

Among these " Poesie " were a few stanzas upon an
iron bedstead, which he desired his old nurse, to whom he
was much attached and who lived with him to the last,
to place in his room at Verona. The couplets described
the bed as made of the same "metal temprato, onde si

---

[8] In his letter upon the death of the late King (Jan. 11, 1878)
Aleardi writes of his successor :—" Di Umberto io spero. Gagliardia
e dignite, nobile orgoglio di seguitare le vestigia de suoi avi," &c.
—*Epistolario*, p. 373.

fan le spade," &c.; but the last verse was prophetic. It ran thus:—

> " E alfin verrà quel dì, che tra le bianche
> Tue coltri, o letto, ove morir desio,
> Placidamente le pupille stanche
> Io chiudirò, per riaprirle in Dio." [9]

And so it came to pass exactly as it is described in these lines.

One night (July 18, 1878) he lay down to rest on this bed, which has now become historical, apparently in perfect health, but in the night, death came upon him without his being aware of that awful presence, and he passed away in his sleep. No end could have been more blessed, more peaceful, more entirely to be envied. After a life of toil and anxiety, many hardships, much suffering in the cause he loved, he lived to see the desire of his heart fulfilled, and died in his own home in his native city, Verona, and surrounded by those he loved. The countenance was so perfectly calm and placid, almost with a smile on the lips, that, when the faithful nurse came to rouse him in the morning, it was long before she could be persuaded that he had entered upon the dawn " di più sereno dì " than any which could have awaited him in this world.

When, on the following day, the coffin which contained all that remained of her beloved " bambino " was borne to the grave, the poor faithful creature watched it from the window till it was out of sight; then her heart broke, and she fell down dead.[1]

All Italy mourned the death of her patriotic poet, and all the city of Verona followed him to the grave.

An elaborate oration was pronounced over his coffin before it was lowered into its final resting-place. We do not know what were the terms of praise or criticism which were bestowed on the departed poet on that occasion, but we do know what he wished to have said when that moment came:—

[9] " Canti di Aleardo Aleardi," ed. 1878, p. 400. This edition contains a fac-simile of these couplets in the poet's own handwriting. They were translated into German for Prince Bismarck.—*Epistolario*. p. 300.

[1] " Prampolini," pp. 3, 4.

"Oh mi sia dato
Tanto di vita e di quest' arte mia
Che un dì si possa dir *sul mio feretro,*
Ella fe batter nobilmente il core
Di santi sdegni e confortò di speme
La mesta gioventù della sua terra."[2]

The love of poetry and the love of his country were the twin passions of Aleardi's soul, and it was his constant endeavour to make the first subservient to the second. Yet he says himself,—

"I saw that by so doing I should circumscribe the flight of my Muse and pluck many a feather from her pinions. Still my country had the paramount claim. I was proud of my nationality, and I had a sure presentiment that, one day, Italy would be free, that meanwhile it was a sacred duty to devote my poetical gifts, such as they were, to her cause. Much of my poetry was written under the watchful, suspicious eyes of a foreign administration, with a vista in the background of some Illyrian, Hungarian, or Bohemian prison awaiting me. Therefore my ideas were many of them nipped in the bud, some were thrown out in the shape of a suggestion, some as outlines without my being able to add the colour or shade which would have give them more evident life. And these restrictions ill become an art which should be as free and unfettered as the soul. Hence many obscurities, a somewhat artificial style, often disconnected and vague, defects which will instantly strike the reader. . . . For this reason I feel that my poems will have but a fleeting popularity, and that if I were to return to earth after the lapse of a hundred years, I should find myself and them as clean forgotten as 'Fra Felice,' on his return from the wood where he had been listening to the enchanting song of the bird, heedless of the flight of time."

So frank and fearless an avowal of faults on the part of the poet himself must disarm any harsher criticism and leave us free to dwell with unmixed pleasure upon the succession of new and beautiful ideas supplied from the inexhaustible treasures of his imagination, and upon his power of rendering them in language and rhythm de-

[2] "Aleardo Aleardi," p. 61.

scribed as "Aleardesque" by his native critics. Nor was this descriptive art, in which he was so great a master, confined to the scenes of varied beauty among which, as an Italian, his lot was cast. We find it again in the faithful delineation of the equally variable passions and affections of the human soul. "I have written," he tells us, "more with the heart than with the mind," and here we have the secret of the strange fascination of his poems, scarcely to be accounted for by their literary merit taken in the abstract "Heart speaks to heart," and Aleardi, out of the overflowing of his love for his country and his compassion for all suffering humanity,[3] strikes so sympathetic a chord that the heart must indeed be cold and dead which cannot vibrate in answer: more especially when touched by one intimately acquainted with those delicate shades of feeling, those depths of passionate tenderness, to which only those who have suffered possess the clue.

This kind of poetry may not perhaps entitle Aleardi to the position of "*Cinque* Poeta Italiano," to which, in the first burst of their enthusiasm, he was elected by his grateful countrymen.· Nor can the rhythm of his blank verse, however smooth and faultless, be considered anything but a poor exchange for the vigorous *terza rima*, or the rolling stanzas, of the fathers of Italian poetry. Still it marks a new capability of the beautiful plastic language; it served a great purpose, and must on these accounts claim an honoured place in the beadroll of his country's literature. His writings in prose show the same fervent imagination, the same originality of thought and expression, to which his verses owe so much of their charm. In his "Epistolario"[4] we read with interest his brilliant letters to such correspondents as Giulio Carcano, Cesare Cantù, and the famous living historian, Pasquale Villari, who revised several of Aleardi's poems by his special request.[5]

Aleardi has yet another claim to the gratitude of posterity in having refused to become the disciple of a

---

[3] "Pietà di tutto cui quaggiù castiga
Lu inevitabil legge del dolore."
        Canti di Aleardo Aleardi, p. 121.
[4] Published at Verona in 1879.   [5] "Epistolario," p. 176.

T

school of Italian poetry at that time prevalent in Italy, which reached its climax in Leopardi; a school whose maxim was despair. To Leopardi the world was covered with a dark pall. It was vain to hope for any improvement from society, rotten at the core, or from a nation sunk in slavish apathy and indifference. And if the present life was dark, that of the future appeared dim and clouded to his faint and wavering faith.

Aleardi would have nothing to do with this faithless discouragement. Often baffled, he returned again to the charge; again and again he revived the people's courage when crushed by defeat; no public disasters could destroy his confident hope in the future restoration of his country, just as no personal hardship could quench the enthusiasm of his soul.

His faith remained clear and bright as the polestar to guide him safe through the journey of life, which he describes in one of his most original metaphors :—

> " Iddio connesse
> In un mistico nodo anima e polve,
> Come cavallo e cavalier, li avvia
> A le venture d' una corsa istessa.
> E perenne è la lotta, e le cadute
> Vituperose, e splendidi i trionfi.
> Cou la valida voce ora i galoppi
> Domina il sire; con obliqui slanci
> Ora il cavallo il cavalier trascina.
> Passan, così congiunti, profumate
> Curve di colli e selve paurose,
> Squallidi stagni e fruttuosi piani,
> Fino e quel dì, che estenuato esangue
> Cade il corsier ; e del nitrito estremo
> Fa il portico sonar d' un cimitero."

> " God hath knit
> The soul and body in one mystic bond,
> As horse and rider, and then sent them forth
> To run their course upon the race of life.
> Along the way the strife is permanent.
> And now the rider with decided voice
> The steed controls, and now with sudden swerve
> The horse has thrown his burden in the dust.
> Yet joined together onwards still they pass
> O'er gently swelling slope, through forest dark,

Flying o'er dreary marsh and pleasant plain ;
Until at last, one day the charger falls,
Worn out, his strength all spent. The hollow tomb
Gives back the echo of his dying groan."

And therefore we feel that we may safely leave him at that moment when—

"Libero il cavalier si leva
Affacciandosi a Dio, che le cadute
E le vittorie numera." [6]

---

[6] "Canti di Aleardo Aleardi : Lettere a Maria," p. 169.

COUNT ARRIVABENE.

COUNT ARRIVABENE, the subject of the present paper, born in 1787, and dying at the ripe age of ninety-three, was an eye-witness of every stage of that last great struggle which resulted in the freedom of Italy.

His earliest recollections, we gather from his "Memoirs," centre round the birthday festival of the Prince of Gazzoldo. It was the last State ceremony of the little principality, which, having existed since 1262, was now about to be swept away by Napoleon and to be absorbed in the Cisalpine Republic; but the splendour of the pageant of the expiring State left a lasting impression upon his childhood's imagination. Nor was the blockade of Mantua by the French a less vivid recollection; the more deeply impressed because his mother, in the absence of her husband, was obliged to fly for refuge to Parma, where she took shelter with her own mother, the Marchioness Malaspina della Bastia.

When the blockade of Mantua was raised, the Countess Arrivabene begged an audience of General Buonaparte, in order to save her husband's goods from sequestration. The General had taken up his quarters in the Ducal Palace of Mantua. The mother and her three sons were admitted into his presence; and, says the Count, in the "Memoirs" which he pens in his declining years:—

"I seem to have Napoleon now before my eyes. 'Small of stature, spare; with hair which appeared in a few scattered locks upon his forehead, and then fell on either side of his eager, haggard countenance; tied behind in a pigtail, and secured with a silver pin, the universal fashion of the time. So that, in this respect, I, a child of ten years old, resembled the General.'"

Three years later, in 1802, circumstances again brought Arrivabene into the presence of the great general. His father was chosen by the Mantuans as their representative at the Council of Lyons, summoned by Napoleon to determine the question of the Cisalpine Republic. Giovanni, with his two brothers, accompanied their father on his journey. The Council was fixed for the first days of 1802. It behoved the travellers to start from Mantua in the middle of the December of 1801, for the passage of the Cenis lay between them and Lyons. The journey was not likely to be forgotten by the young travellers, who rejoiced in the novel scenes and incidents, and despised the accompanying hardships of bitter cold, and slow progress over the rough ascent, in days when there was neither railway above nor below to speed them on their way.

Having reached Lyons, Arrivabene describes the saddening effect of the closed churches, which none might enter, and the difficulty they had in refraining from those marks of outward courtesy inherent in well-born Italians, lest they should be taken for aristocrats. Every evening Count Arrivabene took his sons to the meeting of the Council. There was another meeting with Napoleon. " Are the taxes more heavy in Italy than they used to be ?" asked the First Consul of Count Arrivabene. "' Sire ' (thus anticipating his future destiny), my father replied, 'they weigh far more heavily upon the people.' "

And yet Napoleon was, in truth, the founder of the liberties of Italy, and during the short existence of the Cisalpine Republic the Italians enjoyed at least a semblance of freedom. It is impossible to say how long that semblance would have endured ; but when, at the fall of Buonaparte, they were again placed under the rule of their Austrian tyrants, they sighed for the larger liberty and impartial justice of the Code Napoléon.

Shortly after the return of Count Arrivabene from Lyons Murat was sent to take up his quarters in the Palace of Mantua. When the Count went to pay his court to the French general, Murat asked for the loan of the young Giovanni "that he might make a soldier of him," a proposal which was declined ; happily, perhaps, for the future fortunes of the young Count.

Arrivabene, in a few paragraphs, gives us a brief summary of Napoleon's dominion in Italy, the war of 1809 between France and Austria, in which France came off victorious, and the surrender of the unhappy Tyrolese patriot Andrew Hofer, of whose entry into Mantua Arrivabene was eye-witness. Then came the news of the retreat from Moscow, in 1812, which gave a rude shock to the dominion in Italy. Eugène Beauharnais struggled during the following year, 1813, to make a stand for the French cause in Lombardy; but when Napoleon's power collapsed in 1814 he disbanded his army and gave up the point. The Austrians lost no time in re-entering Lombardy, and Arrivabene's heart died within him when he saw them march back into Mantua. A pause in the "Memoirs" gives an interesting sketch of the social state of Italy at the time. There was a cold splendour, but little comfort, about the palaces of the rich; insufficiently warmed, with floors either bare or covered here and there with scraps of matting. The only carpet Arrivabene had even heard of was known to exist in the house of the Marchese Tullo Guerrieri, a brilliant leader of social life at that time. The discomfort and misery of the lower classes may easily be imagined. The public streets and roadways were in a deplorable condition of dirt and darkness, and until the French introduced a system of illumination with lanterns there was no light save an occasional stray torch borne by a servant before the great "signori." The gutters from the roofs poured water in torrents upon the carriages, or upon the heads of the unfortunate foot-passengers. But if the luxuries and comforts of life were scanty, there was no lack of variety of entertainment among the pleasure-loving Italians. The theatres were always open, with a separate "sala" for games of chance, so that when the audience had listened to the last notes of Marchesi's beautiful voice they might find fresh food for excitement in gambling. Once only Arrivabene was induced to play by a French general, who lent him a louis-d'or to start with. That was soon lost, and nine others shared in the same fate; but, says the biographer, the loss was gain to the gambler, because, like Dante's player at zara, "tristo impara " (he sadly learnt) a never to be forgotten lesson, not to venture again upon a game of chance.

As to politics, parties were equally divided between France and Austria ; and so little universal at that time was the hatred of Austria that there were many who preferred the Austrian domination to that of France, prophesying, even at the summit of Napoleon's power, his fall, and the return of the Austrians to Italy. But in a few months the Austrian Government began again the system of tyranny which made it for ever hateful in the eyes of the Italians. The first victims were officers of the disbanded army of Napoleon, who were arrested under the pretext of having plotted against the State. The same vague accusation was destined one day to serve against Arrivabene, and to be the means of condemning him to a year's imprisonment ; but at this period, from 1815 to 1821, he was free to dedicate the first ardour of his youth to those schemes of improvement in which he delighted. " Pleasure," he exclaims, " a man may derive from various sources, all more or less tainted and soiled, but the draught of happiness can only be drawn from that purest fountain of all—benevolence ! "

This golden sentence was the rule of his life. After travelling through Italy, and founding everywhere schools of mutual improvement, he established himself at Zaita, his property about six miles distant from Mantua, where, during 1815, a year of great misery in Italy, he employed labour freely, and from the beginning of November, 1815, to the spring of 1816 he went out of the city every day laden with a small bag of money, with which to pay the labourers their week's earnings. After nineteen years' exile, on returning to the neighbourhood of Zaita, the door was suddenly burst open by a peasant woman, who threw herself on her knees before him and showered blessings upon him for having given her husband work in those days of famine.

Between the return of the Austrians and the year 1820 the spirit of patriotism had developed itself in Italy, and the prominent figures already so familiar to us in the life of Sir A. Panizzi—of Gonfalonieri, Silvio Pellico, Filippo Ugoni—to say nothing of the classical bards, Niccolini and Vincenzo Monti, were Arrivabene's friends and associates. Monti was his guest at his villa of La Zaita; so also was Silvio Pellico. This last piece of hospitality cost him very dear, for it was the only accusation the Austrians could prove against Arrivabene when they arrested him as a "Carbonaro" in the May of 1821. The horror of that moment was still present to Arrivabene's mind when, nearly forty years afterwards, he describes it in his "Memoirs:"—

"It was two o'clock in the afternoon, the last Friday in May. I was at Zaita, and a few friends were with me. It was so very hot that I had retired to my room, and was surreptitiously taking an afternoon siesta. My house is only removed by about a hundred yards from the high-road which runs from Mantua to Modena. The road is hollow, so that the sound of approaching wheels makes a great noise. I heard the carriages coming while they were yet a long way off; the noise came nearer. I ran to the window, and I saw two carriages coming up to the entrance-drive. I ran hurriedly downstairs, and found five persons in the hall, one in full uniform with his sword by his side. I understood in an instant who they were, why they came, and yet I asked them what they wanted. One of them replied, 'We are Government messengers, and we have instructions to examine your papers.' I took them all over the house; there were no papers to be found, for there were none there. 'Now,' said the first spokesman, 'you must accompany us to Mantua, as we have orders to search your house at Mantua also.' I offered them dinner; they declined. I had refreshments brought up, and these they accepted. Either from an exaggerated idea of the duties of hospitality, or because I felt a pride in showing myself superior to my misfortunes, or from a wish to contrast my conduct with their ungracious office, or from all these motives combined, I made a point of treating them as guests, regardless of the nature of their errand. I assumed an open, cheerful manner; but I suffered much, and now, after the lapse of many years, I can never recall that moment without a shudder."

The search among the papers at Mantua, which Arrivabene had contemplated without alarm, feeling sure of his innocence, had an unfortunate result, and upon some trifling pretext he was informed that he would have to go to Venice to take his trial for "Carboneria." Silvio Pellico tells us that the first night in prison is a most horrible experience ;[1] and all night long the unhappy Arrivabene tried in vain to gather comfort from the reflection that he knew nothing of " Carboneria," and had never had anything to do with it, little thinking that a chance conversation with Silvio Pellico, long since forgotten, was enough to condemn him. His faithful servant counselled flight while his jailers were, or feigned to be, asleep ; but Arrivabene would not consent. At four in the morning they pursued their journey, and midnight found them in Venice. The result of the trial next day can be easily guessed ; Salvotti, of evil fame, was the principal of the four judges appointed to try the case.

One ground of complaint was the school at Mantua, which Arrivabene was accused of having founded for the purpose of instructing the people in revolutionary ideas. This he emphatically denied. He had, indeed, closed it in obedience to the Austrian authorities. After an interrogatory which had lasted nearly five hours he learnt the real "head and front of his offending." " Pellico told you, when he was with you at Zaita, that he was a Carbonaro. It was your duty to inform the Government; you did not do so : you are therefore guilty of the crime of concealment." Then the few words which Arrivabene had exchanged with Pellico when at Zaita flashed across his mind. A cooler and more experienced person would have remained silent, but this course never entered the prisoner's head. "What!" he exclaimed with passionate eagerness, " betray my friend and my guest ! What laws are these? The most wicked that could be devised. Condemn me if you will, but were I a thousand times in the same case I would do the same thing." Imprisonment followed as a matter of course upon this speech, and Arrivabene was consigned to the prison of San Michele at Murano. During the hours of captivity he had time

[1] " Le mie Prigioni," c. iii. p. 6.

to reflect upon the cause of it, and many times the tormenting conjecture assailed him as to how the Commission could have extracted from Silvio Pellico the conversation which, apparently harmless in itself, had been attended with so disastrous a result.

When the two friends met at Turin years afterwards, Silvio Pellico having been released from his ten years' imprisonment and Arrivabene having returned from exile, the same question rose to his lips, but he was restrained by a feeling of delicacy that it was for Pellico to take the initiative, he having been unwittingly the cause of Arrivabene's imprisonment. Pellico did not touch upon the question, and so the mystery remained unsolved.

It would be idle to compare the sufferings of these two victims of Austrian tyranny. Those who are familiar with "Le mie Prigioni" will remember that for more than eight of Pellico's ten years' imprisonment he was condemned to hard labour. The imprisonment of Arrivabene lasted barely a year ; nor were the discomforts of San Michele to be named with the burning heat of the "Piombi" or the horrors of the fortress at Spielberg. The island of San Michele, whither he was conveyed, is close to the larger island of Murano. There had once been a convent at San Michele. and this was the building now converted into a prison. The cells of the prisoners were ill-lighted, ill-ventilated, and yet with apertures large enough to let in the rain, so that at the first shower the floor became a lake. Abundance of insects of all descriptions and scorpions swarmed everywhere, and fetid vapours arose from the mud of the lagune at low tide. All these discomforts became serious calamities as the imprisonment prolonged itself from days to weeks, from weeks to months. For some time Arrivabene suffered from the close confinement to his room, but at length, as his health became affected by it, he was allowed to walk in the garden accompanied by his jailer.

The young Count Laderchi and Maroncelli became afterwards his companions in misfortune, and the hours of their captivity were enlivened by their daily prescribed walk in the garden. It was on one of these occasions—December 10, 1821—when all three were walking to-

gether accompanied by the jailer, that a message came for
Arrivabene, to say that the president of the Commission
had arrived in the island and had asked for him. His
companions prophesied good news, and their prophecy
came true. "You have been acquitted," were the joyful
words which fell on Arrivabene's ears; "you are free,
and may leave the island as soon as you please."

Arrivabene knew how to moderate his joy in the
presence of his less fortunate companions; nor would he
hastily abandon them in their captivity. He spent the
remainder of the day and night a voluntary prisoner, and
the next day parted with them, promising to return that
evening again from Venice and to obtain permission to
dine with them. He kept his word, procured the best
dinner that could be got, and returned laden with books
to cheer their solitude. Doubtless the recollection of this
delicate kindness was present to Maroncelli during his
frightful sufferings at Spielberg, so eloquently recorded by
Pellico.[2]

His return to Mantua was made the occasion for great
festivities; friends, relations, and fellow-citizens all combined to do him honour, and even the Austrian general
Mayer expressed a wish to see him. At Milan also he
met with the same enthusiastic reception, and people who
had never known him personally now desired to be presented to him. Among these was the illustrious Manzoni,
who warmly congratulated him upon his release. It was
the year of Napoleon's death. The soul-stirring lines
of "Il Cinque Maggio," the noblest funeral elegy ever
written, were at that time upon everybody's lips; Arrivabene heard them with awe-struck admiration in Venice.
A few years later, when he read for the first time the
account of "Fra Cristoforo" in "I promessi Sposi," he
tells us that he rushed round the room like a maniac,
exclaiming at intervals, "It is too beautiful! *far* too
beautiful!"

From Mantua he hastened to the beloved villa La
Zaita; but his stay there was brief, and disturbed by the

---

[2] "Mic Prigioni," pp. 156, 157. It is interesting to know that
Arrivabene saw Maroncelli in Paris twelve years afterwards, on his
release from Spielberg.

warning voices of his friends, who reported daily new arrests of members of the Liberal party, and urged him to fly the country while there was yet time. At last the arrest of one of his immediate companions forced him to perceive his own danger, and he tore himself from his home without waiting to be arrested there a second time. Scalvini, just released from prison at Brescia, and Camillo Ugoni joined him *en route*, and their flight, like that of Sir Anthony Panizzi, was a series of hairbreadth escapes. Like Panizzi, when they reached Paris they found they had not made their escape too soon. Within a fortnight of their arrival in Paris Arrivabene read in the *Gazzetta di Milano* the accusation against him of high treason, and that he was cited to appear within sixty days, under pain of sequestration of all his goods. The threat was eventually carried into execution, and followed by the announcement of the sentence of death. Arrivabene's character never showed to greater advantage than in the fortitude which he displayed under this adversity. Far from spending his time in useless lamentations, he turned his mind to extract good out of evil. In his "Memoirs" he dwells, in a remarkable paragraph, upon the fact that he owes to these very misfortunes his subsequent fame and success.[3]

The exile of Arrivabene dates from April, 1822. At the end of the year 1823 he made his way over to England, "the only secure and real refuge for political exiles." Even the well-known resort of foreigners, Leicester Square, was too dear for his reduced circumstances, and he took up his abode in the suburbs, "where the rays of the sun were less obscured by coal-smoke," and where the close vicinity of Ugo Foscolo and Santa Rosa[4] offered another attraction. He is struck by the contrasts of character between these two men : the former gloomy and vindictive, the latter frank, affectionate, and gay.

[3] "Memorie della mia Vita," pp. 111, 112.
[4] Santa Rosa, an illustrious Piedmontese statesman, born 1783, author of "History of Piedmontese Revolution." Fled to England, 1822. Left England, 1822, to fight for the cause of Greek independence. Killed in battle, 1828.

The climate of England in December made a melancholy impression upon the Italian exiles, and a yellow fog, "thick. dense, the colour of an orange, so dark that the traffic was suspended outside and candles lighted inside the houses in the middle of the day, filled them with despair." The little sash windows, "constructed on the plan of a guillotine," pleased them no better ; nor the post, distributed in those days to the sound of a hand-bell, people rushing down to the doors to receive their letters ; nor the watchmen in their long grey cloaks, with their incessant cries all through the night. Moreover the sensitive Italian nature was keenly alive to the want of courtesy constantly displayed towards foreigners by the English of the class among which the exiles were of necessity thrown. At that time, as Arrivabene observes, a foreigner only represented a Frenchman, or rather French *dog*, to the English mind. A general gloom and depression seemed to go hand in hand with this rough discourtesy, and he seeks in vain to account for the term "merry," which he believed to have been at one time associated with England. At first Arrivabene was friendless, but a letter of introduction from Sismondi, whom he had known at Geneva, procured him the acquaintance of William Smith, the friend of Wilberforce, who had interested himself in the great cause of the suppression of the slave trade.[5]

The members of William Smith's large family (among whom was Mrs. Nightingale, mother of Florence Nightingale) vied with one another in showing the exile that courtesy which hitherto he had failed to find ; and, through their means, he was introduced into the class of society to which he naturally belonged. He became a member of the Athenæum Club and of the club of political economists, where he was constantly thrown into the society of the great authorities upon his favourite study— Took, McCulloch, and the elder Mill. Franklin was at that time the lion of the day. Arrivabene had the good fortune to see the hero, and describes him as small, bald-headed, and with eyes of penetrating brilliancy.

[5] "Life of Wilberforce," by Bishop of Oxford, pp. 80, 106, 226.

The country life of England was next the object of his study, and it is interesting to read his account of the journey by coach from London to Norwich : the four fiery horses, each with a groom ready to remove the horse-cloth which covered each animal at a given signal, in readiness for one simultaneous start. Norwich was chosen for the first point because of an invitation from Mr. Gurney to meet his sister, the famous Mrs. Fry. From thence to Holkham, to see the domain of the celebrated agriculturist, Earl of Leicester, described by Arrivabene as "il Signor Cook." A letter of introduction from his friend William Smith procured him admission to this one of the most " splendide dimore dell' aristocrazia Inglese ;" and a drive all through of the domain with its mistress gave him an impression English country life which he was not likely easily to forget. The rich produce of the land in those more palmy days of farming, the fat beasts and the air of general prosperity, the cottages of the tenantry, but above all the kind interest taken in the tenants by the landlords, inspired Arrivabene with wonder and admiration.

The visit to Holkham was repeated in November, when the Count was invited to join a shooting-party arranged for the Duke of Gloucester's amusement. The Duke of Gloucester observed when Arrivabene was presented to him, "I knew Goufalonieri: he was, like you, a revolutionary character ; but we do not make much account of foreign politics, and when people who are presented to us are of good birth and education we give them a hearty welcome." The wonders of the Black Country and the manufacturing towns, the next points in Arrivabene's progress through England, caused him to remark that if the surface of England's soil was abounding in wealth, far greater was the treasure which lay concealed beneath it. In Scotland, Edinburgh, Glasgow, and Newhaven were visited by him in turn ; and returning by Liverpool, he was particularly struck by the taste for letters, science, and art displayed by the great merchants in the midst of their all-absorbing occupation.

His travels revealed to him four of the sources of England's greatness : agriculture, mines, industry, and commerce. He visited the two Universities of Oxford and

Cambridge. The first he describes as Tory "par excellence" and conservative; the second as Whig, liberal, and progressive. He was amazed that, notwithstanding the amount of liberty of action accorded to the undergraduates, they should study so persistently, especially Greek and Latin, even attaining to writing verses in the classical languages.

It was well that he had so much to distract his thoughts, for sad news greeted him on his return to London. His brother Giberto was dead, and the Austrians had condemned to death Gonfalonieri, Castiglia, Pallavicini, and Borsieri, although their sentence was commuted into penal servitude for fifteen years. For those who had refused to appear, among whom was Arrivabene, there was no commutation, and their names were affixed to the gallows by the executioner; but he was not charged, like Sir Anthony Panizzi, with the expenses of his own execution. Happily for Arrivabene, the extreme depression of spirits caused by this news was removed by the arrival of his brother Giuseppe, who brought him, at his own imminent peril, some money to live upon at a moment when he was nearly destitute.

Arrivabene resided another year in England (1825), and devoted himself to the study of those large works of charity and beneficence which had, in fact, impressed him more than any other feature of English life. He wrote a book describing them, entitled "Società di Beneficenza della Città di Londra," in order to make them known in his own country, and the book was afterwards published in Italy.

In the autumn of that year he again employed his holiday in exploring England. He rambled through the Isle of Wight, Devonshire, Cornwall, Wales, and Kent, in most places sharing the "villeggiature" of those English friends who had shown him kindness when in London, and who extended their hospitality by asking him to visit them in the country. Every visit that he paid confirmed him in his high opinion of the dignified retirement of the English country life, while he looked upon the residence of the English landowners upon their estates as another main source of the riches and prosperity of the country.

Although not reduced to the extremity of poverty endured by Sir Anthony Panizzi, he knew too well what it was to be straitened in means, and to be driven by degrees to seek cheaper and cheaper lodgings, where the dirt and squalor hourly offended his refined and fastidious taste.

In the September of 1826, the French Government having relaxed their severity towards the proscribed Italians, Arrivabene bethought himself of trying his fortunes again in Paris, though it was with reluctance that he bade adieu to his English friends. All his life long he cherished the recollection of the hospitality so delicately offered and so liberally maintained which had greeted him when in England.

At Paris he found a friend in the lawyer Teste, who tried, without success, to rescue some portion of Arrivabene's sequestrated property ; and afterwards in "la famiglia Arconati," who received him with so much kindness that he looked upon them as his adopted family. Through their means he became acquainted with Guizot, and attended the course of lectures on political economy given by G. B. Say, a man who, in his unflinching frankness, did not fear to offend the great Napoleon when First Consul, and forfeited his post in consequence.

The Marquess Arconati was the means of introducing him to Belgium, where he afterwards spent many years of unremitting labour in promoting the welfare of his adopted country, and was for some time the guest of the Arconati, with many other distinguished Italians in a similar plight to himself, such as Giacento Collegno, "Poerio," (father of the famous Poerio), and Gioberti, whose remarkable works on philosophy he diligently studied. Van de Weyer, then a young lawyer of Louvain, was also among the guests. Arrivabene relates as an anecdote of Gioberti that he would often walk bareheaded in winter during the falling snow, to cool the burning fever of his brain, hard pressed by long study. In the winter of 1828 Arrivabene returned to Paris, and was witness of the review of the Garde Nationale by Charles X., which delayed, but did not avert, the Revolution of 1830. The winter of 1829 he spent peacefully in Belgium, "never once molested by the sight of a gendarme," and early in the spring of 1830 he went again to England, to collect new materials for the second volume of his book, which had already made itself a name.

His peaceful life in Belgium was disturbed by the Revolution of 1830, which he describes with the vivacity of an eye-witness. There were great hopes on the part of the exiled Italians that the successful and successive revolutions at Paris and Brussels in 1830 would not be without their effect upon Italian affairs, and Arrivabene set off in the dead of the winter of 1831 for Geneva, to consult Peregrino Rossi, the most far-seeing of the exiled Italian Liberals. But Rossi saw nothing to be hoped for from the cold, selfish policy of Louis Philippe ; and Arrivabene returned to Brussels to prosecute his labours in the cause of political economy.

It was at this time, by means of an introduction from M. Van de Weyer, the Belgian ambassador, that he became, acquainted with Nassau Senior, who had been put on a Commission to inquire into the method of providing for, the poorer classes in foreign countries ; an acquaintance which rapidly ripened into friendship, and was most fruitful in advantage to Arrivabene. The second volume of the book was published in 1832, and was quickly followed by other works of the same class, one of which, a statistical account of the little commune at Gaesbek, gives a fair average account of the agrarian condition of Belgium. This last work had been prompted by his new friend, as an assistance to his own researches ; it was written in French by Arrivabene, but afterwards translated by Senior, communicated to the Commission, and engrafted in one of the Acts of the English Parliament passed in 1833.

Through M. Van de Weyer, the Belgian ambassador, Arrivabene became known to King Leopold, and was directed to present himself at Court, where he was received with every mark of distinguished favour. And thus closed, in 1832, the fourth year of his exile. Still his goods remained under sequestration, and it was only through the generosity of two Milanese bankers, who lent him money on the faith of their possible recovery, that he was able to subsist at all.

U

His next work was to translate into French the numerous MSS. of the lectures on political economy by his friend Senior, and for this purpose he made another expedition to England. He arrived to find his friend Van de Weyer on his way to an immense fortune; about to marry the only daughter of "il Signor Bedst"—*Bates.* Having obtained an introduction to Lord and Lady Lansdowne, he was received with a kind hospitality, which was renewed on the occasion of his third visit to England a few years later. It was then that he made the acquaintance of Archbishop Whately, who had succeeded Mr. N. Senior in the Professorship of Political Economy at Oxford. Arrivabene was deeply impressed with his learning, but was quite unable to understand the humour of the "Historic Doubts relative to Napoleon Buonaparte." The author he considers "un poco originale" for publishing a book to prove that Napoleon had never existed!

The year 1838 dawned more favourably for the Italian exiles. Gonfalonieri had been released from twelve years' hard labour at Spielberg; the Emperor of Austria published an amnesty at Milan; and Arrivabene (in spite of the disheartening rumour that he had been excluded from it) hastened to Magdeni, on the borders of the Austrian dominions, in the hope of obtaining the formal leave to emigrate which would relieve his goods from sequestration. After two months of anxious waiting the welcome permission to emigrate arrived. and the sequestration was removed. His property—much diminished in value, it is true, and in a pitiable plight—was restored to him. But he was still an exile, with little chance of being able to return to his country; so, though his heart still yearned towards his native land, he asked to become naturalized in the land of his adoption, a request which was immediately granted. His continued interest in the welfare of his poorer brethren was rewarded with the honour of being chosen one of the four vice-presidents of the Congress of Economists, the first of its kind, which was held at Brussels in 1847, when Free Trade was one of the burning questions of the day.

Once or twice after the removal of the sequestration of

his goods Arrivabene hovered on the borders of his native country. In 1843 he visited Piedmont, and compared notes with Cavour, with whose writings on political economy he was already acquainted. Cavour was then a young stripling, living in his father's house, engaged in agricultural experiments, nor did any one foresee at that time the great position in store for him. Arrivabene made acquaintance also with Cesare Balbo, distinguished not only for his wise policy as a statesman, but for his literary and historical works, and, with his assistance, drew up an interesting analysis of the state of Piedmont at that time, which he communicated to a Brussels paper. He dwells upon the religious character of the King, Charles Albert, and the influence of the Jesuits at Court, to whom he applies Manzoni's lines—

> " Segno d' immensa invidia
> E d' indomato amor,"

adding that, for his own part, he would limit that influence to preaching the truth of the Gospel, laying aside all political considerations.

In 1847 he returned again to Turin, and found the King, statesmen, and people making rapid strides towards the great political movement of 1848. It is not necessary to dwell upon the excitement, the alternations of hope and fear, which agitated the breasts of the Italian exiles while Charles Albert embarked the fortunes of his little kingdom in the gigantic enterprise of freeing Italy from the Austrian domination. But that fear dominated in the end may be gathered from Arrivabene's letter from Brussels in 1848.[6] His prudent calculations as to the little probability of success attending the Italian arms seem tame and cold when compared with subsequent events, which show that a handful of volunteers did indeed accomplish what he had pronounced to be an impossibility. However, for the time being the Austrian victory of Novara quenched all hopes of liberty in Italy, although Arrivabene was a true prophet when a year later (1850) he wrote from Turin :—

---

[6] " Memorie della mia Vita," pp. 257-60.

"In spite of all her misfortunes Piedmont still holds the future in her grasp. The State has not lost vigour, the voice of authority can still be heard, and religion still holds its sway over the people. The King is respected and loved, and he deserves to be so. In spite of a neglected education he is good, loyal, and upright, and his word may be implicitly trusted. He is not the man to overthrow his country or to betray his trust."

With the exception of a few occasional visits to Italy, Arrivabene still continued his residence at Brussels. In 1850 he was invited to take part in the provincial administration as a member for the canton of Lennik St. Quentin, in Brabant. The exile gladly accepted the honour which would serve as an apprenticeship for those happier times when he would sit as a senator in the administration of his own free and independent country. This event was nearer at hand than he anticipated, but the steps by which it was accomplished are too well known for it to be necessary to recapitulate them here, except so far as they are connected with the subject of this memoir. In 1852 he received through the hand of Count Cavour the distinction of the Croce Mauriziana, not only in recognition of his indefatigable labours in promoting the welfare of the people by just principles of political economy, but because the King wished to give some proof of his high esteem for an Italian who had done honour to his country, when an exile from it, at a period and in circumstances of the greatest difficulty and danger.

In 1859 he became an Italian senator, and from that time took an active part in every important discussion, proposing various laws for the welfare of the State, and bringing constantly to the debate the fruits of an enlightened and scientific experience and all the weight of a mind trained in the principles of true liberty, and sustained by an unwavering rectitude of purpose. He was appointed Ambassador Extraordinary to Belgium in 1866, to represent the King of Italy on the occasion of the succession of Leopold II. to the throne of Belgium. On his return to Italy he had the joy of witnessing the freedom of his native city of Mantua, where he was welcomed with rapturous applause. From 1866 to 1880 he continued, on behalf of his native country, those unremitting labours in promoting the welfare of the poor which had occupied him when in exile. In spite of his advanced age he made many a journey to Rome to take part in the duties of the Senate. Here he made, in January 1880, his last speech, warning the Government on the subject of not disturbing the finance of the State. Long after this he was still to be seen every week at Milan, presiding at the Board of Mantuan Railway, every one pausing in the streets and coffee-houses to admire the noble old man, who bore in his countenance the stamp of his eventful career.

There you might read, as in a book, the result of years devoted to study, great recollections, an ardent love of liberty, a childlike simplicity of character, a large and universal benevolence of heart. While preserving intact the great principles of religion and the love of lawful authority, he sought to loosen the trammels of the past century ; so that the new era might embrace with a larger grasp those wise and prudent reforms which promote the welfare and prosperity of nations. The great lesson which his residence in England had taught him was' always present to his mind, and never more so than when he strove, in his turn, to impress it upon his own country in the hour of her triumph and of her freedom ; so that when, at the ripe age of ninety-three, Italy laid him to his rest, she had cause to mourn the loss of one of the wisest and truest patriots who had ever embraced her noble cause.

EDOARDO FUSCO.

THE life of Edoardo Fusco adds another page to the interesting history of the struggle for Italian independence, and the efforts made by individuals to promote that cause, when it seemed a hopeless dream, should not be forgotten, because " Italia Una " has now firmly taken her place as a kingdom among the European States. But, meanwhile, the current of events sweeps on its way; the outlines of a past, scarcely twenty years old, are already fading from recollection; perhaps a few more years will suffice to efface them as completely as the grave of Alaric the Goth, over which the waters of the Bussento have now rolled for fourteen centuries their foaming torrent. To these fading memories belong the pathetic narrative of Sylvio Pellico's captivity, the sufferings of the Neapolitan prisoners on whose behalf. Mr. Gladstone made his eloquent appeal; the passionate strains of Aleardi's lyre now hushed in death ; the noble efforts of such statesmen as Cesare Balbo, D'Azeglio, and Cavour; —even the King himself, the Rè Galantuomo, whom no temptation could turn from his plighted word.[1]   Still, as

---

[1] It is not perhaps generally known that the King owed his popular title of Rè Galantuomo to his firm adherence to the statute entitled " Legge Siccardi," which dealt with ecclesiastical reforms, and was, at the time, a most unpopular measure. But once convinced of its justice, and having given it the royal sanction, he remained proof against the threats of the Vatican and the open disapprobation of the Piedmontese Episcopate. When the turmoil was at its height D'Azeglio observed to the King, " There are so few instances of ' Rè Galantuomini ' in history, that it would be well to add to their number."   " Then am I to play the part of Rè Galantuomo ? " asked the King with a smile.   " Your Majesty has sworn to observe the statute ; your Majesty in so doing has considered the whole of Italy and not Piedmont alone.   Let us continue in the same course, to prove that in this world a King, no less than a private individual, must keep his word when it has once been

one by one the champions of Italy are gathered to their rest, the interest in their gallant struggle for liberty is renewed, and the page of history is turned back to trace the steps by which the battle was fought and won.

Edoardo Fusco, the subject of this review, was a native of Southern Italy. He was born in 1824, at Trani in Apulia, of wealthy parents, and of how ancient a stock may be determined—the biographer says with pride—by the Ode of Horace to Aristæus Fuscus,[2] and his epistle to the same much-valued friend and companion.

> " These lines behind Vacuna's fane I penned,
> Sincerely blest, but that I want my friend." [3]

From early youth the restless fervour of genius showed itself in the descendant of this ancient lineage. Impatient of provincial education, he implored his parents to send him to study at Naples, and, finding his entreaties vain, he formed, for the special purpose of studying the language and history of his native country, a sort of literary society, to which none were to be admitted but those who endeavoured to speak the Italian language in all its purity. Fearful lest the suspicions of the police should be aroused, his parents put a stop to even this mild attempt at patriotism ; and Fusco, vexed, disappointed, and hopeless as to the future, took the extreme step of quitting his Neapolitan home, in order that he might indulge, unrestrained by parental fears and cautions, his patriotic zeal. Already he thought he could discern the future of Italy dawning in the dark horizon, and before his father and mother could recover from the shock of his departure, they learned that he had enlisted as a volunteer in the Liberal cause. His letter to them, while it implored their forgiveness, and their blessing on his self-chosen career, left them no hope of ever recalling him. In the first heat of patriotism, chafing against any restraints which might be put upon it, sustained by all the boundless hopes which belong to the age of twenty-

given." " There does not seem to me any difficulty in following that course," replied the King. " E il Rè Galantuomo l' abbiamo," observes D'Azeglio.—" La Vita ed il Regno di V. E. di Savoia," Massari, p. 107.

[2] Lib. i. Od. xxii.; Epistle x. lib. i.   [3] Ibid.

three, he may have thought that the end justified the
means, and that he was making a noble sacrifice of
private affection upon the altar of his country. But
eleven years afterwards the natural feelings which he had
tried to overcome, revived in all their strength, with the
added poignancy of remorse, when the news reached him
in his exile of the death of that father from whose roof
he had fled, and whose face he never saw again.

Meanwhile the insurrection of 1848 broke out in Italy,
and the young patriot embarked in it heart and soul.
The hopes raised by the temporary success of the Sicilian
insurrection, which caused the King of Naples to tremble
on his throne, only made the subsequent failure a more
cruel disappointment, and the cause appear more hopeless
than ever, while the patriots were again compelled to seek
refuge in exile from the vengeance of the irritated Bourbon dynasty. Fusco was far too deeply compromised for
it to be possible for him to remain in Italy. His escape
was contrived only just in time—for the police were
actually on his track-—by the lawyer Pisanello, and other
friends, who, through the British Ambassador, Sir R.
Temple, obtained a temporary refuge for him on board the
English frigate *Prince Regent*, anchored in the Bay of
Sta. Lucia. From thence he was transferred to a French
steamer *en route* for Malta, and eventually landed at
Corfu.

It was now evident to Fusco that for some years to
come the pen, rather than the sword, would prove the
most effectual weapon for the service of his country. The
persuasive language of verse readily lent itself to a cause
which had inspired the genius of Dante and Petrarch,
and had ever since been the theme of the Italian poet.
Fusco soon won for himself the sympathy of the lettered
inhabitants of the Ionian Islands—a sympathy which
ripened into enthusiasm when deeds of modern Grecian
heroism became, in their turn, fitting topics for the young
and enthusiastic poet. The first of these poems, entitled
"Il Salmista Suliotta," took for an argument the heroic
defence of their country by the Suliots against the Pasha
of Janina. After a resistance of fifteen years, the very
women taking part in the strife, they retreated to the

Ionian Islands (1803). It was not till the year 1820 that they were able to return to their country, when their old enemy, Ali Pasha, finding himself closely pressed by the Turks, was glad to purchase the assistance of the gallant mountaineers. The English reader will be familiar with Byron's allusion to this incident, when, after describing [4]

> "Stern Albania's hills, .
> Dark Suli's rocks, and Pindus' inland peak,
> Robed half in mist, bedewed with snowy rills,
> Arrayed in many a dun and purple streak;"

he speaks of Albania's chief:

> " Whose dread command
> Is lawless law ; for with a bloody hand
> He sways a nation, turbulent and bold ;
> *Yet here and there some daring mountain-band*
> *Disdain his power, and from their rocky hold*
> *Hurl their defiance far, nor yield, unless to gold."*

The title of " Salmista Sulio ta," chosen by Fusco, is explained by his having related the narrative in a style imitative of the Biblical Psalmody. The poem was translated into Greek, *con amore*, by Giorgio Zallocosta, the laureate ; and, the Greek Parliament, looking upon it in the light of a work likely to encourage patriotic feeling, promoted its sale by the immediate purchase of 250 copies. A no less popular poem was " Il Fillelleno di Sfacteria," suggested by the tomb of Santa Rosa, a spot visited by Fusco with lively interest while travelling through the Peloponnesus. " Sfacteria " was the name of the rock on which that accomplished gentleman died, and many incidents of the battle were supplied to the poet by Maurocordato, the friend of Santa Rosa, who was by his side when he fell. Finally there appeared " I Canti Italo-Greci." The title alone would suggest the subject of this last poem without the Preface, which describes " two countries, but little removed from each other, stretching their sunny shores far into the blue waters of the Mediterranean, sharing a past of unrivalled greatness, drawn together by the common bond of present misfortune,

---

[4] " Childe Harold," ii. pp. 42—47.

and linked into a still closer union by the future hope of a common deliverance from bondage and oppression. " Italy and Greece," concludes the writer, with an enthusiasm unquenched by recent disaster—" Italy and Greece, already united by a threefold bond of intellect, valour, and patriotism, will one day find their place side by side at the great banquet of European nations." Such was the argument of the " Canti Italo-Greci," and it is a satisfactory reflection that Fusco lived to see the accomplishment of at least one-half of the sanguine prophecies of his youth. We will not inquire too closely whether the poetical reputation which Fusco acquired after the publication of these " Canti Italo-Greci" was not more to be ascribed to the spirit which inspired them than to any intrinsic poetical merit, an opinion which is confirmed by their author's own subsequent reference to them. But it will suffice to say, that during his stay in Greece, he was held in universal esteem by all the Liberal politicians and *letterati* of the time. Early in the year 1852 he visited Constantinople, and here another and wider field presented itself for literary labours, though of a very different kind. Setting aside politics, and forgetting for a while the elevating themes and heroic deeds of patriotism, he dismounted from his Pegasus and plodded over the comparatively prosaic grounds of philanthropy, with the same energy and zeal which had inspired his political efforts. This ready sympathy was soon enlisted on behalf not only of his own exiled countrymen, but of all the European colony in the cosmopolitan city : and he set himself eagerly to work to ameliorate their forlorn condition.

The result of his inquiries revealed to him the existence of a benevolent society, which went by the name of the Association Commerciale Artisane de Piété à Constantinople ; and, struck by the active, unostentatious labours of the society in all works of benevolence, he drew attention to it in a pamphlet, which was commented upon in terms of high praise by the *Echo de l'Orient.* The pamphlet touched upon the past miserable condition of the Europeans at Constantinople, which had first suggested the necessity of the creation of this society to M. Jacques Anderlich, whose name will be always remembered as a

benefactor amongst the poor of Constantinople; then
narrated the first beginnings of the association, the
obstacles which had to be surmounted, the opposition of
the rich, its various phases of administration: the foundation and ordering of the hospital, the admission of the
Sisters of Mercy, the foundation of schools for the
children, the financial success of the association in freeing
itself from all the debt incident to its growth. It concludes
by paying a high tribute to those who had first set on foot
this pious design. The author, who had the art of enlisting the sympathy of his readers by a clear and per-
spicuous style, received the formal thanks of the association for the good service rendered by his pamphlet, and
was at the same time urged to persevere in dedicating
his faculties to the solution of those great problems of
humanity—Poverty, Employment, and Education. When,
at the end of 1853, he was compelled, by the breaking
out of the Crimean War, to quit Constantinople for
London, he left behind him no inconsiderable reputation
as a writer, coupled with a grateful recollection of the
manner in which his talents had been employed.

But Fusco himself was by no means satisfied with his
literary labours, nor disposed to sit down content with
the laurels which he had won in the East, "terra che
dell' intelligenza è tomba." It is more in the capacity
of "the youth to fortune and to fame unknown" that,
on reaching England, he appeals for help to Giuseppe
Devincenzi, his countryman. Devincenzi was at Naples
in 1848, and had used his influence to forward the escape
of Fusco. Now friendless, and stranded in the great
city, the exile once more solicits his aid. Will he—of
whose generosity Fusco has already made proof, and
whose talents place him beyond the reach of petty envy
and jealousies—be his mentor and guide, and direct his
efforts in the right path, that he may produce some work
of real merit, and possible advantage to his country,
either in her present critical position or at some future
time? Fusco was not mistaken in his choice of a counsellor and guide; for, as soon as he had made himself
thoroughly master of the English language, he was encouraged by Devincenzi to write and publish various

articles upon Turkey. It was the time of the Crimean War, the subject was popular, and soon brought the writer into notice. The public gaze was fixed on the East ; and the "immense" (as Fusco rightly terms it) English Press, eager to give information on this topic to a people thirsting to receive it, was too glad to employ the pen of a writer just returned from the centre of interest. A sketch of Omar Pasha, published in the *Morning Chronicle* of March 7, 1854, was so highly thought of as to be reprinted, the following month, in *Bentley's Miscellany*, with the title of "Omar Pasha, and the Regeneration of Turkey." Thus his position became recognized as that of a fluent writer, whose residence in Constantinople had made him perfectly acquainted with Eastern manners and customs, and he was constantly employed to write on these subjects for newspapers and magazines. The material for these essays was supplied from his Italian papers on "La Turchia, ossia usi, costumi e credenze degli Osmani," arranged and published for the first time in 1877 by his widow.

" Constantinople," perhaps the most charming of all the attractive works of Amicis, with its little pictures, each perfect in itself, of the entrancing beauty of the Golden Horn when seen through the cypress-trees, and the stupendous grandeur of Santa Sofia, has spoilt the reader for the sober disquisitions of Fusco upon the possible reform of Turkish manners and customs. Our interest in these papers, carefully considered and well written though they are, is still further damped by the recollection that thirty years have elapsed since these reforms were contemplated, without one vestige of improvement being discernible in the country. Nevertheless, we must praise the courage of a writer who could open his pamphlet at the critical moment of the Crimean War with the following paragraph :—

" While a new conflict is preparing in the East, while the armies are marching and the fleets are sailing, while the diplomatists are contriving and the statesmen are discussing, while the friends of progress are hoping and the conspirators (either crowned or otherwise) are plotting, Turkey, that apple of discord, cast four centuries ago into the lap of Europe, exhausts her forces and her finance and her last remains of vitality in the effort to preserve an Empire which no human power can sustain, unless those great barriers are removed, which she still obstinately opposes to the march of civilization in Europe." [5]

The success of various articles on Turkey, of a less critical and more descriptive kind, contributed by Fusco to various English magazines, paved the way to other literary work. He was next employed to write on the more kindred subjects of the literature and politics of his own country. The first lecture which he wrote on "Italian Art and Literature before Giotto and Dante," was printed in *Macmillan's Magazine*, with a preface by Matthew Arnold.[6] The Essay is in itself a little work of art, and deserves a permanent position in literature. Commenting on this obscure and difficult portion of the history of Italy, the learned writer observes that "a period when literature is not the result of a public desire for books and novelties; a period when art is not a trade; a period when whatever emanates from the mind is but the spontaneous expression of the new civilization rising among a people who possessed the whole inheritance of ancient traditions, cannot fail to offer a wide field for speculation to a thinking and observing mind." " What is civilization?" he next asks, and borrows the answer from Dante: "Civilization is the development of the human faculties."

Thus guided, he divides the civilization of Italy into four distinct periods, and these periods are to be determined by their art and literature—' the two landmarks by which we can assign to nations their place in the history of the human intellect.' Then passing rapidly over the Etruscan civilization, lingering fondly over the Italo-Greek era of Magna Græcia—which perhaps recalled to him his own recent attempt to unite the destinies of the two classical nations in one common cause—glancing at the civilization of Rome, which he stigmatizes as the

---

[5] " La Turchia," &c., p. 1.
[6] *Macmillan's Magazine*, 1876-77, pp. 228-60.

nightmare of oppression, he begins his theme with the Italian civilization, the first-born child of Christianity which arose out of the ashes of Rome, to keep up the sacred fire of learning and of the arts by associating them with Christianity, the new reviving power of modern life. It was in the Catacombs that this new life began, where figures instinct, despite their clumsiness of form, with faith and devotional feeling, bear witness to an inward inspiration till then unknown to the sculptor or the artist. "There is a whole cycle of art and poetry," writes Fusco, "in the Catacombs. It is not poetry as yet perfect in form, precise in language, elegant in style, but there is in everything an effort to convey a sentiment under an image, to show the ideal in the reality, to give a symbol to architecture, to painting, to sculpture, and to the inscriptions." In illustration of this, he chooses several instances from Christian sculpture, then in its infancy, which, when it could present nothing to the eye worthy of the name, could still suggest to the imagination the idea of life by such emblems as the leaf to express its fragility; a boat with a sail the swift passage over the waves of this troublesome world, and the well-known Christian symbol of the fish.

As with art, so with literature; the influence of Christianity is traced to its source :—

" By the noble enthusiasm born of Christianity, everything is renewed and transformed. The science of Aristotle and Plato revives in the early fathers. The eloquence of Cicero and of the Gracchi adorn the homilies of St. Augustine and St. Jerome. The poetry of Virgil and Horace is renewed in the poems of Prudentius, the singer of the Catacombs in the hymns of St. Ambrose, and in numerous popular poets. The Pagan superstitions themselves give place to legends of miracles, tales of martyrdom, and histories of a supernatural kind."

These were to be succeeded by the golden legend of the Middle Ages, and the vision of the young monk of Monte Cassino, the immediate forerunner of the great poem which was to create the Italian language. In this manner Fusco carries his readers along with him through the obscurity, or, as Dante might call it, the " áer perso,"

of the dark ages, till he brings them to the very threshold
of the golden era of Italian literature and art. This essay
was the most considerable of Fusco's English compositions,
and it was remarkable not only for its deep research, but
for a fluency of style illustrating the writer's perfect
mastery over a foreign language. It is to be regretted
that another essay on Italian literature in the nineteenth
century should have remained unpublished.

Emboldened by the success of his lectures, he ventured
to point out to the editor of the "Encyclopædia
Britannica" several omissions as to Italian subjects,
which might be remedied in the forthcoming edition of
1857. His letter received the immediate attention of
the editor, Mr. James Carmichael, who was glad to
employ an Italian thoroughly acquainted with the history
and literature of his own country, who yet had no difficulty
in expressing himself in fluent and scholarly English. He
was requested to contribute articles upon the philosopher
Vico, Volta, and Paolo Sarpi—names which had hitherto
not found their way into the "Encyclopædia." Gioberti,
Leopardi, Giordani, Giusti, and many others, were also
entrusted to his pen. Besides this purely literary work,
he was employed for two years to write political articles
for the *Morning Chronicle*, the *Leader*, and the *Athenæum*,
on Italy, Italian institutions, and the misgovernment of
the Bourbon dynasty at Naples. It will readily be
imagined that Fusco eagerly availed himself of this
opportunity to plead the cause of his oppressed countrymen with passionate eloquence. Often and often does he
return to the charge, and at last is challenged by a corre-
spondent to declare what is the Liberal scheme for Italy,
to lay, in fact, before England the scheme of the future
they propose for their country.

Fusco retorts with vehement irony :—

"What would be the use of such a proceeding? Is it
likely that the hopes and aspirations of the Italians will
affect England at this moment? Would their feelings be
consulted in the future reorganization of the Peninsula?

"Supposing England were to co-operate with European
diplomacy in suggesting what reforms were necessary in
the government of Italy ; would the wishes of the Italians

be taken into consideration ?   No.   The promised ' Italy for the Italians ' would again be a byword, and the un- happy people held up to scornful derision, just as they were at Naples in 1799, in Sicily in 1812, at Genoa in 1814, in Lombardy and at Venice in 1815, in Piedmont and at Naples in 1820-21, and throughout Italy in 1848.

" The future of Italy can only be decided on the battle- field. A common hatred of Austria, of foreign domination, and of all the tyrants and petty tyrants of Italy, calls the people to arms ; and it is no longer possible that their hopes and aspirations can find expression in any other manner or have any other solution ; nor can the fusion of the various conflicting parties and opinions be effectual, but in the face of a common peril, in front of a common enemy.

" The columns of a newspaper, and of an English newspaper, are not the arena for such a combat."

Thus he wrote in 1857.   Three more years and Italy was once again embarked in the often renewed struggle which was at last to be crowned with success.   Fusco hastened to take part in the liberation of his country. This course involved no little personal sacrifice.   His reputation in England was made : he was Professor of Italian and Modern Greek at Eton and Queen's College ; another Professorship, that of the University of Dublin, was offered to him, but declined because his time was already too fully occupied – a wide literary career was open to him, but he cast it all aside, and did not let even the enforced separation from his wife [7] hold him back from his patriotic purpose.   His letters to his wife from the scene of action have the special interest of being written by an eye-witness of the great conflict.

In August, 1860, he writes :—

" Events follow one upon another with such frightful rapidity that the things of yesterday seem to have happened

---

[7] Fusco married, March 19. 1854, La Contessa Greca, Ida del Carretto, of an ancient noble Neapolitan family, who was widowed in early youth, and left friendless in London.   It is to this lady that we are indebted for the arrangement of her husband's papers, and for the sketch of his life.

long ago. No one attempts to disguise from themselves that these are moments of solemn and awful import; few nations have had a similar experience, but then few nations have wept for centuries as we have the bitter tears of oppression; therefore few nations have as good a right as we have to a future unclouded by perils and endless disappointments, and free from that tyranny which has so often worn the mask of liberty."

Later on we read of the frightful battle, the "Solferino" of Southern Italy, in the environs of Naples, when the soldiers on both sides "si batterono da leoni ed incontra-rono leoni;" and when the battle was finally won by 3000 Calabrians, who arrived on the scene one half-hour before sunset.

The memorable sortie of the Bourbon troops from Capua, when they attacked the whole line of the Garibaldians spread along the Volturno, is described by Fusco as "a terrible and sanguinary drama in which the scenes of individual heroism were swallowed up in the great result of the victory. Young soldiers under arms for the first time fought with the steadiness of veteran troops; the serried ranks of the enemy, the shock of the cavalry, the thunder of the artillery, could strike no terror into the hearts of these volunteers. They had sworn to conquer or to die, and they maintained a front of immovable firmness. The royal troops, divided into three squadrons, marched upon Maddaloni, S. Angelo, and S. Maria; their intention was to scatter our bat-talions, converge towards Caserta, and, thus reunited, to double back again upon Naples. The scheme was daring, but against them stood Garibaldi and the fortunes of Italy. The battle was long and fierce, and for a long time the victory remained undecided; but the Bourbon squadrons of S. Maria and Maddaloni being put to the rout, the remaining troops either retreated across the river or laid down their arms."

Although it is well known that this battle practically decided the fate of Italy, it is equally well known how many shoals and quicksands awaited the ship of the new State before she was fairly launched on her course. A living picture of these has been preserved in the papers

x

published by Fusco in the *Nazionale* at this critical period in the history of the country. The first of these dealt with the appeal of the Southern Italians to Victor Emmanuel to come and be their king, and thus set the seal of his sanction upon their success. Every contribution to the contemporary history of Italy proves more and more conclusively that from first to last this was to be, in more senses perhaps than one, the crown of the Italian hopes. His name alone could bring the elements of order out of a chaos of falling kingdoms and principalities, just as all hope of stability and future prosperity for the State was equally centred in the " Rè Galantuomo," who had made the cause of Italy his own.

The Italians did well to place their confidence in the House of Savoy. No colours had a better right to wave over their united kingdom than those which, riddled with Austrian shot in the national cause on the plains of Novara, had ever since been the polestar of the exile in his hairbreadth escapes from prison and death. When the sinister arms of the Bourbon dynasty still hung their threat over Naples, and the foreign flags of Spain, France, and Austria fluttered from the ports of Gaeta, Civita Vecchia, and Leghorn, Genoa could still display the white cross of Savoy, floating calmly on the breeze—a sight to gladden the fugitive's heart with the prospect of immediate security, and the hope of a better future yet in store.

Fusco never wavered from his opinion that here lay the only true solution of the Italian problem. He despised foreign intervention—it was useless in the day of adversity ; why should it be called in in the day of prosperity, to complicate the question with all the additional petty jealousies and alliances of the various European States ? No less decided were his utterances on the internal divisions and parties which threatened to tear in pieces the newly-made kingdom before it was a year old. He was no Democrat, he shudders when the extreme Republican party brought the country to the verge of anarchy. " One more step, he writes, " and we were over the precipice. A great blot would have stained this wonderful page in our history, and would have involved the destruction of the entire fabric erected at the cost of how many a gallant life, how many a noble intellect, how many repeated sacrifices on the part of the whole nation!" And although Garibaldi receives his grateful homage as the liberator of his country, although no terms can be more enthusiastic than those in which he invites the Neapolitans to raise a monument to the great general, he is not blind to those indiscretions which placed for a time the whole cause in jeopardy, though he would rather ascribe them to the "cattivo genio del generoso generale, che si chiamava una volta Bertani, ed ora lo chiamano Crispi."

Aware that the demagogue politics prevalent all over Europe in 1848 had caused the various States to look with suspicion upon the efforts of Italian patriotism, Fusco avails himself of a paper on Mazzini to rescue Italy from the category of disorganized and revolutionized countries, and to place her in her true attitude before the Continent :—

"No one," he says, "can deny how much has been done by Giuseppe Mazzini for the cause of liberty; but his mistake has been, to refuse to comprehend the real state of the situation; and worse than this, to insist upon the strict fulfilment of his ideas, and his ideas alone. Any one who has considered the present aspect of Italian affairs will perceive at a glance that it is no longer a question of liberty ; the question is now one of nationality. The people of Italy, with far-seeing policy, have agreed to constitute a national independence, and the great power of the Turin Government results from a complete understanding of the will of the nation, and a determination to guide it to that issue.

. . . .

"Mazzini, on the other hand, wishes for a social revolution, and has thus raised against himself the people he desires to liberate. . . . Mazzini has a few adherents, but no following among the people ; on the other hand, the Government of Turin has won, by a judicious policy, the confidence of the whole nation."

Thus it came to pass, that at last the memorable day dawned for Italy when twenty-two millions of Italians signified as one man their choice of Victor Emmanuel as their Sovereign. Fusco was a spectator of the scene, and he wished that all Europe could have witnessed with him the quiet and orderly conduct of the much-maligned Neapolitans on that occasion. Twice only the general joy and self-congratulation rose to anything like a tumult —when Garibaldi's carriage was recognized in the streets, and when Baron Poerio, accompanied by other returned exiles, approached the Municipal Palace to record his vote. At the sight of the gallant old man who had suffered so much, the multitude broke into frenzied applause.

The King's entry into Naples, which followed immediately upon his election, was also witnessed by Fusco:—

"Literature, art, and history," he writes, "will one day vie with one another in describing this crisis in our political life. But no strain of poetry could be too high-flown, no colouring of romance too brilliant. to represent in an adequate manner the boundless enthusiasm, the wild joy of that moment throughout the city."

It would certainly need the descriptive power of Ariosto or Tasso, the glowing pencil of Titian or Tintoret, to do justice to such a scene—the streets crowded with thousands of rejoicing people, eager to catch, if it were possible, a passing glimpse of the Sovereign, whose name had been their watchword for many a long year, and whose presence on that day was the pledge of the ratification of their hopes, the signal for acclamation and "evvivas" which rent the skies. Italian colours fluttered from every roof, garlands of flowers were showered from every balcony, and birds, released in hundreds from captivity, at every stage of the royal progress, were a fitting symbol of the national deliverance from oppression and bondage; the never-ending, still-recurring, inexhaustible source of the rejoicings of that eventful day.

No sooner has the curtain fallen on this the culminating scene of the first act of the drama of Italian independence than Fusco turns to consider the future of his country. The diplomatic position is still critical; but, at all events, the new kingdom has already one ally. Europe, at first breathless with astonishment at the daring enterprise of

Garibaldi, and the no less hardy policy of Il Rè Galan-tuomo, recovers herself to express her opinion by the mouthpiece of her various Powers. After the mild dis-couragement of Prussia, the bitter reproaches of Russia, the muttered vengeance of Austria, the uncertain attitude of France, Italy is thankful to bask in the sunshine of English sympathy, declared in plain, unequivocal terms ; and, thus encouraged, the "Cæsare" of the people's choice begins already to feel himself more firm in the saddle. But the internal organization of the kingdom was a question of even graver importance than her external relations with Europe, and one likely to afford ample scope for the energies of the Italian patriot for many years to come. Fusco describes the new machine of the State creaking and groaning, and working " a balzi" amid the chaos of disorder left by the departed dynasty. His mission as editor of the *Nazionale* being accomplished, he lays down his pen to accept an office in the department of " L' Instruzione Pubblica" under the new Government. He chose that of Inspector-in-Chief of the Schools, primary and secondary, in all the provinces of the old kingdom of Naples ; and he inaugurates his appointment by a striking appeal to the youth of Italy. They have a sacred mission to fulfil, for it rests with them to establish the country on so secure and orderly a basis as to render the return of despotism difficult, if not altogether impossible. The thread of the future destiny of the country, he proceeds, is in the hands of this generation.

"Theirs is the unconsumed fire of youthful energy, only waiting to be called forth, generous enthusiasm, noble aspirations uncontaminated by contact with the world. Turn then from the past, and look steadily towards the future ! Others may dwell upon the glories of past times, we belong to an epoch of living reality, changing from hour to hour ; and the memories of the past are only useful as an incentive to emulate them in our own time "

He would have them consider that the most difficult part of the Revolution is yet to come—the moral and social revolution, which must declare itself in the daily habits of the citizen's life, in the general ideas of order, legality, justice, and national dignity among the populace—ideas which must be as the very heart's blood of the nation if they would complete the regeneration of these provinces, and render the Italian kingdom calm and powerful, respected by other nations, and worthy of such respect.

Agriculture, trade, industries, manufactures, commerce, science, art, literature—even the forms of government itself—he summons to the great work, and his energies do not spend themselves in words alone. He worked unceasingly in his new office, which he had accepted without salary, shocked at the clamorous demand for lucrative official appointments which beset the new Government on all sides:—

"It is perhaps natural," he writes, "that the citizens of Naples should believe everything to be possible to the new Government, but the distribution of Government offices has ever been one of the gravest difficulties of the party in power. There is the new element to be introduced, so necessary in the new aspect of affairs; then, there are the victims of despotism, who have—or think they have—a just claim to demand what they please. Of victims belonging to this class, the Bourbon dynasty may be accounted responsible for so vast a number, that it would take *four Italies* to give them what would be considered a sufficient indemnification for their sufferings. What then is the Ministry to do? We do not see that they can do better than be guided by the consideration of the general welfare of the State, without regard to any other consideration. To suppose that any individual can fill any post is folly. Still greater folly is the belief that the sole qualification of 'Il Martirio Politico' gives a claim to the most responsible and most remunerative office. The good of the State should be the supreme consideration of the statesman, a maxim which cannot be set aside in a free country without weakening the Ministerial authority." (Vol. i. p. 178.)

The financial distress of the country was also a question of momentous gravity, the worst of all the bad legacies left by the Bourbon administration to be dealt with by the new State. The resources of the country had been brought to their lowest ebb by a system which sedulously closed all channels of communication, either industrial or commercial, between Italy and other nations; which reduced the people to the utmost misery, that they might be the more easily corrupted, the more entirely dependent upon the Government. Thus they had lost all power of helping themselves, and every spark of enterprise had long since died out from among them. Bread was dear, labour scarce, poverty and misery on all sides.

In the midst of this general confusion and distress, Fusco's thoughts revert to England, and to his wife, from whom he had been separated several months, and he longs to resume the broken thread of his quiet English life, with those literary occupations which had been the solace of his exile. But then he reflects that this would be a life of egotism which could not satisfy him, which would always leave behind it a pang of remorse in the thought that he had abandoned his country when he might still have been of service to her. He does not hesitate long. The claim of his country is again paramount, the home in London is broken up, his wife summoned to join him at Naples (May, 1861); and henceforth his visits to England are only of a flying character, for the purpose of gaining information—educational, industrial, agricultural, or otherwise—which may be of benefit to Italy. A very little experience in his office convinces him of two things: (1stly) that the whole method of education in Naples would have to be rebuilt, from its very foundation; (2ndly) that it was useless to approach it from the philosophical side alone; that all future success must depend in a great measure upon a precise and clear understanding of the technical method and details of teaching. When the first result of his inspection reveals to him a fearful state of ignorance, he finds that he can bring no practical knowledge to grapple with it, and, conscious of this deficiency, he visits England. The contrast between the two countries strikes him with painful force:—

"When I compare Italy with other countries," he writes, "I perceive that we are in a state of semi-barbarism. Science is unknown in our country, not only

among the middle classes, but among men of education
and intellect. . And science, the exact sciences, with
their innumerable various and wide applications to industry, agriculture, manufacture, and commerce, will command the future. Literature and literary culture must
have a definite and positive aim, if it would preserve its
narrow thread of life; but it must inevitably yield the
ground to scientific culture, the only learning which will
be both effectual and remunerative in the years to come."
This may, or may not, be so in the future, but for the
present we would rather leave the indefatigable patriot to
his researches on behalf of his country, among the industries, manufactures, and scientific discoveries of England,
as displayed in the Exhibition of 1862, till we join him
at the Dante Festival at Florence in 1865. The universal
jubilee in honour of the great father of the Italian language
would, on the contrary, lead us to hope that the delights
of literature and poetry may yet hold their ground a little
longer against the cold, material laws of science. On this
occasion, Fusco was the representative of his native city
of Trani. Trani had reason to be proud of her citizen,
and had welcomed him with open arms when he returned
from exile in 1860; for, as soon as the tumult in Naples
had subsided, Fusco bent his steps homewards, where his
mother greeted with tender affection the son whom she
had never hoped to see again, not to speak of his sisters,
although they were no longer the *sorelline* he had left
behind him when he fled from his home in 1848.

During his tour through the southern provinces of Bari
and Lecce, in the discharge of his office, Fusco had occasion to visit Trani again in the year 1861, for the purpose
of founding a provincial Patriotic Association. The main
objects of this institution were the support of the Government, the maintenance of law and order, the instruction
of the people, either by schools for children, or by popular
addresses explaining the laws and language to the adult
population. It will be remembered that Fusco's earliest
patriotic efforts took the form of inculcating the study of
the pure Italian idiom upon his countrymen. Never was
he roused to greater indignation than when the Austrians
endeavoured to force their language upon the country.

After the reconstruction of the kingdom he was more than ever convinced that it was of vital importance to substitute, by degrees, the pure idiom for the various provincial dialects. He held to his point, in spite of much ridicule of his "Tos-caneggiare," and his adherence to a language which might have been used by his great-grandfather. In the year 1865, on Fusco's return from another inspection of the southern provinces, the Government entrusted him with the difficult task of reopening the clerical schools, which had been suppressed in the ex-kingdom of Naples, and of reorganizing them on the system of the reigning Government. His appointment was signified to the Prefect of Naples in the following flattering terms: "The Inspector (for this purpose) chosen by the Government is l'onorevole Cav. Edoardo Fusco, already known to you, whose noble qualities are in themselves a guarantee to the Government of the success of his mission." This was not the only proof of Ministerial confidence in the talents and principles of Fusco. The faithful and successful discharge of several other offices, of more or less importance, connected with the Department of Public Instruction, won him at last the permanent distinction of the chair of "Anthropologia" and "Pedagogia" in the University of Naples; or, as he describes it in less abstruse terms, "the direction of the human faculties in the study of science, and the best method of imparting education and instruction to the people." This Professorship had been in abeyance since 1860; Fusco was the first appointed to fill it under the new *régime*. The course of study in the University was intended for, and made obligatory in the case of, students aspiring to be inspectors, or schoolmasters, or professors in the universities. Fusco began his lectures in the November of 1866 with a powerful opening address, in which he quotes, with effect, Lord Brougham's remark,— that it was not cannon which changed the face of the world, but the village schoolmaster. He filled this office for seven years, during which time the students gleaned much from those stores of knowledge which—at first accumulated by years of study—were afterwards enlarged by visiting the cities and universities of other nations; by the study of the various technical contemporary works on education, and by the frequent interchange of ideas with the learned professors of either hemisphere.

In this way he was able to approach with confidence the great problems of the nineteenth century—compulsory education, the employment of labour, the dwellings of the poor—to reason upon them in the abstract, and then to consider their special application to Italians and Italy. With such an end in view he edited for four years a paper called *Il Progresso Educativo*, which was first published in March, 1869. The introduction is chiefly occupied with a retrospect of the eight years which have elapsed since the political reconstitution of Italy. The time appears an age, though it is within the memory of us all ; only the brief space of eight years had intervened since the princes and rulers of Italy vied with one another in closing the schools, and in shutting out knowledge from the people, lest the light should penetrate the dense mass of ignorance, and make them desire a state other than that of the corruption and degradation in which they vegetated and " intristissero "—for the word cannot be translated—but now, in the ninth year of the *risorgimento*, it is time to look round and see what had been done.

There is no doubt that the number of teachers, pupils, and educational institutions has increased tenfold, that the State has spent thousands, nay, millions more than had ever yet been spent, but still there is much ignorance left to contend with, many prejudices to combat, no little presumption to check, no small number of errors to correct. Although the country was never more alive to the necessity of educating the people, it is well known how wide is the difference between the mere wish for the welfare of the people and the actual setting to work to promote that welfare, or, as the Italians would themselves express it—

> " Del detto al fatto
> C'è un bel tratto."

And, alas ! for the Italian character, the eager wish for improvement disappears when put to the test of labour and study. With them more than with any other nation " Le mieux est l'ennemi du bien," and the time is spent in condemning what they have, and clamouring for what they have not, because it is so much easier to point out faults and omissions than to remedy the one or supply the other. There is no one thoroughly conversant with the Italian character who would not perceive how deterio- rating must be the effect of these constant complaints and dissatisfaction, resulting from a wrong conception of the meaning of liberty. Instead of these and similar useless lamentations, the object of the *Progresso Educativo* was to grapple with the difficulties one by one, and to suggest some remedy for them, each in its turn. Although Fusco is the first to throw himself in the gap, he does not propose to undertake so arduous a task single handed ; his hopes of success rest in the co-operation of others, interested, like himself, in the moral and social welfare of his country. Their efforts ought to be concentrated upon the South of Italy : these provinces, with their special needs and characteristics, were well known to Fusco ; also, when compared with Northern Italy, how deficient they were in technical instruction, how few and insufficient were the schools, how great was the ignorance of the women, not only of the lower, but also of the upper class ! The papers deal one by one with these difficulties, and in spite of the writer's profound conviction of the necessity of " scuole, sempra scuole, e dappertutto scuole," he cannot bring himself to accept, as a whole, the *compulsory* system of education, which he had made the subject of careful examination during one of his visits to England.

When asked by the Department of Public Instruction to give his opinion upon the subject, he devotes two chapters of the *Progresso Educativo* to the consideration of this question, and comes to these dispassionate conclu- sions :—(1) That the compulsory system is not a violation of the liberty of the subject ; on the contrary, a social guarantee, and a useful guarantee, and a useful safeguard against domestic despotism. (2) That compulsory educa- tion is not sufficient of itself to secure the welfare or prosperity of a nation ; a proof of this fact is furnished by modern Greece, where the system has been in opera- tion since 1830, and has produced no increase of industry, no progress in literature or science worthy of the name.

(3) That the compulsory system cannot be asserted as a general principle to be applied without distinction of country, place, or social class.

With regard to Italy it would be impossible, on the ground of economy alone, to recommend a scheme to the Government; for the finance of the country is at present by no means equal to the enormous outlay which the project would involve. He deals in the same manner with another burning topic of the age : the education— or, to adopt the current phrase, though it is by no means always applicable, "the *higher* education of women."

"Certainly," he writes, "the problem of the education of women is one of the most arduous to solve in the present altered condition of modern civilization. Some change on this point is necessary. The altered condition of society has made this an evident necessity in an age of liberty. No longer the idols of an absurd chivalry" (alas! even from Italy must we hear the echo of the sad truth that the 'age of chivalry is gone !') ; no longer the slaves or the playthings of mankind, women would now prefer either to share in their labours, or indeed to work for themselves, and make their own way without the help of a companion. For either purpose a woman must be better educated, her acquirements must be of a less superficial kind, she must have passed through a more serious discipline of life. Let us then give her the opportunity of instructing, educating, and disciplining her noble faculties ; but let us, at the same time, be careful to avoid the perils which the process may entail. Exaggeration on this point is most common, and the sentimentalists of civilization are apt to overshoot the mark when they discuss this, one of the favourite topics of the time. Chivalry appears again in a totally new and different dress, and descants upon sundry doctrines of equality—with which we agree up to a certain point—but loses sight of certain special conditions, certain educational safeguards, which are important items in a woman's education, and upon which nine-tenths of the success of that education must depend. From the day in which Stuart Mill gave his opinion in favour of women's suffrage, a series of ideas upon emancipation ensued, and found its interpretation in thousands of authors and authoresses, especially among the Transatlantic Anglo-Saxons, where the manners and customs of democracy have predisposed the social mind to give its full countenance to this emancipation (so-called) of women. The rapid spread of these ideas in America, the nature and amount of studies successfully accomplished by American women, would scarcely be credited in Italy, but we cannot touch upon them here, nor can we hope, I might add nor do we desire, to imitate them.

   .   .   .   .   .   .

" We may, however, find in the example of other nations a useful incentive to ameliorate the education of our own countrywomen, that they may assist the development of a civilization of which they are the climax and the crown." (Vol. ii. pp. 228, 229.)

The dwellings of the poor, the care of the blind, the method of clerical education, and the instruction to be given in prisons, are treated successively in the pages of *Il Progresso Educativo* with the same thoughtful consideration, the same careful comparison with the institutions of other nations.

In one of the chapters dedicated to a review of the scholastic institutions of Naples, Fusco laments over the condition of the Royal School of Music, which had taken the place of the old Conservatorios. It would have been impossible for a Neapolitan by birth, proud of an inheritance rich with such musical memories as Scarlatti, Paisiello, Verdi, and Mercadante, to view with equanimity the decay of one of the greatest glories of Naples in past times ; and he made many endeavours to rouse the Government to take some action on its behalf before it was too late. His position and character gave weight to any suggestion he might make upon this or any other point, and sometimes the changes he desired were brought to pass ; but the work of the Government was still slow and painful as that of a machine with blunted and rusty teeth, nor was it his lot to see any immediate, or very definite, results from his unwearied labours. In the very midst of them, in the prime of life and manhood, with the cheering reflection of a well-spent past, the zest of an active present, and the promise of a noble future, he was overtaken by the fatal illness of heart disease, hereditary in his family, and in forty-eight hours he was dead— December 28, 1873.

This brief sketch of his life will have failed in its object if it has not conveyed to the reader the impression of a noble and disinterested nature, of an enthusiastic disposition tempered by judgment, of a rare intellect, which, though mainly self-taught, was free from conceit, ever open to conviction, and ready to learn from all places and all men, so as to gather from the stores of all countries a rich harvest of learning. The fruits of this harvest he poured into the lap of the beloved " patria terra," hoping thus to relieve her from the poverty and distress entailed by centuries of oppression, and to place her, in the first years of her new-born freedom, on an equality with her sister European States. To this end he thrice sacrificed a brilliant prospect in England to return to Italy, and, while placemongers were besetting the new Government, he gave his services gratuitously to his country, and performed the duties of a position of comparative drudgery with cheerful alacrity and un- flagging zeal. Thus he laboured, and thus he died. So unpretending, so little self-seeking was his career that it might have remained in comparative shadow during that brilliant epoch of Italian history had it not been for the efforts of the faithful companion of his labours, his sorrows, and his joys. Hers was the loving and congenial task of collecting the scattered fragments of a life spent in the service of others, and of presenting them to the judgment of posterity in one perfect whole. Should any details be yet lacking to complete the picture, they may be supplied by those ornaments of character which make the charm of domestic life, a ready sympathy, a never- failing courtesy, and a tender affection which could, even from the tomb, command the following pathetic fare- well :—

> " Terra del pianto ove il mio amor riposa,
> Da te io prendo ormai l' estremo addio ;
> L' ultima volta è questa che amorosa
> Lacrima spande su di te il cor mio,

E colgo al suo sepolcro il mesto fiore
Che inaridito porterò sul core.

Addio! terra diletta, che nascondi
Quanto di grande, generoso e bello
Un Dio per me creava nei due mondi ;
Addio, terra del pianto, amato avello,
Or l' universo mio è questo fiore
Che inaridito porterò sul core."

A LEGEND OF "IL CENACOLO."

THE well-known "Cenacolo," or "Last Supper" of Leonardo Da Vinci, was painted on the wall of the Dominican Convent of the "Madonna delle Grazie" at Milan between the years 1494 and 1499.

This wonderful painting has been the subject of numerous writings and commentaries, both on account of its extraordinary beauty and of its rapid decay.

One of the many interesting legends respecting the picture forms the subject of the following lines.

"And call upon Me in the time of trouble: so will I hear thee, and thou shalt praise Me."—Ps. i.

Rude is the structure—plain the whitewashed wall,
Rough-hewn the rafters of that convent hall ;
High from the ground, unfriendly to the sight,
The narrow casement scarce admits the light.
But crowds have thronged around that entrance door,
And many a foot hath trod that pavement floor
With fearful step, as though on holy ground,
While o'er each soul there steals an awe profound.
No matter if the hand of time efface,
No matter if the Form we scarce can trace,
We feel that there, as when on earth adored,
We gaze upon the Image of the LORD.
And vivid thought depicts the Eastern clime,
The upper room prepared at even-time,
The silent night beneath the cloudless sky,
The faithful few who came with Him to die.
The faithless one—It seems as if the sound
Of that dread warning could be heard aroun d;
As if those Lips could speak, the very air,
The Form, the appealing gesture—all are there.

Again the thought recurs—no human hand
That Figure could portray, majestic, grand,
The Glory of that Face, whose rays Divine,
Nor time, nor ruin can forbid to shine.
O great Da Vinci, must thy work decay,
And by the hand of time be swept away?
And doth this matchless fragment only show
That nothing perfect can exist below?
Was it for this thou didst no labour spare,
For this thy ceaseless thought and anxious care?
For this thy restless energy and zeal
Which knew no rest, and ne'er could weary feel?
Was this the hope which fed thy soul for years?
For this the sleepless nights of doubts and fears?
Can this support the honour of thy name,
And, perishing, bestow immortal fame?
Da Vinci—yes—no other work of art
Shall ever speak, as this, to human heart,
Shall wake a chord, although untouched for years,
And cause to flow the pent-up fount of tears.
Ye who have followed in that breathless race
Which would perfection seek, nor yield the chase
So long as life shall last, e'en though each day,
In the far distance, farther still away,
Ever receding, melting in dim haze,
It seems to fade before our longing gaze.
Of earthly joys or sorrows here below
The deepest, purest, you alone can know!
Such, Leonardo, was thy fate—thy hand
Could ne'er accomplish what thy thought had planned.
Rival of Angelo in artist's skill,
If great thy deeds, thy thoughts were greater still.
Still ever pressing onward in desire,
Each summit gained, reveals another higher.
Thus thy great work unfinished stood for years,
Alike the centre of thy hopes and fears,—
Oft as thy soul would steadfastly incline
To paint the semblance of that Form Divine,
Trembling, unnerved, would pause the practised hand,
Nor could the will the failing strength command.
Nor height, nor depth, by thee untried remain,

Y

Thy soul all eager, and on fire thy brain,
For, when thus baffled in its upward flight,
Thy thought would fathom the abyss of night.
Where else could type so base, so vile be found,
For him whose name, so hateful in its sound,
The lips refuse to speak, the hand to trace,
The worst example of the human race,
Shunned as an evil omen, loathed, abhorred,
Judas the traitor who betrayed his Lord.
Unrivalled crime ; therefore nor heart, nor mind
Could e'er conceive this outcast from mankind,
Earth's lowest haunts the painter sought in vain,
Image of fraud ! thou shalt not live again !
Oh native genius, heaven-born ray of light,
Who shall curtail thy lofty soaring flight,
The boundless riches of thy thought control,
Or gauge the depths, unfathomed, of thy soul !
Short-lived thy joy, for doomed by bitter fate,
A jaundiced envy on thy steps doth wait,
Still close pursuing in thy track to fame,
Casting its venom at the greatest name.
" Why should he pause ? " the Prior [1] oft would ask,
" Why can he not fulfil the appointed task ?
See, my Lord Duke, [2] unfinished it remains ;
Where are his former zeal, his care and pains ?
Two years untouched, unvisited it stands,
The painting should be placed in other hands.
Or bid him come and finish with all haste,
Charge him with wilful fraud and reckless waste,
And, as his patron, let thy word proclaim
His honour tarnished, forfeited his fame,
If by a day which seems to thee most meet,
The Picture still, as now, be incomplete."
Oh petty soul ! dost think thy sordid spite,
Can chain a genius in his lofty flight !
Fear rather lest thou rue for aye the hour
Thou turn'st upon thyself a hidden power,
Provoke to wrath an artist's master hand,

[1] Fra Cristoforo.
[2] Lodovico Sforza, who gave Leonardo the commission to paint the picture.

And, as the traitor mid the chosen band,
Thou gain a terrible, unenvied fame,
And infamy for ever soil thy name.
Pause, Leonardo, ere th' unhealthy blight
Of earthly passions blind thy piercing sight,
And thou, entangled in their deadly snare,
Shall find thy labour fruitless, vain thy care.
Swift flew the thought across his angry mind,
Nor arrow swifter sped upon the wind;
Alas! if haply in temptation's hour,
Close on the thought succeeds the evil power,
Ere the weak soul has tottered to its harm,
Stretch, O good LORD, stretch out Thy saving Arm!
Strong as the will, the latent force was there,
He neither stopped for thought, nor paused for prayer;
By passion fierce his eager hand was led,
And soon the form was sketched: the sullen head,
And scowling brow, the dark and low'ring face,
Aptly filled up the traitor's vacant place.
He paused; how masterly, how true each stroke!
None can mistake the likeness. Nay, it spoke.
Thy portrait, Fra Cristoforo, behold—
The traitor who his LORD and Master sold!
Sudden as tempest borne along the wind,
The storm of wrath had burst upon his mind;
Swept o'er his eager nature fierce and fast,
And then the storm was spent—its fury past.
Once more the sun of reason, calmly bright,
Shed o'er his soul its wonted steady light.
Fled are the angry thoughts, nor longer brood
To vex his mind or chafe his calmer mood;
But the unhallowed vengeance of his hand
A lasting record of his wrath will stand.
As when one travelling through a beauteous land,
With eager eye the glorious view hath scanned,
Marking the shadow that across it lay,
Wearied and sad has turned his gaze away,
Where is the sun's glad beam, with golden ray
To kindle all the landscape into day?
Such the dark gloom which o'er the fresco lies
As when the storm-clouds lower in the skies,

Figures but now with master's skill expressed,
Unworthy seem, e'en those which pleased him best.
Cold, motionless, the groups are silent all,
Nor life, nor passion glow upon the wall;
No light shines forth from Countenance Divine
To bid the dead forms live, the darkness shine.
Well might the trembling heart and spirit fail,
For, scarce foreshadowed, yon dim outline pale,
Which once his careful hand had dared portray,
Now foils each vain attempt, and fades away.
Vain years of study! and the hope more vain,
Creative thought once banished to regain,
Sterile the mind and powerless the hand,
To sweep the baffling curve, th' ideal truth command.
Delusive Pencil, speedy to betray!
And faithless Palette! both are cast away—
While o'er his soul in quick succession came
Bitter remorse and fast-increasing shame.
There he beheld with sharpest pang of pain,
His noblest work all marred, the clinging stain
Of earthly passions, vengeance, wrath and pride
Can never be effaced or set aside,
Its heavenly theme it ne'er can now attain,
But of the earth, and earthy aye remain.
Oh, bitter thought, o'erwhelming, crushing blow
Destructive of his fairest hopes below!
Turn, Leonardo, turn thy thoughts above,
The LORD is gracious, full of tender love—
"Oh, ever blessed, ever worshipped LORD,
Who didst our human nature deign to wear,
One pitying glance unto my woe afford
Incline Thy loving Ear unto my prayer.
Hear me, O LORD, of Thy great goodness hear,
My hand is powerless without Thine aid,
Its skill is paralyzed with grief and fear,
My sorrowing soul in lowest dust is laid."
He ceased, and lo, there stood in robes of white,
Encircled by bright beams of heavenly light,
The form of one [3] long dead, whose skilful hand

[3] Andrea Verocchio, the master of Leonardo Da Vinci (b. 1432, d. 1488).

The latent genius of his soul had fanned,
First had descried the gift which hidden lay,
First sped his youthful talents on their way,
Which treading eagerly the road to fame,
Early procured him an undying name.
Then as a meadow swept by passing wind,
With fitful gust, across his troubled mind,
Fear, joy, and hope, their lights and shadows threw,
As ever on their rapid course they flew.
Still as he marvelled if he saw aright,
It seemed as if before his startled sight,
An Angel hand had drawn that Form Divine,
While o'er the Face a radiant light did shine,
Yea, o'er each feature shed its glorious ray,
The everlasting light of heavenly day.
Oh, sacred Beauty, wondrous to behold,
Image Divine in perfect human mould ;
Who shall describe Thy glory, who may show
What neither tongue can speak nor heart can know ?
At length there fell upon his wond'ring ear
A sound of far-off words distinct and clear :
"To those who call on Him the LORD is nigh,
His ear is ever open to their cry,
His Angels ever watch around and wait,
To minister to fallen man's estate,
Swift messengers from heaven they wing their way,
And round the sons of men as guardians stay.
The LORD has sent an answer to thy prayer,
Look on thy Picture and behold it there !
Not as man sees, He saw thy great desire,
Thy ceaseless labour and thy zealous fire.
But never shall a mortal hand portray,
Of that Eternal Sun the faintest ray,
Before whose Face the light of heaven grows pale,
And Angels, with their wings, their faces veil.
Aye, let a speechless rapture fill thine heart,
And shine forth in thine eyes, my child in art,
Oh gaze thy fill with joy and holy fear,
Ere from my lips the Almighty Will thou hear.
Thy evil passions thou didst not control,
When as a storm they swept across thy soul,

Therefore thy work must perish in its pride,
(E'en though far meaner works will long abide,)
And in the midst of glory pass away,
Like as the sun eclipsed at high noon-day.
Nor shall hereafter any copy show,
The light which there shines forth in radiant glow,
A beauty by no earthly power given,
Traced, as GOD willed it, by a hand from heaven.
So when thy heart with bitter anguish torn,
Shall o'er the fading Picture grieve and mourn,
To CHRIST in glory, bid thy spirit rise,
His Face shall shine before thy weeping eyes.
For if such rapture doth thy soul afford,
The Light which is the herald of thy LORD,
Faint not, nor slacken in the race of life
Till the last call shall bid thee cease from strife,
So shall thy spirit to that Presence soar,
At whose Right Hand are pleasures evermore,
Then shalt thou see the beauty of the King,
Whose praise the Angels aye unwearied sing,
The glorious gates of heaven shall unfold,
And that dear far-off land thou shalt behold."

THE END.

www.ingramcontent.com/pod-product-compliance
Lightning Source LLC
Chambersburg PA
CBHW031336070726

47496CB00017B/1143